MEAN BUSINESS

How I Save Bad Companies and Make Good Companies Great

D1026437

ALBERT J. DUNLAP

With Bob Andelman

MR. MEDIA BOOKS

St. Petersburg, Florida

Copyright © 1996 by Albert J. Dunlap
Published by Times Books, a division of Random House, Inc., New York

New chapters 18, 19, 20, 21 and epilogue
Copyright © 2014 by Albert J. Dunlap
Published by Mr. Media Books, St. Petersburg, Florida

First Mr. Media Books Edition 2014
Published by arrangement with Albert J. Dunlap

Visit us on the web!
http://www.MeanBusinessBook.com

http://www.MrMediaBooks.com

Mr. Media® is a registered trademark of Bob Andelman

Manufactured in the United States of America
10 9 8 7 6 5 4 3 2 1

Library of Congress Cataloging-in-Publication Data
Dunlap, Albert J. (Albert John), 1937-
       Mean business: how I save bad companies and make good companies
    great / Albert J. Dunlap with Bob Andelman. - 1st ed.
          p. cm.
       1. Corporate turnarounds. 2. Corporate turnarounds—United
    States—Case studies. I. Andelman, Bob. II. Title.
    HD58.8.D858 1996
    658.4'063—dc20   96-21876

ISBN-13 978-1500498832
ISBN-10 1500498831
Also available as an e-book
Audiobook ISBN 978-0-9911254-2-5

Front and Back Cover photographs provided by Florida State University
Photography Services. All Rights Reserved.
Front and Back Cover Design by Andrew Skwish.
http://www.Skwish.com

For Judy
The joy of my life
My dream.

CONTENTS

WHY DID I CALL THIS BOOK *MEAN BUSINESS*?

Chainsaw Al.

Rambo in Pinstripes. The Shredder.

If you want nicknames, I've been called a million of them. Some were meant as ferocious or grudging compliments, others were less well intentioned. But nicknames are part of image, not strategy. They don't really explain *how* or *why* I do what I do: Make a company and the people who work there the best!

The essence of *Mean Business is* competitiveness—how to become competitive, and perhaps more important, how to *stay* competitive. That's what I'm about. That's what you need to be about because the harsh reality of business life is that what works today won't even be satisfactory tomorrow. The predators are out there, circling, trying to stare you down, waiting for any sign of weakness, ready to pounce and make you their next meal.

Why Should You Listen to Me?

I've been where you want to go and I've worked through just about every kind of problem you'll face, from companies that have lost their focus to employees seeking motivation and leadership.

I'm not an academic or consultant making a living just by *studying* problems. Neither am I an MBA from some fancy, high-priced school, who was anointed into the corporate elite. I started my career at the bottom, literally: I worked the third shift at a dirty, smelly paper mill. I swam my way up through a sea of look-alike, sound-alike middle managers, and stepped onto dry land as Chairman and CEO of Scott Paper.

Along the way I studied how and why products get made correctly. I took note of laziness, good management and bad, and, particularly, an insidious form of ivory tower disease that keeps managers aloof from the gritty world of manufacturing, marketing, and selling products and services. As if anything else in business mattered!

Scott Paper was my most famous challenge. When I took over in April 1994 it was in woeful shape, having lost $277 million in 1993. Its stock price had been comatose for seven years. Scott products had peaked long ago, and the company had not had a proper marketing strategy for several years. However, the deepest trouble came because Scott's management and employees no longer believed the company's decline could be stopped.

That all changed within a matter of months. By December 1995, when

Scott Paper merged with Kimberly-Clark, creating the second largest consumer products company in the United States, Scott was virtually debt-free, its stock's value had improved by more than 200 percent, and shareholder value had increased from $2.5 billion to $9 billion.

Perhaps just as importantly, the people working at Scott had regained confidence—in their company, their products, and themselves.

Besides Scott, I helped turn around many other companies: Sterling Pulp & Paper (1967-77), American Can (1977-82), Lily-Tulip (1983-86), Diamond International, Cavenham Forest Industries (formerly Crown-Zellerbach) (1986-89), Australian National Industries (1989), Consolidated Press Holdings (1991-93), and Sunbeam (beginning in 1996). In seventeen states and across three continents, I've worked with—and learned from—some of the world's great business geniuses, including Sir James Goldsmith.

What I learned was that it's no longer enough to be competent or pretty good. You must be *great.*

But even the great can't rest. At the start of each business day, you must assume that failure is just beyond the next obstacle. You must be vigilant, working as hard today as you did when you were trying to reach where you are today.

Ten Reasons Mean Business *Is Worth Your Time*

1. Business is simple, remarkably simple. In fact, if everyone followed my four simple rules—get the right management team; cut costs; focus on the core business; get a real strategy—the Harvard Business School (and its imitators), as well as most consulting firms, would be out of business.

2. When problems start at a company, they're often traceable to a self-aggrandizing corporate royalty more concerned with its own perks than with the products the company makes or the services it offers. When you must make changes, start by throwing corporate toys (and their defenders) overboard. Squeeze corporate headquarters and shrink high-priced, unproductive management.

3. The most important person in any company is *the shareholder.* Not the CEO, or the chairman of the board, and not the board of directors itself. I'm not talking here about Wall Street fat cats. Working people and retired men and women have entrusted us with their 401Ks and pension plans for their children's college tuition and their own long-term security. If we're not concerned about them every step of the way, they're screwed. Another reason for calling this book *Mean Business:* If you're going to be in business, you'd better understand that, above all, your goal is to make money for the owners.

4. Marketing strategy is a vibrant daily reality. If your company needs a dictionary to define it, you've got a problem like the one I had at Scott. I'll tell you how Scott was transformed from a company that thought of itself as a commodity paper manufacturer to one that believed in itself as a global consumer products company.

5. Everyone in a company needs incentives, but they should be tied directly to the performance of the company. The last dirty secret in the corporate world is how directors live off the fat of a business that is not their employer. I started a revolution by insisting that Scott directors be paid only in stock. They became intensely and personally interested in how to improve performance.

6. Don't turn decision making over to an army of consultants. Use them sparingly, if at all. Don't use outsiders as a shield against risk taking or following your own vision.

7. Reward leadership and outstanding performance at every level in the company. Most CEOs are ridiculously overpaid, but I deserved the $100 million I took away when Scott merged with Kimberly-Clark.

8. Put your money where your reputation is, and have the utmost faith in your own talent. When I accepted the job of Chairman and CEO of Scott, I put a portion of my personal fortune at risk and invested $4 million in Scott stock. I believed in what I was doing and I foresaw that we—all of us—would be successful.

9. Be outrageous—but pick your spots carefully. When you have a good story to tell about results, spread the word, even if it means acting like a bull in a china shop. And when performance lags, stay out front. Take responsibility—and criticism—for your actions. If you're doing the right things, stay the course.

10. You're not in business to be liked. Neither am I. We're here to succeed. If you want a friend, get a dog. I'm not taking any chances; I've got two dogs.

•••

Several years ago, I met Roger Bannister, a man who exemplifies the traits needed for success in today's business climate. But Bannister wasn't a businessman—he was an athlete and a surgeon.

Bannister was the first runner to break the four-minute mile. On May 6, 1954, I was one of millions who cheered and envied his achievement. I ran track and heaved the shot put while in high school, so it was an especially great honor to meet him while I was working in London for Sir James Goldsmith. One of my former executives, Phil Lader, invited my wife Judy and me to a private dinner with Bannister, who was master of Phil's alma mater, Pembroke College at Oxford.

We ate in a 300-year-old dining hall and, while we ate, Bannister and I traded stories from our careers. He spoke modestly of his extraordinary athletic feats and more enthusiastically of his subsequent career as a renowned neurosurgeon.

He told me he had known that the four-minute mile would be broken and that two fellows beside him could do it. When he heard they were running in an upcoming race, Bannister entered a lesser, earlier race because in his heart and mind, he had to be the one to break the barrier. And he did it! Incredibly, the two guys he was concerned about went on to break Bannister's speed record, but they're just historical footnotes. Everybody remembers Roger Bannister and nobody remembers the other two guys.

Bannister had total commitment in everything he did. He studiously trained to become a world-class runner and, later, a world-class physician. He wasn't just a fellow who had natural gifts and moped along, like some of today's star athletes. He had a plan, paid the price, and followed through. Bannister created his greatness by using everything he had.

He was the ultimate competitor. He knew what he wanted and how he would charge after it. I saw, in the things he did, a total application of what I do in business: Create a strategy, follow through, take risks, sacrifice, recognize opportunity, and pick up the winner's spoils at the end.

I want *Mean Business* to provide similar lessons so you can develop your own unique game plan for success in some of the toughest times business has ever known.

PART I

SAVING A FALLEN GIANT

Chapter 1

PAPER THIN:
A MICROCOSM OF BAD BUSINESS

LESSON: TODAY, IN GOOD TIMES AND BAD, EVERYONE MUST BE A TURNAROUND MANAGER.

I was standing in the aisles of a Publix Supermarket near my home in Boca Raton, Florida, when it became shockingly apparent how much trouble the Scott Paper Company was in. Scott's trouble was of particular concern to me. I had just accepted the job as its new chairman and chief executive officer.

After two hours of wandering the store's aisles, seeking out Scott's famous label products and talking to unsuspecting shoppers, I and my friend Dick Nicolosi were alarmed. Scott's packaging was so bad even the products were embarrassed. ScotTowels hid from customers. They seemed ashamed of what had become of them in recent years.

We talked with consumers as they went through the aisles. We asked their opinions about what was going on, why it was going on, and how they decided what products to buy. We were like eager high school students, doing a first public survey, preparing for a big exam.

Our shopping tour was an excellent way of getting firsthand knowledge about Scott's product categories. We found it remarkable that people talked with us easily and gave candid answers to the questions we asked.

We heard a bunch of things. One was that the Scott brands were considered old-fashioned, antiquated, and not particularly innovative. To shoppers, they were just plain boring. And Scott wasn't good at telling consumers how well its products would hold up compared with other brands.

The way Scott merchandise was priced and packaged was confusing. The variety of products and the way they were presented on store shelves and in advertising made it difficult for consumers to figure out which product represented the better value. In short, Scott wasn't keeping up with the competition.

Dick, a veteran of twenty-three years at Procter & Gamble (he became Scott's chief marketing executive), led me through an analysis of our findings to figure out what could be done. For the first time since being offered the job, I had serious doubts about whether anybody could save this company. I experienced the "Oh, God!" factor: I thought, *what have I signed up for?* The Scott people had let their boat take on a lot of water. It was going to take an entire marina of pumps to get all that water out and make the flagship seaworthy again.

Those were the quickest two hours I had spent in a long, long time. They went by like a moment.

The issues we identified were not solvable in a heartbeat. They were not small blips; they were fundamental for a consumer brand, and to change them would be like trying to reverse the course of the *Queen Elizabeth H* when it's at full-speed ahead. We needed time and careful plotting.

The next day, I called Scott's headhunter and warned him that, although I wasn't backing out, I was having second thoughts.

•••

Two brothers, Irvin and Clarence Scott, founded Scott Paper in Philadelphia in 1879. The company began as a producer of bags and wrapping paper, but began manufacturing toilet tissue when indoor plumbing became more prevalent toward the turn of the century.

Some 115 years later, Scott was the eighth largest paper company in the United States, and had the second largest U.S. market share of tissue paper. In the world market, it was No. 1, with 15 percent of the marketplace.

By the time Gary Roubos, chairman of the search committee for the Scott Paper Company board of directors, interviewed me for the CEO job in 1994, he had already spent six months in the hunt. The company had come close to finding its CEO twice before. The first candidate stunned the board. He said, *"Wake up!* This company *can't* be saved. Not only don't I want the job but *whoever* takes this job is a fool."

The initial description given by Roubos to Tom Neff, president of the executive search firm of Spencer Stuart Inc., called for someone who combined a classic consumer packaged-goods background with experience running a business—ideally, a CEO, or maybe a chief operating officer, of a fairly substantial company with international operations. They were looking for people who grew up in companies like General Foods or Procter & Gamble.

Plans were made to offer the job to a second person who fit that profile but he was traveling internationally for a couple of weeks, delaying the committee's action. And based on what the search committee had learned from talking with the candidates and getting their harsh assessments of Scott Paper, something clicked. Roubos suggested that, before making a final decision, the search committee should think "out of the box." How about somebody who could restructure companies rather than just package and sell consumer goods?

That's when my phone rang.

Roubos, whose full-time job is as chairman of the $3 billion Dover Corporation, described the situation as he saw it at Scott.

He didn't try to bullshit me. He said, "This is acute. It's an overly bureaucratic organization, spending too much money on the wrong things. It's so slow-moving that it can't get out of its own way."

He told me that his own corporation has just twenty-two people running its corporate headquarters. It was immediately apparent that we shared an inclination toward leanness.

I asked him how Scott got into such a mess.

"It didn't happen overnight," Roubos said. "When I went on the board seven years ago, Scott was doing pretty well. But the paper business is cyclical. It was at the top of the cycle at that time and most of its big subsidiaries such as S.D. Warren were making money. But as the paper cycle turned down, it became very apparent that it was going to be very, very bad for Scott."

Many of the top management people at Scott hadn't changed in thirty years. It was very difficult for them to see a different way of doing things. The boring, old-fashioned packaging that consumers complained about reflected the old-fashioned thinking that had nearly wrecked the company. They tried, but the management that had grown up in that antiquated culture could never make the kind of changes that were necessary.

Roubos believed that the men and women running Scott knew they were in trouble and were trying very hard to figure a way out of it; they just couldn't see what it was. And having moved away from the company's core tissue business into so many ancillary and unrelated fields—ranging from health care to energy generation—Scott just wasn't a focused business.

The company, he confided, was considering a bankruptcy filing if dramatic change was not made.

As negotiations moved ahead, I told Roubos I agreed that there would be a need for a fairly dramatic change in direction and strategy, and I would only seriously consider the job if the board empowered me to accomplish that.

He didn't mince words with me. He said, "What would you do?"

I told him I would attack costs, put together a high-powered management team, focus strategy around the core business, and get rid of debt.

And that's what I did, from day one.

•••

Once I signed on the dotted line, the next few weeks rushed by like a Chicago Bears blitz. I sold my new house in Boca Raton to Scott Paper for exactly what I paid for it. (The company subsequently resold it.) My wife, Judy, and I put our belongings back in storage and moved, along with our two dogs, into the Four Seasons Hotel in Philadelphia for seven weeks.

As my car pulled up to Scott World Headquarters on April 19, 1994, my first day on the job, I couldn't help but think of those poor orphaned rolls of Cottonelle toilet tissue and ScotTowels back in Florida. Quietly, I resolved that the next time we met they'd look so good they'd be jumping into shoppers' baskets.

Taking in the company's campus, with its three handsome office buildings, manicured lawns, elegant water fountains, geese, and flags representing each country where Scott did business, I knew what else had to be done. In my experience, the success of a corporation is inversely proportional to the size and opulence of its headquarters. Scott's buildings told the world what management thought about the shareholders' money. Running my hand over the marble walls in the foyer, I thought about the self-aggrandizing executives who had built them. I knew their days—and the buildings'—were numbered.

My honeymoon with Scott lasted only as long as it took the elevator to reach the sixth floor. That first week went by in a rush of meetings, ultimatums, and firings. The things I saw and heard were absolutely incredible. If Scott's shareholders had known what I discovered, they would surely have burned the place down.

There were 1,600 people working at the three headquarters buildings known as Scott Plaza, including 500 people with management responsibilities. At the top of the chart was an eleven-member ruling management committee. I ordered them immediately into a meeting.

"Ladies and gentlemen," I said, "this could be the best day of your life, or it could be the worst."

By reputation alone, they knew what I meant. For those who hadn't performed—virtually all of them—it would be the worst day of their professional lives.

I asked them to introduce themselves and explain their duties. One thing immediately caught my attention. There was no chief financial officer in attendance. The chief administrator, an engineer by training, said he handled financial details at these meetings. How absurd!

In due course, the eleven member operating committee was disbanded. Two of its members were given increased responsibilities. The others either resigned, were reassigned, or were fired.

When a business doesn't do well, no one can stand up and say, "Well, *I'm* not to blame." If you were part of the business, you must accept some of the blame. If you were *running* the company, you must accept most of the blame.

Some critics may think I fire people too quickly. But it's pretty easy to discern who is willing to make changes and who will maintain the status quo. I don't want the status quo. The former management screwed up. I didn't want them screwing me up.

When there are problems, I don't blame employees. I pick the right targets: management and the board of directors. That goes over well with employees. They know that if they're not efficient or productive, the fault usually lies above, not below. At my general staff meeting, I practically got a standing ovation when I talked about Scott management's underperformance. "Why are we where we are?" I said. "Leadership! A massive failure of leadership to perform!" It was already quite apparent to people on the inside.

At the same time I go after people who don't perform, I am incredibly loyal to those who do. When I put people in leadership positions, I am very supportive of them. And once I make a choice, I stick with it.

My takeover of Scott Paper was a bloodless coup, a most amazing and effective change in leadership, all done from within. It was peaceful and quiet; no hostile outsiders took part. The result was that no premiums or greenmail were paid to prevent an unwanted suitor from taking over, and in the end, tremendous value was created for the shareholders.

How did we do it?

The remedy started with awareness. In 1993, even before I arrived, there was an effort to look at value creation. How much value was Scott creating for its shareholders? The board of directors looked at the earnings that the business had generated and the cost of capital over the preceding five years. When earnings were compared with costs, the overall results were not encouraging.

No sooner was the board aware of the gap, however, than the gap widened. And it continued getting worse. Forget about just looking at the stock price. The work going on at Scott was not creating value.

The process by which decisions were made to invest capital was flawed and shortsighted. There wasn't sufficient vigor, and the process stank. At last, the board could no longer deny that the return on investment was poor and the course that was supposed to produce future earnings was not being plotted correctly.

At the same time, shareholder groups all across the United States, and particularly in long-depressed companies such as Scott, were becoming more vocal about their diminished investments.

On the positive side, the prevailing view was that the company's product still held great potential. There was nothing fundamentally wrong with the industry itself; the opportunity existed to improve margins. But Scott was being horribly managed, and opportunity was passing it by.

Everything pointed to a need for change, starting at—but not limited to—the top.

•••

I was not the cause of the average Scott employee's discomfort in 1994. I was the result of the previous administration's having created a train wreck out of a once successful company. But people within the company had difficulty accepting that fact, particularly those in what were the company's pockets of excellence and competence.

Everything was not bad. Scott had some terrific people and some great business units, such as the European Consumer and Away-From-Home Worldwide divisions; the latter developed and marketed commercial and industrial cleaning products. Many of those people couldn't understand why everyone had to endure the pain and torture of the restructuring. The answer was that we had to become competitive across the board, not just in one division. We had to be efficient and unload a lot of the rubbish that years of poor management had heaped on itself.

Some of Scott's European operations were rare gems in an otherwise cloudy picture. The first time I met Paolo Forlin, then a senior vice president of Scott's European operations, with thirty-five years on the job, I asked him, point-blank, "Why is this corporation so screwed up?"

He hardly paused to think before answering.

"Philadelphia headquarters," he said. "Those people screw up everything."

Honest answer! I made Forlin—one of the few Scott senior executives in Europe who had performed—our new head of consumer products in Europe. He took over what most people might have thought was a cushy position, with Scott products leading in many categories across the Continent. But his mandate from me came in two words: "Do better."

•••

After my first and only meeting with Scott's existing management committee, I sought out the company's chief financial officer, an amiable young man named Basil L. Anderson. Anderson was one of only two executives of whom the board of directors spoke highly.

"Why weren't you at the executive committee meeting?" I asked him.

"I've never been invited," he said.

"You are now."

Then I asked him about the corporate morale officer who sat in on executive meetings. A pleasant enough person being paid an obscene amount of money, her primary job was to ensure harmony in the executive suite. The hell with harmony. These people should have been tearing each other's hair out, demanding to know why this 115-year-old company was getting its ass beat on supermarket shelves every day. I told Anderson to get rid of her.

He told me that she didn't work for him. Wrong answer. Get rid of her, I repeated, and walked out. Half an hour later, I called him. "Did you do it?"

He got the message. By day's end, Scott was less one morale officer, but I had found the first executive worth keeping. Anderson recognized that if I had made a decision, I expected it to be carried out. And he cared about getting things done.

Later that week, one of our in-house lawyers fell asleep during an executive meeting. That was his last doze on our payroll. I woke him and told him to at least pretend to be interested. A few days later, he was a memory.

•••

Scott Paper Company was a classic microcosm of what's wrong with the American corporation. More than $2.5 billion in debt and bloated beyond recognition, the Philadelphia paper producer was unable to shake off a decadent and dying corporate culture about to implement its third three-year reorganization plan in four years.

Scott was the largest tissue company in the world, but it was living in the past. A decade had passed since it had launched a proper marketing campaign. It had some great tissue paper brands, such as Scott and Viva. Scott, I thought, was a potentially great consumer products company masquerading as an out-of-date, poorly managed commodity paper company saddled with ancillary businesses such as health care, food service, energy generation, and coated paper.

Scott's debt was onerous, resting uneasily during a Dun & Bradstreet credit watch.

On the plus side, Scott had some good products and good facilities. The way I saw it, if I could get this dinosaur back to its core business—tissue paper—sell everything around it that didn't fit, and deal with the debt, I could rebuild it.

It would take massive restructuring, a new management team, asset sales, severe layoffs, and an entirely new marketing department.

All of these are a lot easier said than done. I believe that, when you go into a situation like this, you either get the pain and suffering accomplished in the first twelve months or you don't do it at all. There are no three-year restructuring plans in my line of work. If a restructuring is done over three years, moods and corporate directions change. The longer it takes, the greater the opportunity for the old corporate culture to corrupt it. Employees and strategies are held hostage; it's a tortuous process. The restructuring must be done in the first twelve months. (See Chapter 11, "Real Jobs, Real Cuts.")

What Scott Paper had lacked was a leader. It had seven different technologies to make paper, some excellent, some lousy. But instead of settling on the best, it continued applying all seven. That was crazy.

Even setting aside all the ancillary businesses, it was still in two different, high capital-intensive paper businesses: coated and tissue. Few companies could afford to do both, and Scott wasn't one of them.

But the biggest sin was that Scott Paper, the biggest manufacturer of tissue in the world, wasn't capitalizing on its reputation and the sales potential of its assorted household brand names.

A similar situation faces every company, every day, not just those teetering on the edge of the volcano. If you're successful and prosperous today, don't take it for granted tomorrow. My specialty has been saving companies on the verge of collapse, but I don't just pull them away from the brink. I give them strength and systems for surviving the long days and nights ahead.

Mine is not just a "turnaround" strategy. It's a smart business approach that will profit any manager or executive as business expands from regional and national to global opportunities. Run a tight, moneymaking ship today, and you can sail the world tomorrow.

CHAPTER 2

SHOCK THERAPY

LESSON: THE PRICE OF LEADERSHIP IS
CRITICISM.

An effective business management strategy is like a workout.
If I work out regularly, I get fit. If I stay with the workouts, I'll
get fitter every year. But if I just work on my arms this year, my
legs next year, I might not live long enough to get fit.

So many companies, for one reason or another, totally lose
their way. Many were great household names at one time. Along
the way, their own people forgot the entrepreneurial spirit that
created them. The managers became custodians. They lost the
ability to lead. They totally acquiesced to being members of the
club. People want to be liked; they don't want to do what's right
if it costs them entry to the clubhouse.

By the time I arrived at Scott, I had turned around seven
corporations in my career, including Lily-Tulip, Diamond
International, Crown-Zellerbach (which a 1983 *Fortune*
magazine survey of executives ranked as having the 195th worst
reputation out of 200 corporations), and, in Australia,
Consolidated Press Holdings and Australian National Industries.
But I had never before started so close to flatline. Scott didn't
need a quick fix, it needed defibrillating.

Bam! I put into place my own form of shock treatment. It's a plan that can work in any kind of business. And it's simple:

1. Get the right management (*see Chapter 3*).
2. Pinch pennies (*see Chapter 4*).
3. Improve the balance sheet by focusing the business (*see Chapter 5*).

Get a real strategy for success (*see Chapter 6*).

•••

I took charge at Scott on April 19, 1994. Not long after, I spelled out the new reality at a meeting for 1,600 headquarters staff in the company's largest cafeteria.

CFO Basil Anderson spoke first, laying out in real numbers the ugly turn in Scott's performance, sales growth, profitability, and capital. He presented all the problems so the staff could see the need for change. I could have done what Basil did, but Scott's very credible and well-respected CFO better communicated the gravity of the situation. We spent a lot of time in making sure the right messages would be given, and he was very effective.

Then I stepped up and told the assembled staff that, in the coming months, I would be cutting thousands of jobs and selling billions of dollars' worth of assets. But, I added, come December 31, the worst would be over, and then we'd get on with building the company.

Scott, a once inspiring corporate giant, was lumbering behind its competition, bloated beyond recognition, grossly overweight and sluggish, I said. To compete effectively once again, it needed to shed fat and think of itself as the entrepreneurial company it once was. And that's exactly what Scott employees wanted to hear.

The speech I gave to the staff that day was just the warm-up for the big event, my first annual meeting as CEO, held at the Radisson Hotel in Essington, near the Philadelphia International Airport, on June 3, 1994.

Once again, Basil Anderson delivered the bad news: 1993 sales were off by 7 percent. Income from operations had fallen by 19 percent. Net income had declined by 30 percent on a normalized basis (i.e. before restructuring charges). Pulping facilities in Chile, Canada, and Spain had contributed heavily to another $20 million of the company's $277 million total losses. Prices and volumes had dropped at S.D. Warren, a boom-or-bust company we owned that manufactured coated paper products.

Then Basil brightened considerably. Since I had been hired, the stock had risen 30 percent to $49 because the market believed in what we were doing. We had Wall Street's vote of confidence in our management and direction. That's when he turned over the floor to me.

I started off with some of my background, describing how I started my career in the industry at one of Scott's chief competitors, Kimberly-Clark. I worked in the paper and pulp mills as a machine tender, a back tender, a third hand, a fourth hand, a fifth hand. I worked in the beater room and I ran a converting winder. My hands-on experience gave me credibility within the industry and with anyone who knew how hard it was to work your way up from the bottom.

I changed gears in my speech soon enough, making it infinitely clear that the business had not been run well of late. "The last four years," I said, "Scott's average annual shareholder returns were down 1.9 percent, while the Standard & Poor's 500 (over the same four years) was up + 10.6 percent and the rest of the paper and forest products industry averaged +9.6 percent. That's dismal."

The shareholders took my no-nonsense approach well. They knew the company was in serious trouble and, if something didn't happen, they were going to lose a lot of money.

Shareholders respect strength, and that's what they got from me. I announced publicly my intention to sell Scott's coated paper manufacturing company, S.D. Warren, and detailed my plan for shearing one-third of the company's workforce by year's end. I told them that, on a percentage basis, our reorganization would probably take out more salaried people than hourly people.

There was no subtlety in my remarks. It was a rousing speech before 300 people, not at all like what typical annual corporate meetings are known for.

I made some key points about what had gone wrong and what was going to be done about it. Then I presented my four-point turnaround program: (1) get the right management; (2) cut back to the lowest costs; (3) improve the balance sheet by selling noncore assets; and (4) above all, have a strategy.

"A business plan is like a laser, not a shotgun," I said. "Our business plan is to build our position in tissue and rebuild our core business. I'm talking about developing a strategic plan that is a road map, a road map to Scott's success, a living document!"

In twenty minutes, it was over, and everyone in the room was on their feet, applauding.

I knew I was playing to an unusual audience for an annual meeting. In addition to the retirees who often compose the bulk of the shareholders in attendance at these get-togethers, we had attracted a large number of curious analysts and business reporters who heard something electric was in the air at Scott Paper. They wanted to meet me, look me in the eye, and get an indication of what was in store.

There was one strongly worded question after my speech. John Brody, a union representative of the United Paper Workers International Union and past-president of Local 448 at our Chester, Pennsylvania, mill, said, "1 haven't heard one word about the worker and where you're coming from as to workers in the plants. Do you believe in 'jointness?' Is this the direction you're going in or do we go backwards to the old traditional way of management versus worker?"

"If jointness means working together for the mutual benefit of Scott's workers and Scott's future," I answered, "then I am for jointness." We continued the jointness process and worked with the unions as Scott was restructured back to its core business.

After the meeting, I was mobbed by shareholders and analysts who congratulated me on what I said and planned to do. Strangely absent from the group of well wishers were many members of the Scott board of directors. I was dumbfounded by their lack of visible support.

Rather than dwell on it, I made an unscheduled appearance at a small luncheon that Basil Anderson and investor relations director Michael D. Masseth had organized for analysts and major shareholders. Present was a representative cross-section from the major Wall Street investment firms that followed the paper industry and Scott. Among them were Linda Lieberman of Bear, Stearns; George Adler of Smith Barney; and Kathy McAuley of Brown Bros. Harriman—three outstanding analysts whom I came to greatly respect.

McAuley quoted my line about focusing "like a laser." She mentioned it in her report, and just about every business publication in America picked up on it.

•••

The bottom line at Scott Paper Company: We cut back 70 percent of upper management and eliminated more than 11,200 total jobs, 35 percent of the Scott payroll. Another 6,000 jobs became somebody else's payroll responsibility as I sold off assets such as S.D. Warren (for $1.6 billion), and a Mobile, Alabama, co-generation power plant (for $350 million). I sold the company's corporate headquarters for $39 million.

When December 31 came around, I was true to my word. The bloodletting ended and 20,000 people had secure jobs once again.

Despite this kept promise, the media in Philadelphia (the City of Brotherly Love) bitterly attacked me and started using a nickname I had been tagged with in England and Australia, "Chainsaw." It became clear that Scott needed a new setting in which its managers could gain a fresh perspective and a new start. I relocated the rest of Scott's management team to Boca Raton, Florida. Instead of a lavish spread of 750,000 square feet, we leased 30,000 square feet and saved $6 million annually. It was a great way to break the back of Scott's plodding, consensus-driven corporate culture.

To me, the real news was the way Scott's market value came roaring back. Stock prices rose and rose, from $38 the day I arrived to $89 a year later (pre-split). The stock continued to rise every month I was there. In December 1995, I received a congratulatory commendation from the board. The stock had increased in total value by $6.5 billion during my 603 days. That's more than $10 million per day!

Almost anyone can shred a corporation down to size. And although I'm known for taking businesses down to their core operations, more importantly, I also built Scott back up. The increase in the value of Scott's stock came about not only because it was leaner but because it had a promising future.

•••

In my first twelve months we marketed 107 new product initiatives across twenty-two countries. Every existing product was repackaged and most were reconceived, reformulated, and/or relaunched. We firmed up the Viva paper towel brand and, for the first time, made its quality consistent across the United States. Cottonelle bath tissue became an upscale, advanced personal hygiene product sold with a variety of value-added enhancements ranging from baking soda to hypoallergenic ingredients.

Scott Consumer created some "new" products by borrowing certain heavy-duty items created by Scott Away-From-Home and introducing them to the home bath and kitchen markets. This was done under the direction of Dick Nicolosi, a veteran of more than twenty years with Procter & Gamble. He had hired fourteen new marketing directors, whose experience included years at P&G, Kimberly-Clark, Colgate-Palmolive, and Coca-Cola.

Dick retained three world-class global advertising agencies to drive our brands in the future: J. Walter Thompson for Scott bath and facial tissue worldwide; McCann-Erickson for ScotTowels and Viva; and Bozell Worldwide for wet wipes and Cottonelle. These three replaced the fourteen disparate agencies that had previously handled our advertising around the world.

In our Away-From-Home division, fifteen new products were introduced in 1994 alone. (More went on the shelves in 1995.) We also responded to long-standing customer requests that we bundle products within our Windows, Scottfold, and WetTask lines of washroom and workstation sanitary and cleaning supplies. (*See Chapter Nine, "Look Under 'M' for Marketing," for the complete story of our marketing strategy at Scott.*)

We engineered a total global strategy and entered new markets—for example, in India, China, and Indonesia. Scott, which already had operations in twenty-one countries and sold product in eighty countries, became the first international tissue company to have a presence in China, thanks to our joint venture,

Scott Paper (Shanghai) Limited, with the Shanghai Paper Company.

We also formed a joint venture agreement with Pudumjee Agro Industries Ltd., India's sole producer of tissue paper. Scott was the first international tissue manufacturer with operations on the Indian subcontinent.

In Brazil, Scott's Away-From-Home products and systems were launched via a marketing and technology agreement with Dixie-Toga, that country's leading distributor of commercial tissue products. The agreement served as a platform for future South American expansion.

And our affiliate in Mexico invested additional resources to better position Scott in the growing Latin and Central American markets. *(See Chapter Six, "Rule 4: Get a Real Strategy," for the complete story of Scott's global strategy.)*

•••

We built a new state-of-the-art manufacturing facility in Yucca, Arizona, and expedited another in Owensboro, Kentucky. In September 1994, Arizona Governor Fife Symington joined me for the groundbreaking ceremony for a new $40 million tissue paper converting plant at Yucca. When completed, the plant would serve our markets in the West and Southwest.

And by November 1994, when we cranked up the first new paper machine at our $240 million state-of-the-art manufacturing facility in Owensboro, its capacity—devoted to Away-From-Home products—had already been sold out and we had earmarked another $80 million for a second unit there.

Owensboro was the prototype for future manufacturing operations. Its advanced design and work concepts promoted low-cost, quality production.

These important investments in marketing and manufacturing were part of an overall strategy to transition Scott from a paper company to a fast-moving packaged-products company. They were key elements in the development and implementation of a new, stronger, and more effective strategy for Scott's core tissue business.

Could anyone believe we would commit $400 million in

capital on new equipment in key markets around the world if we were short-term-oriented? We were planning for the long-term right up until the Scott Paper/Kimberly-Clark merger on December 12, 1995. (See Chapter Sixteen, "Impressing the Analysts.")

Besides looking out for shareholders' future return on investment, I delivered short-term improvements to our owners—and set off a revolution in the corporate world at large. (See Chapter Fourteen, "Boards of Directors, God Forgive Them.") I changed the compensation of Scott's board of directors. Instead of being paid in cash, they received 1,000 shares of stock in the company. They became shareholders, just like the teachers, police officers, and moms and pops they served.

As for myself, I bought $2 million worth of shares of Scott stock at $38 on the day I took over the company and another $2 million worth, at $50, in June 1994. In October 1994, 1 urged my new management team to demonstrate confidence in our restructuring plans by doing the same, even though some had to borrow money to do it. Collectively, they invested $10 million of their own money in Scott Paper shares. Every one of them became multimillionaires as a result.

After twenty months of intense work—and thanks to my own stock purchases, options, and other incentives—I took my leave of Scott $100 million richer than when I arrived.

That amount is astronomical to the average person. Even I have moments when it's hard to imagine. But it was compensation for my performance at Scott. Only my $1 million salary was guaranteed. Of the rest, approximately $80 million was based on the stock that I bought out of pocket and the options I had—an incentive program directly tied to improving Scott's performance. The last $20 million came from a five-year non-compete agreement I signed with Kimberly-Clark, effective upon completion of the merger.

My contract with Scott provided for a salary of $1 million per year for five years. When the Scott merger with Kimberly-Clark was finalized I received the balance of the $5 million guaranteed in the contract. Another $13 million came from the increase in value of the stock I had purchased from my own funds ($2 million worth of shares bought at $38, and $2 million at $50). My contract with

Scott also included options for 750,000 shares (pre-split). Given the huge improvement in Scott's stock (from $38 pre-split to $120 pre-split) the options were worth $55 million. Restricted stock options[1] were worth $5 million based on 100,000 shares I received after the stock split. My non-compete agreement with Kimberly-Clark was worth $20 million, an average of $4 million per year for five years. Finally, I received $2 million for an advisory role with Kimberly-Clark, based on 5,000 shares of stock per year for five years.

People love comparing my $100 million against the 11,200 Scott Paper workers who were laid off on my watch. But the two totals are unrelated. The jobs were eliminated because the company couldn't afford them. The people were unproductive—not as individuals, but within the bloated corporate structure Scott had become. In a smartly managed operation, they would never have been hired in the first place because their jobs didn't make economic sense.

My chore was to make sense of the company, force it to live within its means, and bring payroll back into line with current revenue and future projections.

If I hadn't saved the company, *everyone* would have been out of work, not just a percentage of people.

And my compensation *did not* come on the laid-off workers' backs. It was earned as a fraction of the increased shareholder value—$6.5 billion—that was created while I was chairman and CEO. I was paid on the basis of getting costs in line, selling assets to reduce the debt by $2.5 billion and relaunching Scott's core tissue projects, thereby protecting a 115-year-old franchise and rebuilding the company's goodwill on Wall Street. My $100 million was less than 2 percent of the wealth I created for all Scott shareholders. Did I earn that? Damn right I did. I'm a superstar in my field, much like Michael Jordan in basketball and Bruce Springsteen in rock 'n' roll.

My pay should be compared to superstars in other fields, not to the average CEO. Only a handful of chief executives are

---

[1] See Chapter 12, "The Best Bargain Is an Expensive CEO," for an explanation of the difference between stock options and restricted grants of stock.

worth the big bucks they are paid. Many are grossly overpaid and should be fired and then replaced by CEOs whose pay is strictly performance-based. *(For more on my views on CEO pay, read Chapter Twelve, "The Best Bargain Is an Expensive CEO.")*

Mike Mullaney, a fund manager at Threadneedle Investment Management Company, once commented on my work in a *Palm Beach Post* story: "This man is an animal, but he seems to know how to make share prices go up."

Still, I get criticized a lot. People say, "Dunlap is out of there in a year, he doesn't stay and build the company." Look, if I can create enormous value in a year or two years and I can get done what someone else takes five years to do, hurrah for the company.

But if I did take five years, intellectuals would say, "My, isn't he a deep thinker!" My answer to that? Rubbish. I think most people agree with my results but they're put off because I move so fast. *If!* did the deed over several years, it might be more palatable to critics but it would also be less profitable and more painful.

Yes, I slashed Scott Paper. But *I* did so selectively. I didn't cut into the muscle of the company, I cut the flab. There was just so much of it that few outsiders could tell which was which anymore.

Even the Kimberly-Clark people, during merger negotiations, suspected that I had pared away too much and that the company couldn't operate over the long term. But once they got under the corporation's skin, they arrived at a different point of view. Kimberly-Clark Chairman Wayne Sanders told a reporter from *The Wall Street Journal* that his company would adopt many of Scott's ways.

I have received my share of favorable press, but I still get criticized all the time for my rough, indelicate handling of companies. That's the price of success; I accept it. I didn't hide behind a public relations machine, even when I was reviled and ridiculed over the years. Newspaper and magazine writers and TV commentators have painted me as the worst SOB. ever. Current and prior government officials such as Clinton Labor Secretary Robert Reich and Nixon speechwriter turned presidential candidate Pat Buchanan have also joined the anti-Dunlap, anti-shareholder-value bandwagon. But I accept the heat because I am my own biggest critic. Every day I'll ask myself, "Did I really do a good job?" So long as the answer is yes, somebody else's criticism doesn't bother me much.

The harshest critics call me a bastard and say I have no heart. I'm probably a much nicer guy than most people think, but who's going to hire a nice guy to turn around a failing conglomerate? I'm well aware that my brashness draws antagonism. But don't mistake my commitment to being successful with heartlessness. If you need someone at whom to shoot poison arrows, look for my predecessors at any company I've turned around. They are your villains.

Scott, under the leadership of my predecessor, was in serious trouble. But he still made millions by the time I engineered the merger with Kimberly-Clark because I gave value to the worthless stock options he collected while helming the company toward oblivion. Who criticized *him* for causing the problems?

The media and politicians don't criticize the proper people and don't understand why I do what I do. The amount of money I get paid, which is so often criticized, comes as a result of the free market. My compensation is always tied to the profitability of a company, not to layoffs. Plus, I invest my own money. I could have *lost* money at Scott. The whole thing could have collapsed, costing me $4 million in out-of-pocket cash and my job, and costing 20,000 other people their jobs. The 11,200 layoffs would have looked like a blessing.

The Al Dunlaps of the world would not be hired if top corporate people did their jobs. But because some executives can't make decisions or consistently make the wrong decisions, their incompetence virtually screams out for an Al Dunlap.

When I become "Rambo in Pinstripes" or "Chainsaw Al," who sells assets and fires people, I have empathy for those let go. But what I keep uppermost in my mind is not that I cut away 35 percent, but that I saved 65 percent. I think that's terribly important. If I don't take action—if I back off as most chief executives do, and fire a nominal 10 percent of the workforce— that's nothing. It's a tease. I could do less and avoid the criticism. But then I'll have to go back and slash again and again. That is a fraud imposed on employees.

Criticism is the price of leadership, in government, sports, business, or the arts. People who effect major change will be severely criticized and vilified in the early stages. Everyone will be against them. Human nature's defense mechanism tells the change agents: "Back off." Most do. I don't. When you back off you lose momentum. The window for change closes. Proponents of the status quo win out.

AT&T Chief Executive Officer Robert E. Allen stunned the business world, in January 1996, by announcing plans for 40,000 layoffs as part of the company's split into three operating units. He was severely criticized in the media, and, by mid-March, Allen had knuckled under, reducing the planned cuts by more than 10,000. A significant portion of AT&T's problems could be laid at Allen's doorstep. He attempted to fix them, drew heat, and wrinkled like a cheap suit.

Many observers point to AT&T's $7.48 billion (in stock) purchase of NCR (once known as National Cash Register) in 1991 as an important cause of the recent layoffs. NCR, a leading manufacturer of computers and business machines, was an acquisition the telecommunications giant never meshed with and never should have engaged. Less than five years—and more than $2 billion in losses—later, AT&T acknowledged that the two companies were a lousy fit and announced plans to spin off NCR.

What was so wrong with that deal? For one thing, NCR was making money before AT&T took it over. AT&T's computer business wasn't. It lost $200 million on computers the year it grabbed NCR.

Following the breakup of the old Bell Telephone System monopoly in 1984, AT&T desperately sought a way into the computer business. To reach that end, it charged Robert Allen with the job. As the years went by, computers and telephones—via modems—grew inextricably closer, which should have meant magic for Allen's computer division. Instead, it lost money from the beginning, digging an ever-deeper hole for itself. According to *The Economist, AT&T* lost $2 billion on computers between 1985 and 1990, and laid off 50,000 workers.

Allen, meanwhile, fell upward, miraculously becoming chairman and CEO of AT&T. When he began his run on NCR in

1990, then-NCR chairman Chuck Exley saw AT&T's future and it bled red. He resisted the telecom company's advances.

"We simply will not place in jeopardy the important values we are creating at NCR in order to bail out AT&T's failed strategy," Exley wrote to Allen.

After the takeover, with Exley out of the way, NCR briefly put AT&T's computer business in the black, but the sensation lasted barely a year. By September 1995, when Allen announced record layoffs at AT&T, NCR itself laid off 7,200 employees, reflecting its own $720 million loss. Thanks to AT&T's deep pockets, it had stayed in personal computers long after the market had surged past it.

Look at AT&T from a different angle, as *Fortune* magazine reporter Carol Loomis did. She noted that in 1984, the year of the Bell Telephone breakup, the new AT&T had $12.4 billion in stockholders' equity, ranking it just ahead of General Electric's $11.3 billion.

In the dozen years that followed, GE earned $44.6 billion in profits. Its market value in January 1996 was an incredible $117 *billion.*

Loomis pointed out that AT&T, during the same period, took "more than $23 billion in pretax restructuring charges—not including another $13 billion of special charges for changes in accounting rules... AT&T made bottom-line profits of only $14.5 billion on its shareholders' capital, a dismal performance."

Newsweek told a joke going around AT&T in early 1996: Allen would soon fire everyone but himself, and AT&T would stand for "Allen & Two Temps."

That's the mess Robert Allen helped create and now sustains, the legend that is forever his. The tens of thousands of workers he periodically lays off every few years to make up for mismanagement and lard probably sleep better at night knowing they're at last safe from him. At least when I do a restructuring, I do it once. When it's over, everyone can move on. I develop a real, practical strategy that addresses the business problem at hand, and employees never worry about the same thing happening over and over again.

Executives must tackle the doubters and the scathing criticism head-on and not avoid them. If their actions are right and correct, they will also be eminently defensible. There will, of course, be great suffering. But in the cool of the night, we must know that if we don't do what we're doing, all these people will lose their jobs.

The number of people I have fired and the assets I have unloaded have been over-reported. What goes underreported is the fact that I took limp, lifeless outfits such as Scott Paper, Lily-Tulip, and Cavenham Forest Products and rebuilt them into real businesses. Look at the operating earnings improvement, quarter to quarter over the years, at any of these companies. That is what the people who write about me miss but the people who hire me depend on.

The final, recurring criticism of me is that I have never proved myself as a long-term manager, only as a turnaround specialist. Our emphasis at Scott Paper on marketing, developing a global strategy, and building new manufacturing facilities shows we were planning for a long-term future. But there is some truth to this polemic as well. I crave the challenge of a major restructuring. There's nothing better than being handed a ton of clay and assigned to mold and shape it into a beautiful piece of art.

By contrast, when things are going well, where's the challenge in that? Eventually, I have gotten bored every place I have been.

Once a company becomes business-as-usual, it loses its appeal for me. I honestly feel that the infamous Al Dunlap doesn't exist except when confronted with extraordinarily difficult situations. I am entranced by situations where I can make great change, have a major impact, challenge my abilities, and create enormous wealth for shareholders.

So I make no apologies for making money. I earned every penny of my $100 million by increasing the overall value of Scott Paper by $6.5 billion. And I wouldn't have made a penny unless the company and its shareholders made money. I was paid to perform and I did.

On July 17, 1995, I capped the turnaround of Scott Paper by announcing a stock swap merger with Kimberly-Clark (see Chapter Sixteen, "Impressing the Analysts") that created the second largest consumer products company in the United States.

By the time the companies merged on December 12, I had transformed a sloppy, incorrigible conglomerate worth $2.5

billion in shareholder value into a focused, highly desirable—and profitable—$9 billion corporation. Not bad for less than two years' work.

PART II

FOUR SIMPLE RULES

Chapter 3

RULE 1: GET THE RIGHT MANAGEMENT TEAM

LESSON: MAGNIFY YOUR OWN ABILITIES BY SURROUNDING YOURSELF WITH GREAT PEOPLE.

The term "to Dunlap" has become a verb in the business lexicon. It means someone is focusing on what that person does best and is eliminating everything that is not the best. If you focus on the best, you will have the best *management,* the best *employees,* the best *products,* the best *marketing,* the best *payroll system,* even the best *jani*tor—the best of *everything.* Being the best is the most basic goal a business should have.

Management is the spine around which all the rest takes shape. Leaders and teammates pull together on game day to win and achieve mutual goals. Some captains have come up through the farm system; others are free agents who have signed on with the highest bidder.

For the most part, I don't believe a company can fix itself solely from the inside. Management has too many friends, too many vested interests, too much baggage. If a correction is too painful, the managers won't have the backbone to do it. They must have a catalyst—perhaps a new executive or manager brought in from the outside—someone who can say "No" and who is driven to do what's right for the business no matter what the hurdles, or who gets hurt, or how it shakes up the company's structure.

Criticism causes managers to fail because no one wants to be criticized. Why do leaders fold their tents? They can't take the heat, which comes from both within the company and outside. They don't want to make change because that draws criticism. They want to go along; they want to get along. And if they rose up through the ranks, they know what the culture allows and what it doesn't.

People want to be liked. And when they take difficult positions, they're going to alienate people. They don't want to elevate themselves and become targets. Anyone separated from the herd can be taken down by predators.

In talking with one corporate leader, I laid out what I thought had to be done at his company. He said, "I can't do that because I'm part of the culture."

To me, that sounded like the truth. He was entrenched in what was, not what could be.

Look at Scott: three restructuring plans in four years, but they still didn't get it right until the company brought in its first outside CEO in 115 years! Still, a restructuring is not just people; it's all the other things that go with improving the productive output of the company.

The heart of my approach to leadership, whether in a turnaround or a simple course correction, is a seven-point plan.

1. Develop an Inner Circle

Unlike some people, who have a revolving door for executives and managers, I put together a team *one time*. If I keep changing the team, how will I ever know the players' strengths and weaknesses?

I build teams that work and fight like hell—with each other, with me. We drive each other to plateaus we never before dreamed possible. I hire mature men and women who know how far to push each other and when to say when. They come to the table as individuals and leave it united for the good of the company. I know they're after what's best for shareholders because their own salaries and incentives are directly tied to shareholder returns.

At Scott, there wasn't a single person on my management team who left. Many were people I had worked with previously—people who could work in tandem with me. Two were executives under the previous managements whose broader talents had been untapped or underappreciated. And one I met, by luck, on the tennis court.

Whenever possible, bring in people who have been with you before, men and women who will be responsive to you and not your predecessor. They will be a general reflection of you and, without asking, will do things the way you would—without being carbon copies or "Yes!" men and women. They are used to your style and can hit the ground running. They will not be blown sky-high by instant and startling change.

If you've been promoted from within, don't just bring along friends from the lunchroom. Look for people who challenge you and who have ideas. They will stimulate you and the company.

You want people who have been through change before. And don't be afraid of people who speak up when you go off the deep end! Have faith in their judgment. That's very important.

A business leader needs an inner circle, a management or operating committee. I've always found that *small* works best. At Cavenham Forest Industries, I had a committee of seven, which we called "The Magnificent Seven." They earned it, too, by whipping that company into shape through cost cutting, re-engineering of production, and upgrading of outmoded equipment and practices. When Cavenham was sold to Hanson Industries, the new owners didn't change a single person at the top. The Cavenham operating committee I put in place stayed for the next decade and continued squeezing every possible profit out of that company.

At Scott, I put together a "Magnificent Five,"—Russ Kersh, John Murtagh, Basil Anderson, Dick Nicolosi, and Newt White—who couldn't possibly be more different from me in temperament and style. But I took these people, each very different and with very specific skills, and melded them into another great team. We were helped along in no small part by being strangers in a strange town; relocating Scott to Boca Raton, where I had lived before, albeit briefly, encouraged us to frequently socialize together and discover mutual interests—we all played either tennis or golf or both.

Each member of the operating committee played an equal role in each major decision, even if it was outside his area of expertise. They knew I wouldn't just use them in their discipline, in their expertise; I would apply them across the board, challenging each other.

You read about marketing director Dick Nicolosi in Chapter One. We met on a tennis court, but hiring him because of his serve would have been irresponsible. Instead, I turned to Tom Neff, president of New York-based Spencer Stuart, the executive recruiting company that recommended me to Scott's board of directors. I asked Neff to independently rate Dick's qualifications and ability to do the job. Dick came back with the highest of marks.

The role of a headhunter is not only to find people but also to check references and maintain contact with the client about developing needs. I used Neff's expertise in all of these situations.

Now let me tell you about my other four wizards.

Senior Vice President P. Newton White, one of two executives I kept on from the previous management, was a good hands-on guy, but in the early stages he disagreed vehemently with what I was doing.

Newt ran Scott's Away-From-Home, Worldwide, business, which sells products particular to commercial washrooms and workstations. He had actually been one of the people the board considered as a successor to the CEO and chairman of the board. He had often complained to the board about how difficult it was to get anything done because too many people stood in his way. White thought a lot like me.

Joining the sales force right out of college, Newt had been with Scott for twenty-eight years when I took over the company. He rose up through the ranks in sales and marketing, and ran operations in the United States and Asia for a time before taking over the worldwide Away-From-Home business in 1990 and joining the executive operating committee.

On my first visit to Scott before actually taking the job, Newt was the only guy I was introduced to beside the board members. The commercial Away-From-Home business had a history of good performance, growth, and earnings improvement under Newt. He had survived Scott's cockeyed culture by going his own way and doing his own thing. He had good people working for him and a track record of innovation in the market. That's why the board of directors had recommended so strongly that he should be one of the few executives I keep.

We talked for an hour or so about where the business was going, and he told me about the things that needed changing. Newt was blunt about what he called the company's "pretty horrendous strategy in the consumer business" and how it didn't make much sense to him to sell consumer products without an organized marketing strategy.

He looked me straight in the eye near the end of the conversation and asked me why he should stick around if I was going to clean house.

"It needs to be done," he said. "Maybe I should just leave with the rest of the gang and get on out of here."

At that point, I decided to fill him in on my background, the companies I had turned around, my philosophy of restructuring. He listened patiently, asked a few questions when appropriate, then looked me in the eye again and rephrased the same question.

"That's great, Al," he said. "But why should I stay?"

"Because," I said, "I'm going to make you rich."

I said that I had every intention of turning Scott around and that the people who participated alongside me in that process would be well rewarded.

Newt said he'd stick around a while and see how it went. The next six months were incredibly hard on Newt, a solid operator in a company populated by incompetents, but a man who had never worked anywhere else and never felt the fury of a corporation in turnaround.

We butted heads often during that time. It didn't end until Newt understood that I was going to restructure the company with or without him, but that I preferred to do it with him. And that after I did that, I would once again let him and the other senior executives operate the business.

Chief Financial Officer Basil Anderson, the only other holdover from previous management, joined the company as an internal consultant in 1975. At that time, the company would hire people to work for a year or two in the consulting group, a management science/operations research team that helped Scott's business managers with problem-solving. Consultants then moved on to whatever area of expertise they developed in the group.

The experience served Basil well. He helped senior executives solve particular business problems and was promoted two years later to the newly created position of manager of international finance. That was significant because Scott already had operations (mostly joint ventures) in sixteen countries at the time. But no one at Scott was overseeing all that activity and helping those companies finance themselves. Some were very sophisticated, such as our venture in England, but others accepted terms and conditions that were lousy and paid high rates for everything. Basil restructured many of these operations and helped them develop long-range plans.

In 1983, he became Scott's first director of investor relations. That assignment made him an expert on both the company and the paper industry. On the road constantly, visiting money managers and analysts he gained a tremendous insight into shareholders and how they think.

Despite his vast—and growing—familiarity with the intricacies of the company, and despite being promoted to chief financial officer, Basil was still treated as a junior executive until I arrived in 1994.

Russ Kersh was one of my old Lily-Tulip gang who joined me at Scott. When I tore up Lily-Tulip's fragile structure in the early 1980s, he was the only financial analyst who understood how to reorganize the company's structure, a concept his own supervisors couldn't grasp. He found himself telling them how to do their jobs.

He got my attention because the people between us couldn't stop talking about him. And every time I walked into the CFO's office, Russ was usually there. When we moved Lily-Tulip from Toledo, Ohio, to Augusta, Georgia, I promoted him to corporate treasurer. He handled many of the financial intricacies of taking the company public and later was involved in its sale to Fort Howard Paper Company. Fort Howard offered him a job but he chose to come to Hilton Head, South Carolina, with me instead. We continued working side-by-side over the next six years for Sir James Goldsmith's GOSL Acquisition Corporation.

When I went to Australia in 1991 to take over operations at Consolidated Press Holdings, a media conglomerate, Russ took over Adidas America, the running shoe manufacturer. He spent about eighteen months leading their restructuring effort. When he arrived, Adidas was coming off four consecutive years of annual losses totaling hundreds of millions of dollars. But Russ had learned his lessons with me and put them to use. Just for starters, he fired the company's marketing group (to start fresh) and half its finance group.

Adidas made $6 million in its first year under Russ, after losing $30 million the previous year. And it was profitable again the next year. He told me later that if he hadn't worked with me prior to taking the job, he probably would have listened to more of what the existing Adidas managers said was wrong, rather than saying, "I don't want to hear it." Everybody there tried to tell him the history of how the company got where it was. But Russ told them, "History is George Washington, not Adidas. What are we going to do tomorrow? How are we going to get today's company turned around? I don't care what happened three years ago. I don't care what happened *last* year. I care about where we are going to go tomorrow."

Russ is gregarious and has a good sense of humor, but he is tough as hell. In the many companies where he has worked with me, Russ has been my alter ego. If I am about to take action, particularly one of the toughest decisions, I usually bounce it off Russ first. I trust him without hesitation.

John Murtagh, about whom you'll learn more later, is a very serious and quiet fellow, quite unlike myself. He's been a mitigating force when we work together because he provides executives with an emotional counterbalance for my own bombast and rhetoric. But, like me, he has an unbelievable capacity for hard work and long hours. John was our general counsel at Scott, yet he played an equal role in all the operating decisions.

Russ Kersh and I tend to be very go-go, and once in a while John steps between us and says, "Stop!" Everybody has a role to play; that was his. In a well-conceived, well-oiled organization, there is someone like John.

2. *Compress Very Difficult Objectives in Time, Resources, and Achievement*

Once the right team is in place, I'm ready to really make things happen. I take a yellow legal pad crammed with notes to operating committee meetings. I attack each item with relish, specifying the day when I expect each assignment to be completed. If something is supposed to be done by Thursday, on Tuesday I'll start asking if it is done. I always move the dates up, always move the target up. One of my key management styles is compressing very difficult objectives in time, resources, and achievement and assuming that my managers will meet or exceed expectations. This forces them to always stay sharp. On a 1-to-10 scale, no one working for me is a 6. They're 10s and will produce like 10s.

One-on-one, I'm probably easier to deal with, because in any group a certain amount of posturing takes place. I'll tell managers some things over and over, because people never "get it" the first time. It's the old saw: "You only remember 10 percent of what you hear." I believe if you hear it ten times, you are likely to remember 100 percent of it.

At Scott, whenever we decided to make a move, we'd announce what we were going to do, set a time frame, and paint ourselves into a corner. For example, I announced that our restructuring would be completed in eight months, a goal many thought was not only ambitious but impossible. But working against the calendar brought great discipline to the process. We never left ourselves an "out." We just performed.

3. Develop Fast Opinions about the Competency of the Managers and Staff

When you move as quickly as I do in hiring and firing, you develop fast opinions about the competency of your managers and staff. I don't believe I ever thought someone was good and my managers disagreed. And I always test people. One of my techniques is to ask the same question on different days in different ways, looking for conviction. I'm also, indirectly, asking: "Do you really know what you are talking about?"

Early on, I tested Basil Anderson by assigning him the task of reforming Scott's reporting process. His job was to eliminate reports that made no sense and nobody read anyway, as well as to cut back on the number of people compiling and receiving reports. He was brutally effective in cleaning up a paperwork nightmare.

By contrast, my early attempts at straightening out human resources were fruitless. I'd hand them an assignment and they were constantly studying it—even if the idea was to cut back on studies. The logjam didn't disappear until I put John Nee in charge. He cut to the core of a task and always got it done.

I cannot keep the people who created the debacle I'm expected to fix. That is a mistake made by timid executives. Existing managers are not all of a sudden going to change! They are *afraid* of change! They'll insist they were doing the right things all along, right up to the front door of bankruptcy court. That's what got them in trouble to begin with. Flush them out of the system.

4. Remember That Business Is Simple: Don't Overintellectualize It

Here's a maxim I'll repeat until the day I die, and some people still won't get it: Business is simple. It is not complicated. Like the football basics of blocking and tackling, there are a few simple things that you have to do.

In 1995, 1 spoke to students at Stetson University in DeLand, Florida. During my talk, a student stood up and said, "Mr. Dunlap, how could you be so successful doing such simple things?" I said, "It *is* simple. The people trying to make it seem complicated—to them it may seem complicated; therefore, obviously they don't get it. To me, it's unbelievably simple."

Here's what you need to do:

1.   Set major goals that make a difference, goals that are attainable.

2.   Don't let people stray from these goals. Hold them accountable with great tenacity.

3.   Focus, *focus, focus* on your handful of goals. If you set too many goals, you will fail. Your intentions will become diffuse.

4.   What complicates business? For one thing, managers

and employees do. Rather than solve problems, they put their energy into all the reasons why the company *can't* do something, Then they hire outside consultants who conduct studies. Then, recommendations in hand, they pass the problem on to a committee. By the end—if there is one—it's so complicated that the company misses its opportunity.

5. I remember reading through the minutes of past Scott board meetings. The directors were always studying something. And rather than reach a conclusion or take a stand on something, they'd hand it off to another subcommittee for further examination. It was a defense mechanism, not a decision-making process.

6. I believe in small executive staffs. When a company has a small staff, everyone is part of a team. They all work together and are more accountable. Large staffs aren't as attentive and they're always pawning responsibility off to somebody else. Small staffs are much greater contributors and they must stay on top of projects.

7. The two major business heads at Scott—Consumer's Dick Nicolosi and Away-From-Home's Newt White—were part of the small staff with which I consulted on most major decisions. So were general counsel John Murtagh, CEO Basil Anderson, and Russ Kersh, who specialized in strategic objectives and overall operations. I coordinated the group. Everybody knew everybody else's expertise well enough to keep fully up on all decisions. In other places, I've seen executive staffs so large that *they* needed staff. Discussions in those meetings go on and on and nothing gets done. The nitty-gritty of their business is busy work.

When a staff is too large, everybody has to wear safety glasses so they don't get poked in the eyes because everybody is poking fingers at each other.

6. Never Rely on Large Meetings for Important Decisions

Don't make decisions in rooms full of people. It's horribly inefficient. The result of the meeting is usually, "Let's have another meeting." By contrast, in every company where I have had a very small staff, we could always make major, tough decisions with just a couple of people sitting around a table.

Put twelve or more people in a room—nothing happens. They all think they must look smart, and therefore they play at one-upping their counterparts, looking clever, playing "Got ya!" I demand a cohesive approach. Here is the problem, how will we—all of us—fix it?

When I was chairman of the board and chief executive officer of Lily-Tulip, one of the companies we thought would buy us was Scott Paper Company. It was a perfect fit, a natural product extension that would augment Scott's "Away-From-Home" business.

We dealt with Scott for months and months *and months*. We saw total indecision. Scott wasted unbelievable sums of money studying the deal. They brought more people to our headquarters than we had working there. I said to myself, "These people are paralyzed. They can't make a decision."

They ultimately did not do the deal. They couldn't.

It was a small group that concluded Scott should either acquire Kimberly-Clark or merge with it. The decision to sell or keep one of Scott's important businesses—wet wipes—was made by Nicolosi, Kersh, and me.

When I was at American Can, large staffs and large meetings were routine. This pattern no doubt helped push the company into unrelated, unwise ventures in the record, fashion, and reclamation industries. Most of those ventures didn't fit with the plastics and canning giant. There was a group dynamic—everybody wanted to present ideas, guessing what the boss wanted—but nobody wanted to stand out by opposing a dumb idea.

By contrast, when six people in a room have been brought up to speed by their staff, they come to a meeting looking for ways to get the job done and not waste time. They're not there to hear the sound of their own voice resonate in an auditorium.

7. Create Opportunities to Develop Your People

When the slashing and burning are over, you've got a business that is sized right and creates enormous new possibilities for people. They've got more authority than they have ever had before. There's tremendous pressure, but the rewards are better. We offered stock options far deeper into management than anyone had before. My people received stock options and stock possibilities that they never dreamed of. Thanks to the stock's dramatic appreciation, we created sixty-two millionaires at Scott! The people who had a hard time with my handling of human resource issues related to restructuring will look back in three years and tell their friends, "Gee, that was a pretty damn exciting thing, and by the way, I made a lot more money than I ever thought I would." Some things need a little time and distance.

In every company, and I don't care how bad the company is, there are some good people buried by layers of corporate politics and bureaucracy. Identify them, remove the shackles of bureaucracy and let them flourish. The bad people are those who say everything has been tried, or they can't do something, or they did it all before, or they can't implement something. They spend hours arguing instead of making something work. I want the people who can show me things that *can* be done.

As may be obvious by now, I expect people to do a lot. In the years I ran Sir James Goldsmith's U.S. holding company, GOSL Acquisition Corporation, Russ Kersh, general counsel Vic Stronski, Phil Lader, three secretaries, and I, working from a small, 3,000-square-foot office in Hilton Head, South Carolina, oversaw an operation that controlled 4.5 million acres of land across the country, and had assets approaching $3 billion.

I believe in sharing secretaries. At Scott, Kersh, Murtagh, and I shared two, Marguerite Hamilton and Karen Jerome. As a result, they became much more than secretaries. They were extensions of us, setting meetings, dealing with the media, being up-to-the-minute in business decisions, and following the ups and downs of our stock. They knew so much about what was going on, they knew what was urgent and what could wait. They could even determine and suggest, among the operating team, who should be in a particular meeting. They got a marvelous business education and could probably run a corporation better than many sitting CEOs.

Business books and the "experts" who write them are always

promoting some fad. Once it was conglomerates. A favorite today is consensus management. Tomorrow it will be something else. But consensus management doesn't work; it's a disaster that pushes its smiling, happy practitioners to less than the best solutions for their companies. To placate everybody, consensus managers sacrifice what's important. On the other hand, strong managers willing to risk failure and criticism will make very different decisions. Better decisions. And their companies get their total commitment to carrying through.

If you operate by consensus, you're not making hard decisions. Instead, you're looking for something easier, something less. Scott's old eleven-member executive committee always worked by consensus, and their record was dismal!

However your management is organized, the operative word remains: *manage*. Take responsibility, make decisions, take risks! No matter how you carve it up, that's what management is all about. Anything less is just seat warming.

Chapter 4

RULE 2: PINCH PENNIES

LESSON: COST IS ALWAYS YOUR ENEMY.

Cost is always your enemy. You must attack it. Whether your company is in trouble or you're just searching for ways to increase profitability, cost should be No. 1 on your list of enemies. Cost will kill you even if you come out with better products. If your cost to make something is your competitor's price for selling it, you lose. You can't stay in business. You must attack cost in every way, shape, and form.

Sir James Goldsmith acquired an industrial parts supplier as part of his acquisition of Crown-Zellerbach. In 1985, the year before he took it over, the company lost $19 million on sales of $56 million. Over three years, it had lost an astounding $50 million. Closing it down would have cost another $25 million; Sir James asked me to take a crack at making it run in the black.

The first thing I noticed about the industrial parts division was that it had the infrastructure of a billion-dollar company. It's a common mistake: Instead of staffing according to levels appropriate with today's business, managers over-hire based on their potential in the future. That wastes money and narrows profit margins. At this particular company, every time sales increased, the existing infrastructure was expanded, which constantly added more cost. Out of every sales dollar, the gross cost of buying goods was 75 cents, on top of which they spent 60 cents on sales, marketing, and administrative costs. Add it up: The company spent $1.35 for every $1.00 sale, a net loss of 35 cents on every dollar. It made no sense.

In the very first meeting I sat in on at the industrial parts division, the president said, "We don't have too much cost. What we need is more sales. To keep growing! Growth, growth, growth!"

Finally, I cut in on him.

"This is ridiculous," I said. "I don't want to hear you use the word 'growth' any more unless you use it in conjunction with the word 'profitable,' as in *profitable* growth.' Until you've contained your costs, even if you grow, what's it matter? Your margins aren't improving, you're not going to produce any more profit. In fact, the more you *grow*, the more you're *losing*."

The division head left the company. We found that with him out of the way, cutting $10 million in costs was much easier. How? I reduced the number of distribution centers from twenty-two to four. Employment—mainly office staff and jobs related to the closing of eighteen distribution centers—was cut by one-third, but sales were not affected. Margins improved, and sales actually increased by one-third.

Then I tackled inventory. The company stocked 11,000 items, 90 percent of which rarely sold. That frequently made our inventory obsolete. Worse, each of our original twenty-two distribution centers bought and sold what it wanted. I centralized purchasing, dropped 9,000 products, and wrote off $7 million in inventory.

By 1987, annual losses dropped from $10.6 million to zero.

At Scott, we had a 71 percent staff reduction at headquarters, a 50 percent reduction in managers, and a 20 percent reduction in the workforce. We sold our headquarters for $39 million and saved $6 million a year in costs. We cut out $30 million in consultants' fees and $2.9 million on compensation experts. Also eliminated were $3 million in association fees and newspaper and magazine subscriptions. We cut out charitable donations entirely, saving almost $5 million.

You have to get to a good cost position and get there quickly. Then you must find a way to keep that good cost position through regular budget reviews, cost control analyses, and frequent rebidding of materials, supplies, and services.

In cutting costs, success will sometimes be measured as much in how you do it as in what you do. For example: Never cut an hourly worker before you deal with the headquarters staff.

If you cut costs at the expense of Joe and Judy Paycheck, they will rebel. But they'll know you mean real business if you slice the real fat first: Get rid of nonproductive senior executives and middle managers, headquarters, airplanes, and so on. That sends a clear message that you are serious. Deal with unions and workers last. They want the company to succeed as much as or more than management does. In my experience, they'll be more supportive of cutbacks if it means the general health of the company will be demonstrably improved.

•••

I'm terrific at beating up suppliers and negotiating more favorable contracts. One time, I thought Lily-Tulip's paper suppliers were charging us too much. I called one of our primary vendors with a challenge.

"I am going to consolidate all of our paper suppliers to one or two vendors," I said. "You could get this big contract and here is what I am willing to pay for it."

The guy I selected turned me down flat.

"No way," he said. "I'm not shipping product to you at that price. Forget it."

The guy hung up.

I went into Russ Kersh's office and said, "Boy, do I have a problem—we have no paper supplier."

At the time, we had about a two-week supply of paper on hand. And a company can't just switch suppliers overnight. Suddenly I was facing a crisis of my own invention. Years later, I don't mind telling you: I was sweating bullets that day. With existing contracts nearing their expiration dates, every day would mean another game of brinkmanship. I enjoyed it, but it made my senior executives' stomachs churn. If the suppliers told us to go stuff it, we had nowhere to go for paper.

I rationalized that, in a reasonable world, the other side would not knowingly shut us down. And we always assumed they didn't really want to lose our business.

Our offer, in return for price concessions, was an increased share of our business. If the supplier wanted volume, it was on the table.

Late that afternoon, he called me back.

"I'll accept your offer," he said.

He figured out that Lily-Tulip was too big a contract to walk away from. A golden opportunity had been tossed in his lap. It would double or triple his business but he'd get less than his normal margin. It was agonizing for us both, but the right thing to do.

That phone call literally saved us a ton of money and became the most crucial cost savings that we accomplished at Lily-Tulip. We leveraged our position by throwing out a myriad of suppliers, cutting down to three vendors from about eight. Production lines were consolidated, and we gained price concessions from the guys with whom we decided to continue doing business.

For at least a few days, my guys thought I walked on water. And as a result of that incident, I believed we could renegotiate with anybody.

Most people just go through the motions in purchasing. They buy everything at list and have too many suppliers. Minimize the number of suppliers for any commodity and drive your organization to obtain the most advantageous prices using a competitive bidding process. When you have ten suppliers for every item and you're paying list—full price, in other words— you're not doing the job. Make them competitive. That will make you better.

Scott's top purchasing agent wanted to introduce me to Scott's suppliers at a big meeting she had planned. "Who's paying for it?" I asked innocently.

"We are," she said.

"Do we purchase advantageously?"

"I think so," she said.

"Wait a minute. We pay for a meeting to bring these people here, feed them and you *think* we're buying advantageously? And you want me to entertain them? Nonsense."

I couldn't believe the person in charge of saving the company money was so out of touch. A smart CEO wants purchasing executives who know the company can improve profits more quickly by purchasing well than by improving production or significantly increasing sales at the same margin. I brought in a new head of purchasing.

I have guided every one of my purchasing departments through the following principles, which saved Scott $100 million. This is the easiest money you will ever make, like taking candy from a baby:

• Leverage volume as much as possible.

• Narrow suppliers to a handful.

• Encourage multiple vendors to bid on requirements.

• Negotiate hard contracts.

• Practice brinkmanship. Let vendors know that they don't have an eternal lock on your business.

• Significantly challenge the procurement organization to take cost out and support them in doing so.

• Ask vendors to help reduce costs by utilizing their own expertise and resources.

Everything we did fit a "common denominator" strategy: What is the minimum amount of change we had to make to everything, to reach the same common specifications?

Take something as seemingly benign as the board test weight of carton material. We used many different weights of cardboard across the company. Some units paid lavishly for corrugated containers that were strong enough to stand on. In some instances, marketing personnel had not reviewed competitive requirements in a number of years. In others, manufacturing processes needed to be selectively improved in order to run lighter weight standard materials. With the various functional areas working with

44

purchasing, we were able to produce better, more cost-effective products.

In Europe, we had eleven suppliers of poly (the film that wraps packages) for the eleven different countries where we had manufacturing. Each international Scott unit had its own specs and its own supplier. Each had its own justification why its spec was better than everybody else's. The units were competing more against each other than against the competition. They wanted to look good among their in-house peers and didn't care so much about beating competitors such as James River or Procter & Gamble.

We consolidated: one supplier for all of Europe—with one spec.

Solving these problems means religiously asking: Why do I have to do this? Or, Why do I have that? If I don't have to do it, or if I don't need it, then I'm going to get rid of it!

It's equally important to define the best practices in your industry and benchmark them for your business. There were fifty-two papermaking machines in the Scott manufacturing system. Five of those machines, the top 10 percent, clearly performed better than the next 90 percent. So we took the best practices, in terms of chemical uses and online reliability, and applied them at every plant.

And one more thing to think about: Don't let the people who buy raw materials and supplies for you constantly lunch and fraternize with suppliers. They may feel like they work for the suppliers.

When purchasing people get so close to vendors that they choose the vendor's side in an internal debate, something is wrong. Employees should never become too comfortable with suppliers.

How do you know if your people are too comfortable? The surest way is to look at the supplier base. When was the last time the company made a change in its purchase of a major commodity? There may be good reasons for not making a change, but when was the last time an item went out for competitive bidding? With purchasing people who aren't aggressive, you often find the company has been riding along for years with the same vendor and nothing has changed.

And, crossing the street, what have you done to encourage the vendor?

What we found at Scott was a hesitancy to maintain leverage and drive real hard bargains. There were some preconceived notions that our procurement agents couldn't take risks that might shut down operations for any period of time. The previous management never gave these employees enough support so they would feel comfortable taking a risk.

I can remember being at dinner one night with Jack Dailey, our vice president of logistics, procurement, and distribution, and a vendor's reps. We weren't getting anywhere with these people. When they went to the salad table, Dailey leaned over and told me a few more details about the proposed deal. What he told me about their reticence to budge upset me. When they came back, salad plates piled high, I proceeded to tear them apart. Dailey couldn't believe my anger. But I backed up his authority to walk away from the bargaining table in no uncertain terms. They knew now that we spoke with one voice. If Dailey told them, "This is the deal, take it or leave it," they shouldn't expect to sweet talk me later. There were no end-run plays around my execs.

Procurement has to do with buying and negotiating for products, supplies, and services across the corporation as well as contract issue resolution. Procurement should be a headquarters responsibility to assure the best price against the greatest volume.

Replenishment, on the other hand, has to do with ordering against the contracts that procurement has already set in place. You could take an army of corporate procurement people and assign them to making sure trucks arrive on time and that you aren't running out of product—but why bother? We sent that responsibility back to our local plant operations. If they needed product, they could order it and follow through on delivery.

In many companies, purchasing is seen as an unimportant staff function. But you can make more money buying right than you can possibly make selling right. How much product do you have to sell, at what margin, to match a savings on the purchase of a major item you buy?

If a company generally pays too much for things, that is rather easy to fix. Everything that costs money is negotiable: travel arrangements, audit, all the purchasing, all the moving people, the airline fees, people who run your pension.

At Scott, as at Lily-Tulip several years earlier, we looked at leveraging volume to consolidate suppliers. One of my goals was to drive the organization together toward a common goal, and the way we spent money was every bit as important as the way we earned it. That meant outsourcing, cutting incidentals, consolidating, and simplifying specifications, which makes life easier for the vendors.

It's not necessarily easy for any of the functional areas of a company, such as marketing or manufacturing, to change designs, but I drove the entire Scott organization to support cost cutting in this way.

Within Scott, one of the major areas of consolidation was specialty chemical suppliers. Specialty chemicals go into the manufacturing of paper and, on a worldwide basis, Scott probably used $18 million worth of these chemicals annually. They are consumed by paper mills and pulp-making operations and were purchased by Scott in the past on a very localized basis. Vendors showed up with coffee and doughnuts, established allegiances, and all of a sudden nothing in the plants would run except with a certain vendor's product.

We consolidated specialty chemical procurement on a worldwide basis, signing on with a single vendor we thought had international potential, even though the company was not a global entity at the time. Naturally, there were others who were already performing on the world stage, but we chose the vendor we thought we could develop and bring along, netting ourselves a lower price than if we had gone with one that was established.

To reach this decision, we put together a team of manufacturing, engineering, and technical people whose assignment was to evaluate the viability of vendor products and make sure potential new or replacement products were quickly scheduled for mill trials and were given a fair opportunity to work.

We had as many as 200 specialty chemical suppliers worldwide, and we used this process to narrow them down to just three. Then we gave one of them, Calgon, an 80 percent position and retained the other two in lesser roles.

Calgon was the newest supplier on the scene, and our choice surprised everyone. Calgon itself was surprised because of the magnitude of the offer and the fact that they got it. They were very aggressive in their pricing; it will probably take them two years to recover their costs in the deal. But it was worth it because the deal catapulted them to worldwide significance in the paper industry.

When we began the process, we held out the possibility of a single supplier consolidating 80 percent of our business. That was the carrot in all of our negotiations. Some companies were not enthralled with the price we demanded, not to mention our expectation of quality and service. Calgon had a very strong presence in the United States and none in Europe, but it wanted to grow there. The company didn't know at first whether we were serious about importing so much volume, but we made it clear that Scott was not afraid to put most of its eggs in one basket.

(You don't do that without being comfortable that the supplier can hold up its end of the bargain. We always had a couple of backup suppliers that we would have gone to.)

The smart procurement executive looks for not only what the company needs but what the vendor needs in a deal. Any time you can find a match between vendor and customer, sparks will fly. Scott was a very large and visible papermaking company. Calgon wanted to demonstrate to the world and the marketplace that it could and would be a very viable supplier. In bidding on our business, it had an opportunity to become just that. Now, Calgon has volume that allows the company to expand its technical and sales expertise into Europe.

Of our three vendor finalists, Hercules was the most firmly entrenched because we didn't have a good alternative supplier for at least a few of the chemicals they make. Still, our negotiator had the authority to press as hard as she could to make our best deal. She also had the authority to tell any company—including Hercules—that it was not a player. During this whole process, one company actually had the temerity to propose a price increase. We said no, even though we didn't have a viable short-term alternative supplier for that product. Naturally, we didn't tell that to the bidders.

We bluffed our way through the crisis by telling them that we were changing processes and doing other things. We made it appear as if we could take or leave their product—even though we couldn't. Negotiations are negotiations; there is always a certain amount of

BS on the table.

Sometimes, a bluff gets called.

We had a separate negotiation with a major supplier of folding cartons. The fiber market was loosening and we had gone out looking for price concessions. Our existing supplier did not want to recognize the decrease in its own costs as something that could be passed along.

The reality, we learned later, was that the negotiation had an extenuating circumstance: the supplier's agreement with Kimberly-Clark.

We knew the company was a Kimberly-Clark supplier and suggested that this might be the problem, but the supplier still refused to lower the price. We went to a brinkmanship negotiation process and said we were about to change suppliers. Meanwhile, we were scrambling to find an alternative supplier. We finally found one and moved our business, at which point our original supplier explained its deal with Kimberly-Clark. Kimberly-Clark was a bigger purchaser of the product than we were, and the supplier was afraid of repercussions after the merger if Kimberly-Clark learned it was paying more than Scott.

Fortunately, the new supplier worked out.

•••

I empowered Scott's procurement organization to help make change. If procurement could get a lower cost for something, the functional areas, such as manufacturing, had to prove why it wouldn't work, rather than to just turn it down, deny it and let it go.

I encouraged and allowed procurement to take risks but demanded it be held accountable.

One of the biggest differences between our vendor selection process and that of other companies was speed. We made our decisions, ran the mill trials, and instituted changes in processes in half the time it would have taken the previous management.

How?

Because of the demands we put on our people. I drove everybody toward making things happen as a positive action, not a negative one. The message was: Change is a good thing. After a while, the entire organization became enthusiastic about what it was doing toward change.

Overpriced vendors were not necessarily the only casualties in this process. People who didn't go along with at least trying to make things change lost their jobs. Complacency was not tolerated. People who have not been exposed to change often don't think they can do it, so they have to be encouraged and prodded—in certain cases, kicked—to move ahead.

Even when Scott made dramatic changes in vendors, we were still cautious not to intentionally burn bridges. We obviously upset people, but if they knew why they were losing our business—because of cost factors, primarily—then they had to accept that. If they couldn't, we didn't want to do business with them anymore, anyway.

We also negotiated consignment inventories. This meant our vendors owned the inventories, and accountability was passed on to them. Not only were they responsible for supplying a product at a certain price, they were also responsible and accountable for making sure the product was where we needed it, when we needed it.

Since the inventory in our locations now belonged to them and they were paying for it, they were not out to push any more inventory on us than we needed. By the same token, they made sure we didn't run out.

•••

You can outsource just about anything today.

As a matter of policy, I directed Scott management to outsource as many functions as possible. This directive covered everything from human resources to corporate security officers. Outsourcing allows you to be more focused on a few things and not consumed by things that really don't have very much to do with whether the business succeeds.

For instance, everybody in a company needs a paycheck with the proper payroll and other deductions accounted for. Why do you need to do that in-house? What value does that add to your company when somebody else can do it better and for less, actually *saving* you money? Even if you have the best damn payroll system in the world, it does not give you a competitive advantage in the marketplace. Scott would not have sold one more roll of toilet paper. You should only do, in-house, what gives you a competitive advantage.

Some people might consider outsourcing and worry about the security of their corporate secrets. For us, that was dealt with and assured in a sophisticated legal process. Were we still at some risk? Perhaps, but no more or less than if we had a bad apple or spy on our own payroll. The size and scope of the vendor's operations are such that security is not likely to be an issue. You must be willing to bypass a certain amount of inherent corporate paranoia to outsource.

An awful lot of Scott's traditional human resources work was out-sourced under the direction of John Nee, vice president of human resources worldwide. Nee replaced hundreds of staff positions by contracting out all of the administrative and record-keeping work, benefits management, and international assignee tax work. He also outsourced domestic employee relocation.

Personnel or human resources groups are a crutch between management and the workforce. Woe unto the consultant not wise enough to realize that. A good manager will keep his or her people happy. The minute management installs a human resources manager, a crutch is erected for both sides. A human resources director, to justify his or her existence, must create problems, which means ever-larger staffs.

Scott had a wonderful woman heading that department when I arrived, but her staff was overinflated by about 60 people. Why did I need that many human resource staffers at corporate headquarters? There was no good answer. They existed strictly to establish policy, coordinate benefit issues, and set up compensation plans. Scott needed human resource people on-site in its mills and plants, because of the unions, but even there we only needed one or two credible people per installation. We kept five or six of them at corporate headquarters, outsourced transaction-oriented processes, and released the rest.

The rest of the company's human resource needs were easily

and efficiently outsourced to companies that specialize in this field.

Scott saved $2.5 million annually by sending our management information systems (MIS) work to Computer Sciences Corporation, which was selected over two other companies. It was a specialist in the field and took over our operations and software maintenance. Computer Sciences also had an opportunity to bid on any new development projects. In the United States alone, the firm replaced 150 MIS workers. All but two of those positions were eliminated. On the other hand, many of our people joined the outsourcing firm. We contracted with companies that supplied 100 percent of our needs on a worldwide basis.

That was drastic by most corporate standards, but I decided MIS wasn't a core competency or one that was so well performed within our own organization that we couldn't outsource it with professionals who could do a better job.

An awful lot of work that corporations do, such as pension administration, doesn't add value in the making or the selling of a product or service. Pension administration doesn't help you make a better product or improve customer relations. And if you do it badly, morale will be negatively impacted. Hire an outside specialist firm to do it and then just manage the contract. What work is generic to all businesses and what work is really specific to your company? Take those two concepts and you can get to the root of work that corporations should not be doing.

Scott also outsourced truck scheduling and load consolidation of customer and transfer shipments. The vendors' personnel were located at our sites and interacted on a daily operating basis with our manufacturing and warehouse personnel. They had access to our customer order information so they could schedule shipments cost-effectively, taking into consideration customer requirements. We negotiated a contract that, had Scott continued independently (*i.e.*, not merged with Kimberly-Clark), would have saved $16 million a year against the $120 million we annually spent on logistics.

It was a gutsy move—if the outsourcing went wrong, we'd no longer have the staff or capability to take it back in-house.

Most companies would study this sort of thing forever, getting caught up in analysis paralysis. We got what we thought was enough information and made the commitment.

Russ Kersh, John Murtagh, and I discussed all the possible implications of our various outsourcing programs. We assessed the risks and the cost differential and agreed that they were more than acceptable.

I said to Russ, "What if it goes wrong?"

"You'll have a serious problem," he said.

After listening to the pros and cons, I said, "Do it."

Bidding wars broke out over much of our work because the service providers saw an opportunity to make Scott Paper an example of how outsourcing could work for other corporations. This saved us even more money.

We attracted good prices, and the transfer of the work was extremely smooth. We never thought twice about our relationship with a single contractor. Outsourcing was more efficient and made all the sense in the world.

Best yet, several vendors hired our own experienced people to manage these same functions.

Outsourcing all these functions—particularly in the midst of a restructuring—isn't easy. It's tough to understand how to do it if you haven't been through it before. We made the outsourcing process a competitive one by getting to know the top players as well as we possibly could. The learning curve was not insubstantial; the first time a corporation thinks about this stuff it usually doesn't know much about it. And an enormous amount of research, discovery, and negotiating must go on with potential providers, to understand their capabilities, the quality of their work, and their charges.

The second reason it's tough is that culturally, the company will be breaking ties with people who had been depended on to administer and provide certain services that now will be in the hands of strangers and outsiders. Confidences may have to be rebuilt, but the workforce must understand that it can be done.

Any consideration of outsourcing must deal with temps. In the past, Scott used temporary employees as a way of controlling head counts. They weren't counted among full-time staff, so temps gave the illusion of job reductions. My belief is that either there's a job that needs doing—which necessitates a full-time staffer—or there isn't. We didn't need temps, and hiring them was a real expense. Their pay comes from the same place as everybody else's: the shareholders' wallets.

The employment relationship is one of the most important relationships people have in their lives. A corporation shouldn't just hire because it has a temporary need or when it is unsure of its needs.

•••

My team followed "The Rule of 55": 50 percent of a company's products typically produce only 5 percent of its revenues and profits. In addition, 50 percent of a company's suppliers provide only 5 percent of the services and products that the company buys. Therefore, almost half of the business, whether it be products or services, represents less than 5 percent of the company's profitability. How many people would not be needed, and how much cost could be realized by eliminating those items?

Eliminate from the company the excess baggage that is not producing profits and adding value. That means brands, suppliers, inventories, working capital—all the things in business that need to be shed so you can focus on things that make money.

Scott, for example, reduced its domestic warehouses from 70 to fewer than 10. We reduced the number of products in our business by more than 500. We looked at all of our plant operations, found the ones that were cost ineffective, old, and obsolete, and got rid of them, either by taking write-offs or selling them. We looked at our plant sites for noncompetitive operations. We looked at our material flow for production bottlenecks. If we couldn't conquer a technology, we unloaded it.

•••

What never ceases to amaze me is how some executives still get away with spending shareholder money on themselves as if they were kings and queens and the business was their royal domain.

The latest poster child for corporate excess must be Paul Kahn, recently deposed chairman of Ideon Group, a Jacksonville, Florida-based credit card registration company. Kahn had previously introduced AT&T's Universal credit card, for which President George Bush presented him the Malcolm Baldrige National Quality Award in 1992.

Kahn, as *New York Times* reporter Kurt Eichenwald disclosed in March 1996, had a propensity for indulging himself and his friends at Ideon's expense. According to Eichenwald, Kahn's behavior included handing out six-figure consulting contracts to friends, hiring a convicted felon as a financial adviser, and putting his inexperienced brother-in-law in charge of a new division. Kahn also paid out $13 million to sixty-eight different consultants in just the first nine months of 1995.

When he was hired, Kahn had told the Ideon board of directors that he would move from Jacksonville to Cheyenne, Wyoming, where the company's corporate headquarters had just relocated at a cost of $17.5 million. It had previously been based in Fort Lauderdale.

Instead, Kahn insisted that the company move—again. He brought it back to Florida.

He bought a corporate jet and spent $1 million to refurbish it, stocking it with Waterford crystal, sterling, Lenox china, and $10,000 worth of handmade place mats.

Kahn had not one but *three* secretaries. He hired a newspaper reporter to write a book about the company. He had a travel department of forty-three people and a dozen more devoted to winning the Malcolm Baldrige Award for Ideon.

Why didn't his board of directors rein in Mr. Kahn sooner? After all, they were well paid to oversee the company's business: $50,000 in annual compensation plus options to purchase 15,000 shares of stock. And three of the Jacksonville-based directors, nominated for the board by Kahn, received funding from Ideon for their own pet projects.

"This shows how American business really works. And it's outrageous," John Westergaard, president of Westergaard

Financial services, told the *Times.*

Confronted by the newspaper with evidence of his excess, Kahn—who had already been fired by Ideon after nearly spending it out of business—acknowledged he was swimming against the tide.

"I don't think I can function in today's corporate environment," he said. "There's too much emphasis on shareholder value."

Too bad it took a newspaper exposé for him to figure that out!

Some businesspeople mistakenly think of corporate indulgence as just country club memberships and flying first-class. I have found perks that dig much deeper and more insidiously into the corporate treasury. When we looked for areas to cut at Scott, we found a hunting lodge and a Paris apartment on the books. I sold them, along with a corporate jet. And before we moved the corporate headquarters from Philadelphia, I closed the company's luxurious executive cafeteria, the one with linen napkins, fine china, and crystal drinking glasses.

Those were all things Scott executives took for granted. Here are some more perks that can go at almost any company:

• Company cars, except for salespeople because transportation is part of their jobs. I've seen companies assign cars to executives who have no need other than getting back and forth to work. They can buy their own; that's why we pay them salary. But a car is a salesperson's tool.

• Subscriptions. If you want to read general magazines, you buy them. If your primary responsibility is finance, why do you expect the company to buy you an office subscription to *Sports Illustrated?* If you need a trade journal and it can be shared with others, fine. But many people order subscriptions for their offices as status symbols. They have nothing to do with business and they cost money. That goes for all publications and seminars. Why do we pay money to send people to classes that have nothing to do with their jobs?

• Trade associations. They don't get membership money out of my companies. Not only will that be controversial within a company, it will also be controversial within an industry.

Scott spent $2.9 million on trade associations such as the Business Roundtable. Most of the people in those groups are round-shouldered because they're all busy patting each other on the back. What does any of this do to improve the bottom line?

• Charitable donations. They should also be history, as is discussed in Chapter Thirteen, "Whose Company Is It, Anyhow?" I don't want to hear any crying about an executive's cash pledge, on behalf of the company, to some charitable or community organization.

Several months after the turnaround at Scott, a woman stood up to ask a question at an employee meeting.

"Now that the company is improving, can we restart charitable donations?" she asked.

"That is a very personal choice," 1 said. "If you want to give on your own, that is your business and I encourage you to do it. But this company is here to make a buck. The stockholders and the board have not empowered me to give away the company's money. My job is to make sure you have a secure future, and the best way for you to have a secure future is to have a healthy company.

"The answer, in a word, is no."

•••

Becoming more cost-efficient means looking at all the company relationships you have. When they're disadvantageous to you—even those enshrined in contracts—you must take steps to change the terms.

Lily-Tulip had two unfavorable supply contracts in place with its former parent company, Owens-Illinois. One of them was a three-party deal involving them, us, and McDonald's. We technically had a contract to sell coffee cups to the fast-food company, but when Lily-Tulip was spun off, Owens-Illinois retained the plant that actually made the cups.

Based on purchasing leverage of McDonald's and the contract we had with Owens-Illinois, we didn't make anything on the deal. It was a large volume of sales, but it didn't generate much profit.

The other contract between Owens-Illinois and Lily-Tulip required us to take the entire output of foam cups from another plant they kept. Naturally, they were producing cups like crazy because they didn't have to sell the stuff. Their mills were running at 150 percent of capacity, including Saturdays and Sundays, cranking out as much as they could. We took it all, filling warehouses full of cups, shutting down our own machines that made the same product, to keep taking it from them. It was a terrible contract, stuffing us with product at a higher price than we could sell it. And the market was not absorbing foam cups anywhere near as fast as Owens-Illinois was churning them out.

Making matters even worse, we had the same kind of cup production plant. We already had too much inventory and capacity without the Owens-Illinois output.

McDonald's settled the first problem for us by applying pressure to get us to lower our price—something we couldn't do because we didn't control cost. Fortunately, they short-circuited our own internal debate about honoring the contract at all by choosing another manufacturer's cup, and we weren't sorry to see them go. We'd have made nothing or lost money had we continued, because Owens-Illinois wouldn't cut *its* price.

Meanwhile, four of us sat around a conference table at Lily-Tulip one dark day, discussing the second production contract. I said, "We're going to go down the tubes if we don't change this contract. We should at least take a shot at pushing back and telling them we don't want any more of their damn product."

We were already in dire straits financially. The debt structure of Kohlberg Kravis Roberts & Co.'s leveraged buyout was onerous, and having to buy product that we couldn't sell was yet another extreme problem.

We reasoned that Owens-Illinois didn't really want Lily-Tulip to fail, nor did they want to be in the cup business. The upper-level management in Owens-Illinois had, after all, *sold* the cup business. So, for a while, we stopped taking their product, even as they continued manufacturing it and filling up their own warehouses all over town. But it was the difference between the business failing or succeeding. It was a pretty gutsy decision.

In a move that we thought would settle the issue, we bought out the second cup contract, only to see Owens-Illinois enter the business as a direct competitor.

That's when I had my first face-to-face meeting with the CEO of Owens-Illinois.

"This is ridiculous," I said. "I will buy the business out from you." He said he wouldn't sell the business.

I said, "I've got a bigger, better sales force and better marketing. You want to compete with me? I am now going to bury you."

The guys running their division intended to compete with us. But we reasoned that, in the sale of Lily-Tulip, we ended up with all the best sales people and all the marketing expertise. So they really weren't dealing from a position of strength. We proceeded with the most vigorous marketing campaign in which I have ever been involved.

No sooner had they filled every warehouse they could than they realized sales weren't materializing. They had no choice but to shut their equipment down. They couldn't continue to run with no place for the product to go.

Two months later, the same CEO called me. Only this time we had the upper hand. "Let's talk about selling you the business," he said.

In the end, he got less money for it then than he would have gotten on the first day I made the offer.

There were still disputes about us not taking the product, but we did agree to buy their manufacturing equipment. So what started as a major hassle turned out very well for Lily-Tulip in the long run because we took the initiative to change the status quo.

•••

Most companies use people strictly according to their defined function—lawyers, for example, interpret the law. They offer their input on legal proprieties and they go away.

Not when they work for me.

As John Murtagh first learned at Lily-Tulip, the general counsel in a Dunlap-operated company plays a role in operating decisions and policymaking that is equal to those of the CFO and senior vice presidents.

I expect the same broad overview of corporate issues from the corporate lawyer as I do from every other player. What problems do we have? How will we solve them? If you're part of my team, you don't just make spot relief appearances; you're in for the whole game.

When we resolved to close a million-square-foot paper cup and paper plate manufacturing facility in Holmdel, New Jersey, saving millions of dollars, it was Murtagh's first real test as one of my lieutenants. Once home to 2,000 employees, the plant roster was by then down to roughly 800. It was far bigger than we needed at the time—so big, in fact, that a portion was leased out to another company. It was a beautiful place, but the site never made the company a cent. In fact, we lost a bundle operating it. I never understood why it was even built when we had excess capacity at existing plants. We closed it and a smaller plant in Old Town, Maine, at about the same time.

I assigned Murtagh and Jack Dailey, who had been plant manager there before being bumped up to corporate, to go to New Jersey and sell the plant.

They spent a week unsuccessfully looking for buyers in the Northeast before returning empty-handed to Toledo.

"Did you sell the plant?" I asked when I saw them. "No? Well, what are you doing here? Both of you go back to New Jersey and don't come home until you sell the plant."

I didn't see them again for weeks. But when they finally came back, a deal had been made.

On the face of it, their job was simple: Sell the facility, lay off or transfer the employees, and move the equipment, some to Missouri, some to Georgia. We needed riggers to tear the equipment down and set it back up quickly so we didn't lose much production. We didn't need Holmdel, but we did need its output.

That created another layer of problems. There was room in Missouri for new equipment, but we needed infrastructure and an entirely new building in Georgia. The existing Georgia plant had only made paper products until then—cups and plates. Besides adding the Holmdel equipment there, we would need new facilities for much more sophisticated foam cup-making machines, and the Georgia plant had no infrastructure for handling the plastics and attendant electronics.

As Murtagh and Dailey soon learned, there is no book you

can study to learn about the ten steps to shutting down a busy industrial plant. There were unions to mollify, and state and federal labor and compensation laws to be followed. And within Lily-Tulip itself, not everyone was pleased with the plant's shutdown. Our sales director, for instance, said, "How the hell am I going to service all my big customers in the Northeast without New Jersey?" That was a bona fide problem. Our Northeast United States customers would no longer be able to call up and get a familiar voice on the phone assuring them that, in less than eight hours, product would be on their dock. Instead, customers would hear a voice dripping honey that would say, "Don't worry, *sugah,* it will be there in about three days."

That was a real big problem because Lily-Tulip's sales strength was in the Northeast. So there was a real customer confidence risk to moving production that far away.

We considered leaving behind a skeleton customer service crew of people who knew the market, knew the customers, and were used to arguing with those Northeasterners. We also discussed establishing a warehouse dispatching facility.

In the end, our southerners charmed the northerners, and we relocated some of our experienced people from New Jersey to Georgia. We also contracted for an emergency distribution warehouse in New York to handle overnight delivery demands.

And, most important of all, Lily-Tulip unloaded an enormous asset and substantially reduced its debt.

•••

All kinds of business and legal relationships get stale if they're not examined regularly.

In Australia, I reviewed Consolidated Press Holding's legal expenses and thought they were way out of line. Kerry Packer and his father, Sir Frank, had had the same legal firm for decades. I went to the firm and said, "We're going to put our legal work up for bids. Whoever gives us the best rates will get our business."

The managing partner was aghast.

"You can't do that!" he blustered, treating me more like an

employee than a valued client. "We have serviced Mr. Packer's companies for thirty-some years and we are not going to bid!"

"Fine," I said. "You're out."

The next day, I went in to see Packer and the very same head of the law firm, whom I had sacked the day before, was sitting in Packer's office. The man, who had been a director on our own board, was pleading his case with Kerry.

"What is going on?" Packer asked me.

I told him, detailing what I considered excessive billing and other cost-related problems with the firm's work. I explained how I had simply asked the man to bid on our future work.

At the end of the meeting, Packer looked at the lawyer.

"Al's right," he said. "You're out."

I cut off many other relationships of the Packers that had gone on for years—personal, business, legal, and accounting. Some of these involved very difficult situations. If you are political and worry how your probing will go over, or if you worry about whose feelings will be hurt, you will fail or, at the very least, become mediocre. It is always easier to compromise. It is easier to go slow. But if I did that, you wouldn't be reading this book.

Sometimes, Packer would say to me, "Al, I have had this relationship my whole life! For God's sake, there goes the relationship! What are you doing to me?"

"Kerry," I'd say, "I came over here to do a job, the job you asked me to do."

He would hem and haw, but he always hung in there and supported me because he knew it needed doing and he didn't want to do it himself.

I fired entire boards of directors, men and women who had been very close to Packer, very big personalities in Australia and Europe. Several undoubtedly went to him and asked why he was letting me do this. I think there were times when he wanted to kill me but he never said, "Take so-and-so back."

People wondered where Packer's loyalties lay, to me or to his friends and family. But in business, loyalty must be earned by merit.

I am loyal to people who I believe are doing meritorious work. I give loyalty to people I respect. To get that respect in business, you must be doing something that has real value. If you are doing something that isn't helping me, then my company can't be loyal to you.

Packer was surrounded by hangers-on and sycophants who were there because he was rich and powerful. Had these people been doing things that were meritorious, adding to the wealth and well being of the enterprise, then Packer would have had every reason to protect them. But you can't protect somebody who is living off the enterprise without contributing to it.

I remember another day I walked into Packer's office and had more news for him and his son James.

"I am going to cut our headquarters staff at CPH," I said. "The new organization will be me, you, and James."

"Isn't that nice," he said, "me and the kid still have a job."

Chapter 5
RULE 3: KNOW WHAT BUSINESS YOU'RE IN

LESSON: FOCUS LIKE A LASER.

Two questions you should always be asking yourself: "What business are we in, anyhow? What business are we in, anyhow? What business should we be in?" When you have the answers, sell everything else and focus on the core business.

Every company I've been in, we've created a "dirty laundry" list. We list all the assets that don't help us, every single one, and then sell them. We free ourselves from having to manage them. We free ourselves from having to worry about them. We free ourselves from having to maintain them. We redeploy our funds into the things we should be doing.

Try this process and you'll discover your company's "hidden" corporate bank, the money raised by selling non-core assets. I call it a "bank" because of its inherent cash value. When we wanted to raise capital at Scott, we went to the best bank we could find: our hidden bank. The rates are great, they cost you nothing.

Most of this stuff sounds so simple, but it's the simple stuff that executives won't see until it pokes 'em in the eyes. Business is simple. It's about doing the right things on a consistent basis.

Scott's greatest hope for success was not going to be as a conglomerate. We sold $2.4 billion worth of assets and took ourselves from credit-watch status to one of the best balance sheets in America. What did we miss by doing this? Nothing. We were an enhanced company.

On the surface, Scott was in two businesses: (1) coated paper and (2) facial/toilet tissue and paper towels. At that level, it was very easy to say what we were in. But when we peeled back the onion and looked within those businesses, we had some fits that were far from perfect.

On the tissue side, we were in the timber and energy businesses, because we were completely integrated vertically. We should have been just working the end product, which is where we eventually focused. The tissue side also had a health care business and a food service business. There was no logic to that product extension.

The coated paper business supposedly focused on coated free sheet, the paper frequently used by the magazine industry. But S.D. Warren was also in a variety of specialty paper businesses, including papers for quick printers and for corporate and institutional in-house publications. So, although we talked about being in two businesses, quite frankly Scott was in seven or eight different ones.

With all those businesses and only a few doing well, we couldn't possibly be successful on the whole. The money required to support all those capital-intensive businesses didn't exist, so *each year management negotiated trade-offs*. One year it supported the tissue business, the next year it supported coated paper. Neither got the attention or resources it needed to get well again.

To me and my team, it came down to a simple choice: Are we a coated paper company or a tissue company?

The decision in favor of tissue was easy. That was the company's history and heritage, the market in which the company had a global presence. Tissue was also more stable, had the best performance and, once its marketing problems were straightened out, the most promising future. Scott tissue— under a variety of names such as Scott, Cottonelle, Viva, and Baby Fresh— enjoyed significant market share around the world. Our brand names were recognized by consumers from Bangor to Bangkok.

By contrast, coated paper had a very volatile history. Scott bought S.D. Warren—which sold paper under brand names such as Somerset, Lustro, Warren Recovery, Warrenflo, and SPectralech—in the late 1960s, and it rarely excelled in profitability. In 1982, the previous management instituted a strategy that produced promising results for a six-year run but then fell apart again. It was always cyclical, but less malleable than the timber resources I handled at Cavenham. It was also an expensive business, requiring billions in capital.

Our announcement that we were considering strategic alternatives for S.D. Warren raised a lot of eyebrows among investors in the company. S.D. Warren brought in $1 billion in annual sales and certainly had its strong supporters. It was a good company and I knew the pricing cycle was about to go up. This was exactly the right time to sell.

When I pressed the core business argument, Warren's supporters went so far as to tell me, matter-of-factly, that we weren't a very good tissue company! We lost market share for four years in the United States, they pointed out. Margins were down. "My God," someone said, "we're going to concentrate on *that* business?" And I said, "If we're not very good at that, we're not going to be very good at anything. We won't exist."

If we had kept Warren, it would have had a couple of good years and many bad years. It would have kept going through cycles and soaking up capital like a sponge. We would never have reached our potential as the premier tissue company. We had to sell it.

The previous management had engaged Goldman Sachs to find a suitor a year earlier, without success. The project was then abandoned. Goldman didn't have much credibility with me. It had been trying to sell S.D. Warren for a year, and it had been part of the old Scott regime. I preferred to start over with somebody I knew and liked.

Goldman Sachs was kept on as an agent for S.D. Warren, but the lead responsibility was transferred to Salomon Brothers' Mark Davis.

Mark's job was doubly difficult: not only had Goldman Sachs been unable to sell S.D. Warren, but I had announced publicly, to shareholders, our intention to dump it before negotiations with a single bidder had begun, potentially weakening our position.

If I jumped the gun, it was because I believed that the best way Scott shareholders would begin to feel good about the company again was if we understood what was our core business and what wasn't.

Mark's global search identified seven buyers. He pursued them, and the process ran smoothly until near the end, when one of the interested parties *publicly* told us it was withdrawing, which was kind of a low blow. They put pressure on us early to cut a favorable deal, and then, some weeks before the final bids were due, they announced to the press, "We are not interested in this property."

History repeated itself when a big European company, Ado Wiggins Appleton plc, publicly stated that it wasn't going to bid either. The last two weeks before the bids were due were very painful.

That left only an investor consortium led by a South African company, Sappi, Ltd., a group known to Salomon Brothers but one I had never heard of.

Despite the apparent lack of competing offers, Mark kept a very firm hand out to the South Africans and told them that they couldn't lower their bid. It had to be at least $1.6 billion. That took iron nerve on his part, with no other bidders in sight, but Sappi didn't blink. We did the deal and shocked a lot of people with the huge price we received.

With that success under our belt, I gave Salomon Brothers another assignment: a co-banking position with Chase Manhattan in the selling of our Alabama co-generation power plant.

The company had committed $300 million in 1992 to building and operating, in Mobile, Alabama, an energy recovery system that would produce power from waste. That $300 million was more than Scott's annual budget for capital expenditures over the whole tissue company. It locked us into a given level of spending, and it drained resources away from other projects.

Working together, Salomon Brother and Chase Manhattan sold the co-gen plant to a subsidiary of The Southern Company for $350 million. The best part was that we would continue buying electricity from the plant's new owners at preferred rates for our remaining Scott Consumer tissue operations at the site.

Selling assets didn't make the tissue side any less challenging. We moved to divest ourselves of food services and a health care joint venture—ancillary businesses in which we were small players in a huge market. It didn't make sense for us to compete in those arenas. We didn't have the best cost positions or the best products. They just drained our resources.

Analysts asked, "Why aren't you doing more with the tissue company?" The answer was that we couldn't afford to. After committing so much cash to the energy facility, there wasn't any left over. By keeping that plant, we prevented ourselves from spending money more advantageously.

If you believe the future of your company depends on profitable growth, you must find those areas where you can make money today but also grow the business tomorrow, so there is natural unit growth over time. Overseas, American companies can often find that kind of growth, but in the United States, the consumer market is growing at only 1 to 2 percent annually. Unless you can come up with startling innovations that push you higher, 1 to 2 percent growth just isn't going to cut it. At Scott, we had the technology, which gave us the potential to grow; we just weren't funding it. We shed the nonproductive assets to free some resources that could fund more productive future growth.

Another problem was a severe rift between Scott's Consumer and Away-From-Home businesses. Consumer products were sold in convenience stores, grocery stores, and mass merchandising markets. Away-From-Home's products were distributed to hotels, hospitals, restaurants and stadiums. Unlike Consumer, Away-From-Home was virtually an independent business; it was innovative and watched every penny.

From what I'd heard, the troops were entertained every day by the next round of the Consumer vs. Away boxing match. It was an often nasty combination of pugilism and chess: Who would outpunch or outwit whom, to get what they wanted? And the overall business did not benefit from it. The clash distracted everyone and was out of hand when I came on the scene.

Disagreements about principles and beliefs were massive, and there was no process to come to closure. I brought closure. If a critical decision needed to be made, it got made.

One of my real accomplishments was getting Newt White, the head of Away-From-Home, and my new Consumer marketing executive, Dick Nicolosi to lock arms and present a common posture to the Scott troops and culture. The marquee then carried three words: accountability for results.

The pair's thoughts became so well aligned that they began to issue jointly signed memos because the key messages were the same. I think that helped bring along more progress in a shorter period of time.

Newt came up with the idea of bundling Scott's Away-From-Home cleaning and paper products to address the multiple needs of workshops, commercial kitchens, and washrooms. Products were sold as groups, in addition to being sold individually.

He also argued that we shouldn't sell the integrated pulp mills, the ones that were connected to a tissue facility, but we should unload the stand-alone pulp mills. He felt—and probably still believes—that we needed a high level of integration for cost-effectiveness. I, on the other hand, believed we should sell the chemical pulp operations and invest in recycled fiber.

At issue was how much we should integrate backward. Should a steel company integrate backward by owning the mines that produce the raw material in steel? The next logical step was to ask, "Do we need to produce trees to be in the tissue business? What competitive advantage does that give us?"

Newt actually shared my commitment to recycled materials. He believed that Scott had made a big mistake years earlier by not getting into recycled fiber. The only really profitable company in the tissue business was using 100 percent, fully integrated recycled fiber. Our entire operation should have learned from that, but only Newt did. The Away-From-Home operation moved into recycled fiber as fast as Newt could squeeze the money out of corporate coffers to do it.

I supported him fully on this because the capital costs per ton of recycled fiber over time are significantly less than virgin fiber. You don't have to have timberlands and you aren't taking down trees, so it's more environmentally friendly and there is no supply problem. I have long believed we underutilize waste paper in the world, and this is one way to do something about it.

Opportunity presented itself with another asset sale, Promise adult diapers, when it became clear to me that we didn't have a competence or enough critical mass after ten years of being in the business. Scott was trying to compete with Procter & Gamble and Kimberly-Clark, both of whom had huge R&D investments in these technologies. We were just dabbling in them. It was too late to be a player, so we sold the business to Molnlycke AB, the tissue division of the Swedish concern SCA AB.

In the process of divesting assets, we looked for whole product lines that could be sold off. One I zeroed in on was wet wipes, a moistened product used to wipe a baby's behind.

On the surface, it didn't seem like an intuitive product for Scott. It was a baby-focused product in a company that was primarily tissue-and towel-oriented. Baby items are a completely different product category, often stacked in their own aisles of a supermarket. I decided to sell the line, and an actively interested buyer was offering a good price. The operating people in the wet wipes division had gotten wind that they might be spun off. Frankly, they liked the idea of getting away from Scott's cultural chaos and were actively pushing for it.

The wet wipes crew represented yet another separationist group within Scott. They had been structured and cultured as an independent worldwide entity who thought their destinies were apart from the rest of the corporation. That was tolerated in—or beyond the control of—the old Scott culture, and they were zealously pushing forward arguments for why wet wipes *didn't* belong with Scott.

But Dick Nicolosi and Russ Kersh talked me into keeping the product.

"We could use this to launch multiple product extensions," Dick said. "We could not only have a baby product, we could have a teenager product. We can apply perfume. We can apply dermatological cream. We can do all kinds of stuff with this product; take it from cradle to grave."

Wet wipes were premoistened and embedded with microcapsules that release different fluids. They had applications for babies, teens, and adults that we had not yet exploited. Dick believed the technology had potential beyond babies. He said that wet tissue performed better than dry tissue and that we shouldn't give up technologies that we could nourish into new products. He concluded that the reasons given for divesting the line were the very reasons we had to have it succeed. Wet wipes had enviable brand strength and recognition within mass merchandising outlets. Nicolosi laid out all these arguments, and I looked him in the eyes and shook my head.

"You really believe we ought to keep this business?" I said, knowing I could easily sell it and bank millions.

"Yes," Dick said. "I think it has far more potential, even

beyond its current business, both to the Away-From-Home and Consumer businesses."

"OK, let's keep it," I said.

In hindsight, wet wipes became one of Scott's more successful businesses before the merger with Kimberly-Clark.

Wet wipes were important for another reason: My team members learned that I would listen to them.

I want to see spirit. If they had just said, "Yeah, we should sell it, you have to sell it," I would have said, "Why didn't you do it before?" There's no possible answer for that, so my next question is, "Why the hell do I need you?"

I want people who will challenge me. There is no forbidding hierarchy around me. My people know they can say, "I disagree," and I'll consider their objections. In the early days of the Scott deal, we had sessions in which you had to hide the sharp objects. People said to me, "If you do that, you'll destroy the company!" To which I always answered, "How can you destroy something that's already dead?"

The worst thing you can do is hire people who sit back and say, "Boss, that's a good idea." You will die. The chief executive—indeed, every manager—must have strong views, but you've also got to have people who will challenge you. Sometimes they'll say, "Al, that's a dumb idea." And sometimes, guess what? It *is* a dumb idea. But in most of the corporate world, the chairman comes in like he's reading from the stone tablets. He pontificates and everybody says, "Oh, great idea." Bullshit! They're not all great ideas.

The best thing you can do is surround yourself with the smartest, toughest people you can find. When a decision is made, all challenges are over and they must recognize they're over. But up until the final decision, they should challenge you. Then I expect them to go 100 percent and get the job done. If they can't do that, they're out.

•••

When Kerry Packer, whom many call the richest man in Australia, bought a 47 percent interest in Australia's largest engineering company, ANI, for $380 million in April 1989, he asked me to go Down Under and take the company over.

ANI was a cheap buy for Packer because it had been rocked by the Spedley merchant banking group's collapse. It was a once-strong operation facing more than $200 million in losses, so Packer picked it up for a pittance.

I did a quick study of ANI and immediately reported back to Packer. "Kerry," I said, "this is just a terrible mess." Which was in stark contrast to what his own people were saying. I said the company lacked focus, costs were too high, and management was running wild with perks. ANI's managers were out of touch and had no vision of the future. Its cost system was bloated beyond recognition. Packer chose to believe me. As he led me around, he told his top executives, "This bloke is in charge. Listen to him, do what he says."

Over the next three months, I went through ANI, one of Australia's largest engineering companies, like Godzilla through Tokyo. Its interests were, literally and figuratively, all over the map. Besides steel manufacturing and processing, the company had a heavy equipment leasing division and two outfits manufacturing railroad car wheels. We proposed selling everything except five core businesses, closing the least efficient plants, and dramatically reducing overhead. Total employment would be reduced by 47 percent. I recommended firing virtually all of ANI's senior management, shuttering and selling nine disparate headquarters and six warehouses, cutting headquarters staff from 200 to 23, and relocating operations to offices in Newcastle that weren't being used. All told, debt was reduced from $570 million to $240 million.

The question for Packer was: How long would it take to complete the plan? He called a meeting attended by the two of us, plus Evan Rees, one of just a few directors who stayed on from the previous ANI board.

"Is the plan doable?" Packer asked us.

"Yes," Rees said.

"It is eminently doable," I agreed.

"Right then—how long?"

"Well," Rees said, heading into territory where we disagreed, "bearing in mind that we will go from 14,000 employees to 6,000, with the unions, I think it will take twelve months."

"What do you think, Al?"

"Six months at the absolute most!"

Packer stared at Rees and me for a long moment.

"You have twelve months."

In that same meeting, Rees told Packer that this would probably be the most daring business plan that had ever been set forth in Australia. We were both concerned that some of the ANI directors might get nervous and fiddle with the plan.

Packer looked me in the eye and said, "It has to be done precisely to this plan. If any of my directors try to interfere, they will be instantly sacked." He said he would vote his stock against them if they didn't go along with me.

I remember flying out to one of ANI's plants and being met by a company executive driving a fire-engine-red Ferrari. "Either this guy is independently wealthy," I thought, "or this company is nuts."

When I asked, he nonchalantly informed me it was a company car. You could have knocked me over with a feather. I told him I wanted to visit the ANI steel mills.

"Fine," he said, "but I don't do tours."

As we drove, he went on to tell me, in great detail, all the other things that he didn't do, so I added one more to the list. "You don't collect paychecks here anymore," I said.

And we sold the Ferrari.

The company had two plants, hundreds of miles apart, both making wheels for railroad cars and both operating at 50 percent of capacity. For some reason, the two operations made their wheels two different ways; the same company was not making interchangeable parts! Why? No one had any better answer than "That's the way we've always done it," so we saved millions by shutting down one plant. The other one became a great success.

Besides Rees, I found one more high-caliber guy at ANI, Paul Redding. I worked with them on the restructuring: we combined their familiarity with the engineering industry with my techniques. Focusing on ANI's steel business, we visited all the mills and facilities, met with managers and employees, and assessed ongoing projects.

One night, when the three of us were sitting in the Regent Hotel in Sydney, Rees and Redding said, "Al, we have gone too far. This thing can't work; it will destroy the company."

We argued, and the meeting broke up with all of us mad as hell. It was a very tough meeting, and I went to bed thinking I would probably have to get two other people because Rees and Redding couldn't possibly engineer a change as dramatic as I envisioned.

The next day, they thought better of it. "It's a high-risk strategy," Rees said, "but it is the *only* strategy we can see with a chance of working." That's how dire ANI's situation had become. But they believed it was better to go down kicking and screaming than to just give up. And they were well compensated for their unease with the plan: $1 million each was their incentive for succeeding. I know these men too well to think they pulled this job off just for a fat payday, but it was certainly a powerful inducement to do right by Packer. And they did, beyond anyone's wildest dreams. Rees went on to become ANI's managing director, and Redding became its chief financial officer.

Rees and Redding were not the only ones with incentive to deliver.

On my recommendation, $6 million in all was set aside to incentivize everybody in the system. Some of the main players eventually picked up $200,000 bonuses based on reaching our goals of job cuts, zero debt, asset sell-offs, and $100 million a year in ongoing savings.

As a result of all this cutting and dealing, ANI was refocused on its core business, engineering. And the restructuring was accomplished in eleven months, not twelve, with only one day lost in one plant due to industrial trouble. Packer eventually sold out his ANI interest in 1991 for a $180 million profit.

In a few months, the ANI mess was cleaned up and I returned to London. But Packer soon invited me back to Australia to improve his main business, Consolidated Press Holdings (CPH).

CPH was a huge conglomerate, the biggest octopus of Packer's 413 different businesses.

My assignment was to pare Consolidated down to a core media business, primarily television and magazines; make Packer as liquid as possible; and, along the way, train Kerry's son, James. CPH was hemorrhaging red ink because Packer had spread himself too thin buying businesses that were losing money and kept requiring additional capital. In the first six months alone, I unloaded more than fifty companies that were not contributing to his core business, thereby reducing debt and strengthening the overall company.

Fortunately for Packer, CPH was a world-class media empire in terms of content and reputation. A top-rated national TV network, Channel Nine; good magazines such as *Cleo, Australian Business Monthly, Australian Women's Weekly, Woman's Day,* and *Picture;* and Australian editions of American magazines such as *Cosmopolitan* and *People* were at its center.

I steered clear of editorial content and followed the money at CPH. Executives were directed to repay low-interest home mortgages granted by the company. Company cars were taken away. Country club memberships paid by CPH were canceled. Packer's people were spending his money without regard.

As I plowed through his assets in the next eighteen months, the only time Packer told me, "Hands off!" was when I wanted to sell his nine-million-acre ranch. It had only made money in two out of the eighteen years he had owned it.

"I am an Australian," he told me. "Australians have ranches. I am a wealthy man; I am entitled to a ranch. You can't sell the ranch!" There were plenty of other assets, of course, so why quibble? Packer was a billionaire who was entitled to his choice of indulgences.

When I arrived in Australia, Packer's empire was carrying about $2.2 billion in debt, a figure Packer wanted reversed. It was supposed to take me five years, but when I left in less than two, I had sold off 300 companies and showed a turnaround from a $25 million loss to a $623 million profit. The Australian press referred to me as "Chainsaw" because of the way I cut through all the fat and left a great sculpture—and Consolidated Press Holdings had a billion dollars in the bank.

•••

Selling noncore assets will improve any balance sheet.

Some people think bigger is better. If your company is losing value and losing shareholders, and the vultures are circling, bigger only means digging a bigger grave. When you are in too many businesses, it is distracting. People don't focus.

As I told Scott shareholders at my first annual meeting, businesses run best with a laser, not a shotgun.

There was a theory in the 1960s that you had to conglomerize because as one business would go down, another business would go up and offset the cycles. That is a failed philosophy. Totally failed. It's like communism. In theory, it's great. But in practice, it doesn't work. The flaw in that thinking is that shareholders are quite able to diversify on their own, thank you. Management doesn't have to do that for them.

Conglomerates—with rare exception, such as General Electric—do not work. Most spread their capital and management skills over too many businesses. They don't focus on a single business, and, as a result, they don't do any of them terribly well. There is no synergy.

When I talk about conglomerates, I mean dissimilar businesses. The Disney-ABC merger was a union of core businesses: Disney's programming feeds into the ABC broadcast television network and Disney's own cable channel, so it works as one business. By contrast, the Westinghouse-CBS merger does *not* fit. Westinghouse has radio stations, but Westinghouse manufactures industrial and commercial products such as transformers, refrigeration equipment, light bulbs, and radar equipment. It makes no sense to combine that kind of operation with the prestigious CBS television broadcast network. In my view, Westinghouse should have cleaned up its ancillary businesses first. Why didn't it get down to just its broadcasting business and then merge? Now, a fire sale of its industrial products may be needed.

But executives and boards don't want to hear about becoming a smaller company. They think bigger is better, which isn't true. More successful is better. More earnings is better. Higher stock value is better.

Why don't people pare down? Because anyone who pares down is going to be criticized. "We used to be a $5 billion corporation, now we're a $4 billion corporation." Who wants to hear that?

Consider W.R. Grace and Company. It's a loose conglomeration of businesses that make no sense, from manufacturing specialty chemicals to running dialysis service centers. Its true value will only come if it sells off unrelated businesses and gets back to a core chemical business. But corporations don't do that, except under the most extreme circumstances. It's only done by the very strong and only under the highest duress, as when the shareholders finally say, "Enough! We want our money!"

Getting small is not in human nature. Human nature is to *acquire* things. People like to acquire stuff so they can have more stuff. They take great pride in saying, "We're in all these businesses; look at all this *stuff!*" So what? You're doing a mediocre job with them all.

It takes a whole different person who would rather have a great $3 billion or $4 billion company than a mediocre $6 billion or $7 billion company. That person will take the risk for selling and will be criticized for selling.

Why did Scott Paper get into so many ancillary positions?

There is a cyclical process that takes place in industrial companies. They start out small, under focused entrepreneurs, and build up a healthy business. But lurking in the shadows is always some strategic planner with an MBA degree who steps out long enough to menacingly say, "You need to be diversified because you can't solely depend on one source of revenue or income." When executives hear that line, they should turn in the other direction and run!

But some managers still think they need to diversify. They're successful and the business generates cash. What should they do with it? They could give it to shareholders, either through higher dividends or a stock buyback. They could expand an existing line of business. They could expand geographically or get into other related businesses.

Instead, they often decide to get into a completely unrelated business.

Bigger can only be better if you are in the same line of business. Conglomerates fall under their own weight. They do well for a while but they're not ideal in the long-term.

BAT Industries, which Sir James Goldsmith pursued in a hostile takeover for more than a year, started out as a tobacco company before it went off into retail, insurance, and facsimile machine paper manufacturing. And it did everything significantly below the quality and sales of its competitors in each area.

As a tobacco company, BAT's market value wasn't great, perhaps six to eight times earnings. But among its divisions were individual assets that should have been valued at much higher multiples. Those were being depressed because of the tobacco business. Some of the companies should have been valued at fifteen times earnings—or more. Their value was forced down because BAT as a whole was thought of as a tobacco company, which the market sets as having a lower value. For example, if a BAT tobacco company made $1 million, the market would multiply that times six and come up with a value of $6 million. But if its Saks Fifth Avenue retail chain made $1 million, its multiple might be fifteen, setting its value at $15 million. So BAT was forced to acquire high-priced assets using low-valued equity. Conversely, if you can individually get everything valued at the higher number, then you make great buys. That's why conglomerate bust-ups are so profitable; individual pieces have higher total sales values than a company as a whole.

Another flaw in conglomeration behavior is those businesspeople who are not doing well in their chosen business and rather than fixing it, say, "Let's find something else to depend on." Weak companies diversify when that is exactly what they *shouldn't* do.

•••

An example of conglomerate mismanagement was Crown-Zellerbach, which Sir James (who put up $100 million) and his partners—including Jacob Rothschild's Rothschild Investment Trust, Elie de Rothschild, Marshall Field heir Ted Field, Kerry Packer, John Aspinall, Albert Frères, and Gerald Eskenazi of Banque Lambert Bruxelles—acquired for $600 million in a 1985 hostile takeover. It was a conglomeration of businesses— timberlands, coated and corrugated paper products, oil and gas, and industrial supplies—that an outsider might have thought bore some relationship to one another. They didn't.

Crown-Zellerbach was bloated and top-heavy, and it lacked focus as to its mission. Once among the biggest and oldest businesses in San Francisco—the philanthropic Zellerbach family had, over the years, endowed an orchestra, a symphony, and three museums—the corporate entity had lost its zip.

Its eighteen-story San Francisco corporate headquarters at One Bush Street was a good example. Big headquarters are there for one thing, to stroke the ego of the CEO and most CEOs already have big enough egos. Something like 700 people were on staff in that office tower, top-heavy as it was with executives doing who knows what. Everything ran smoothly only because nothing was happening. There were meetings about meetings; decisions and risks were deferred and deferred. Talk about meetings: the first one a Goldsmith attorney walked in on was actually a fifty-player strong Trivial Pursuit championship!

On another occasion, Ian Duncan, Sir James's CFO, and I couldn't get any answers in the eighteenth floor executive suites so we went down four levels until we found the men who had the answers, assistant treasurer Bill Spencer and timber comptroller Dave Harris. We promoted them immediately to positions of greater authority and responsibility.

How could the corporate custodians get away with recklessness and pissing away the shareholders' money? In part, because Crown-Zellerbach had seven incompatible computer systems, so the left foot didn't know what the right foot was doing.

Sir James wanted Crown-Zellerbach's timberland assets—which gave him control over 3 million acres nationwide by the summer of 1986, an area the size of Massachusetts—as well as its oil and gas resources but not the rest of the company, the pulp and paper divisions, so we went through the process of splitting the company up. We bought the land under the San Francisco tower for $15 million then sold it and the building to Equitable for $57 million. We relocated corporate headquarters for Cavenham Forest Industries, as Sir James renamed the company, to Portland, Oregon, where we already had operations. I operated everything else from Hilton Head, South Carolina, under the name General Oriental Securities Limited Acquisition Corporation.

Crown-Zellerbach was in a state of turmoil following a strategic shift in the mid-1980s. The company was in the process of moving away from old mills in the wrong locations to new mills. Overall performance had been very poor.

The timberlands company—which had a northern division operating in Oregon and Washington, and a southern division in Louisiana—was treated like an orphaned child. It had difficulty getting capital approvals and attracting priority status. I found that a lot of the guys at the top of Crown-Zellerbach didn't understand the business, didn't understand the numbers. But below them, guys such as Russ Carson, Lee Alford, Harris, and Spencer did.

When I took over, Carson was the vice president of Northwest operations, in Oregon and Washington. He reported to one of four Crown-Zellerbach group presidents. When his boss took a golden parachute, a fat executive separation payment triggered by the purchase of the company, Carson stepped in and filled the void, overseeing timber operations in Louisiana and Mississippi as well as the Northwest. He did such an excellent job that I gave him the assignment for good.

The timber and wood products division had made progress toward being more competitive. But the industry was at the low end of a down-cycle when I arrived. I made it more competitive by cutting 30 percent of the administrative staff—people mostly responsible for answering to San Francisco, a function no longer needed.

I also shifted 40 percent of Cavenham's hourly employees from payroll to independent contracts, tying their income to their individual production. While this made them responsible for their own medical and other benefits, it also gave them the opportunity to make more money than they would as hourly employees. Our wages up until that point had been noncompetitive, thanks to poor labor contracts that were completely out of line with other companies in the industry. So we told the unions that they had to lower their wages or we'd be happy to take a strike. It was either make the change or lose the jobs entirely, as far as we were concerned.

If we were going to pour capital into the sawmills, we were going to do it with a cost structure that made sense for us. We let the unions know that, unlike Crown-Zellerbach, Cavenham was not going to throw good money away on capital equipment if we couldn't operate it economically. If we couldn't get a labor structure that could compete, then the other factors wouldn't bear fruit.

After our saving-jobs-versus-losing-them message was understood, renegotiations with the union yielded $4.1 million a year. Between that and staff reductions, we realized an $8 million savings. In all, $15 million was gained through cost-cutting alone.

With downsizing and layoffs behind it, the division was ready to build up again. We rethought the business, focusing our priority on the timberlands and not on ancillary operations, set grueling agendas, and promoted operators who met our goals.

Sir James's timing in acquiring the timberlands was perfect; with fine-tuning, it became a cash machine. In 1987, Cavenham Forest Industries produced $71 million worth of pre-tax income. That compared quite favorably to the division's best performance under Crown-Zellerbach: $20 million. Incredibly, we did so much better with virtually the same revenues. In 1983, under Crown-Zellerbach, the timberlands generated $270 million in revenues; four years later, under us, the revenues were only slightly higher, $278 million, but income had increased by $51 million.

Crown-Zellerbach's mistakes had been financial and strategic: They paid too much for the sawmills and timberlands. And the mills they bought were poor quality. Costs were inflated because the business was being micromanaged and over-administrated in San Francisco instead of in the Northwest and South, where the facilities were. Too many activities weren't generating revenue.

When prices fell, Crown-Zellerbach was afraid to cut production because the unions might picket their pulp mills. Their solution to poor performance was to overcut the timberlands, selling more product at lower prices to mask sinking profit margins.

My style was a tremendous shock for Crown-Zellerbach employees who weren't performing and a real blessing to the Cavenham people, such as Carson, whom I put in charge. I gave them more latitude and authority to succeed, and they did.

Carson and his people would give me a presentation on some new capital expenditure, like when they wanted a new chipping saw to get better utilization and more production at our stud mill in Holden, Louisiana. The chipping saw converts logs into lumber. I looked them in the eye and said, "OK, but it better work." They rarely let me down, and we invested $20 million in new capital equipment.

During one quarterly review, I asked a detailed question. We were installing laser equipment to position the logs and get maximum yields. I asked Carson how long it would take to set up. He answered me with a bunch of fluff. I said, "That's a lot of nonsense! You can do it in four months and we can start enjoying the advantages much sooner." They were just giving themselves a lot of latitude. That caught Carson by surprise. He looked at me with disbelief written all over his face.

"You're a helluva lot smarter than I thought," he blurted out without thinking. His associates turned ashen, thinking Carson had just insulted the boss. I laughed it off, but they never tried blowing anything past me again.

We stayed very close to the market and looked at what it was dictating. Then we identified the species of wood that we could get the best return on and invested in the equipment we'd need. We were very opportunistic; if the market wanted two-by-fours instead of four-by-eights, and we could make more money giving the market what it wanted, two-by-fours were what we cut.

When export prices were high, we shipped all our export wood in the first three months and sold into the teeth of that demand. Overall, we did the opposite of whatever Crown-Zellerbach had done: we cut more when prices were high and less when prices were low. A facility is no better or no worse than the strategy employed to run it.

The biggest surprise for Carson and his team was how quickly I reached decisions. They had done research on silviculture improvements to increase timberland yields, but could never get the approval to try. I gave them the go-ahead in minutes, and it worked. As an extension of this farming style, they also began fertilizing trees by helicopter.

Speaking of helicopters, I must share the story of the day I met Carson. Cavenham executives in Louisiana often took visiting VIPs on a tour that began on the ground and finished in the air, where you could get an overview of the company's 700,000 acres of timberland. The day I went to Louisiana, the weather was god-awful.

"I'm not going up in that damn helicopter," Carson said. "But I'm sure *you're* not too chicken to go."

So I went. Once in the air, the helicopter shook and rattled, thanks to vicious lightning, thunder, and a horrendous downpour. I thought Carson was trying to kill me. It was the kind of thing that would have cost other executives their careers, but I appreciated his spirit, intelligence, and sense of humor, and later made him CEO of the company.

●●●

Conglomerates are less an issue of how good the finished product or service is, and more one of ego and numbers.

The previous Scott management had the same debt load but, instead of paying it off, they must have spent all their time talking about it. They were mired in endless meetings, bickering about what should be sold, how it should be sold, what should be done, when, and so on, as opposed to just *doing* it.

Any businessperson worth some oats should be able to look at a balance sheet and say, "There's too much debt!"

I look at a financial situation like a surgeon examining a patient's symptoms. Scott's most deteriorating indication was its balance sheet, steeped in $2 billion of red ink—arguably $3 billion, It had to be fixed within a year. That's a leading reason why we moved fast to sell assets. We sold the ones that were least strategic and for which we could get the most money.

Hacking away at debt does wonders for your standing with the investment community. The analysts following Scott applauded our swift and decisive approach to getting out of the red. How hard is that to understand? Bigger is quite a distraction. Analysts reward companies that cut debt with higher ratings.

Most divisions that get spun out of a conglomerate do infinitely better afterward because if they're an out-of-favor corporate stepchild, they're not getting the proper funding or attention anyway. S.D. Warren got off to a wonderful start under the new ownership of a group led by Sappi, Ltd., a South African paper company. Sappi was already in that business on a global basis; it was a perfect fit. They're funding it, they're running it, and they're doing great.

We sold Scott's energy plant to a utility company; it was a great match. When you sell an asset to somebody in the same business, it should grow and be fruitful.

If a conglomerate has six businesses but only enough money to support three, the others must go. In business, if you're spending capital across the board instead of focusing it, the result is mediocrity everywhere.

Chapter 6
RULE 4: GET A REAL STRATEGY

LESSON: ENVISION THE FUTURE AND PLAN A ROUTE TO IT.

If you don't have a vision of the future, you are going nowhere. The first three of my four simple rules—get the right management team, pinch pennies, and know what business you're in—are the building blocks of an overall strategy. Rule four is a strategy that imparts to the rest of the company your vision of the future and how to reach it.

Scott's first step on this path was the implementation of a global growth strategy for the first time in years.

The central focus of my vision was Scott as a global consumer products company on a par with Procter & Gamble and Kimberly-Clark. Until I arrived, Scott saw itself as a paper producer that manufactured as much paper as it could, but it was as focused on providing generic product for grocery store private labels as it was on Scott's own brand names. The higher margins were in Scott labels, not store brands, but that required a marketing strategy, something unheard of in the company for years.

Explaining the difference between being a commodity paper producer and a consumer products company is as simple as pointing out the players. International Paper, Mead, Fort Howard, and James River are commodity producers known primarily within the paper industry. Household names such as Procter & Gamble and Kimberly-Clark are consumer products companies recognized by anyone who ever set foot in a supermarket. I set out to reinvent Scott as a member of the second group by emphasizing brand name products over generics.

Making it happen required what we called a 20/20/20 strategy: 20 percent earnings growth, 20 percent return on sales, and 20 percent sales growth. Inside of a year, we met or exceeded expectations in every category.

Our strategy was to become a global household name in existing markets in the United States, the United Kingdom, and Europe, but also in the new markets opening in Asia, India, and South America.

•••

Achieving that vision on an international basis required building more state-of-the-art manufacturing plants around the world to increase our total output of tissue products. In the past, Scott executives knew they weren't gaining on the competition in the United States, so someone had a brilliant idea: We'll grow the company overseas, instead.

Did I say brilliant? I mean ridiculous.

The idea was good and the company made some money, but that seemed accidental to me. Overseas operations, particularly on the Scott Consumer side, were slipshod and inconsistent.

But is that really surprising? If you can't succeed where you speak and understand the language and culture, by what height of arrogance can you succeed where you don't speak the language? That's crazy.

Europe is not one country. It is several countries, each with its own distinctive personality and point of view. And the mentality of the people is different, whether they speak English or not. Americans assume that because they can communicate with most Europeans in English, they are being understood. Not necessarily. In many cases, the Europeans nod their heads and say "Yes" because they are polite.

Procter & Gamble successfully moved overseas by creating a mix of culture that was 90 percent European and roughly 10 percent American.

We learned from their winning example. We reduced by tenfold the number of expatriates (who were three times as expensive to employ) and replaced them with nationals. Paolo Forlin, an Italian with more than three decades of experience at Scott Paper, became our head of consumer products in Europe.

Under Forlin's direction, we improved communication between countries and regions, and sped up growth through innovation. Fortin, who was well-known after all these years in most European countries, convinced his managers that something successfully done in one country could be done in another.

We transformed overseas operations further by eliminating individual fiefdoms and their competing administrative staffs. With the new European Economic Community rules, there are no boundaries, and we were tremendously successful in applying our existing resources to increase sales and introduce Scott products in new markets.

In most of Scott's overseas operations, we had joint venture agreements, which guided us through the local culture, language, and otherwise hostile distribution networks. We became the first Western consumer products tissue company to enter China, India, and Indonesia. When I'm long forgotten, that will last and be a legacy for the future. For example, we owned 56 percent of the best paper producer in China, Shanghai Paper Company. How great is the potential for a company such as Scott Paper in Asia? We installed a state-of-the-art tissue machine in China. Ours was a gigantic, fast-moving piece of equipment compared with what our new partners had experienced. Their machines were so slow that Russ Kersh said, "If that was newsprint, it's going so slow you could read it." They had a room where 200 women were interfolding tissue, putting one sheet inside the other. By contrast, we had a machine that did the same thing, finishing thousands of cases a minute. That's potential.

But while our technology is light-years ahead of theirs, if we had gone to China on our own, we would have failed miserably.

The previous heads of our European and Asian consumer divisions managed operations as a series of businesses instead of as one. And each of their managers wanted to be king of the assigned country. These businesses had different branding and different package designs, different sourcing of product, different sourcing of raw materials and packaging materials, and the like. And each had a different strategy for building the business, with vastly different results. In some countries, Scott lost money; in others, it made an inordinate percentage of the profits in the region.

There was obviously much work to be done.

Our first step was to change the mindset of the person running Scott in Europe; running fiefdoms had to change into being accountable for the business in its totality. Second, and with rare exceptions, we decided that what was good for country A was also good for country B. Enormous economies of scale and advantages were to be gained from executing one great idea everywhere, rather than creating eleven good ideas.

Next, we decided that the various country managers would have to operate in a spirit of close collaboration and interdependence. We wanted one country manager counting on another country manager for creating the best approach to building the wet wipes business in Europe; another country manager would focus on paper towels or tissues; and so on.

We consolidated our European finance, administration, human resources, and back-office functions at one location, Paris. We also closed unproductive mills and shipped the equipment to the Pacific Rim countries, where we needed more production.

Until then, they were all independent mills, nobody had really run them as part of an integrated company. Each mill manager did what was thought best. So if there were ten mills, there were ten ways of doing things.

In international and domestic operations alike, it was almost impossible to compare results for different businesses because the way each was organized was different. The definitions and language they used were equally incompatible. The head of an international unit always had the excuse that "No one else understands this environment so things have to be done my way."

We realigned management at the mills so that each operated with the same staffing, human resources, and financial controls.

This streamlined the mills and their way of reporting to corporate headquarters.

Finally, we decided there would be one business strategy for all of Europe and Asia, just as there was one across the United States. Marketing Scott brands above all else was our domestic focus, and it became the strategy overseas.

At some point in time, a company as big and broad as Scott is either overly centralized or overly decentralized. We tried to strike a medium where we could take the low-hanging fruit of centralization—getting all the economies of scale; reducing staff; improving design, manufacturing, sales, and delivery. For the first time, each of our country operations followed roughly the same organizational chart for its manufacturing and marketing processes. They were linked as one company, multiple spokes driving a single hub.

What we didn't want to lose was a local understanding of competition because competition in our business—just like politics—is always local. It's all about turf battles between brands. Issues relating to brand loyalty often turn out to be about power and control; people feel, "I've got to have something just this way."

Scott's problems were primarily internal, not external, so the only change the public saw was the evolution of our branding from regional names to "Scott the World Over." Paolo Forlin put consistent business operating systems in place across Europe, but allowed country managers enough leeway and local decision-making authority to keep their markets and customers satisfied.

The old Scott was always making issues more complex as opposed to simpler. Business is simple, black and white. These are the choices that we have, and the worst decision is not making a choice. It is worse than making the wrong choice. With that in mind, we quickly resolved issues that had been hanging over Scott/Europe for years.

As a result of this new strategy, Scott moved way ahead of most other American consumer product companies operating in Europe. We became the industry's low-cost producer. In the eighteen months preceding our merger with Kimberly-Clark, Scott was the most successful tissue company in Europe, outselling the competition—a fact that played no small part in attracting Kimberly-Clark.

•••

A second step in my strategy for Scott was acceleration of product innovation, marketing, and extension in both consumer and commercial businesses.

Most good solutions for any company already reside within that company. I didn't invent Softkins wet toilet tissue or conceive of adding Arm & Hammer baking soda to Cottonelle toilet tissue, but I pushed those products to market.

We created individual strategies by business, by category, and by product. Every business and project leader was required to submit three-year development plans. Mind the difference; these weren't turnaround plans, they were *growth* plans that sought better products and increased profit margins, which would create growth and volume streams. Where the company before had no strategy, now each operation and each product was required to have a plan. Scott became committed to at least two marketing or product initiatives in key categories in every market worldwide, every year.

Make sure you are focused on areas where you have competitive advantage. If you don't have a competitive advantage, know how to get one. You need a plan that capitalizes on your strengths so you can differentiate yourself from competition in the marketplace.

Strategy has to be clearly plotted for growth over time, innovation, technology, and capital expenditures—all with an eye toward profitability. It should focus on when and how products or services are being brought to market, what cash flows or sales will come from that, and how capital investments will keep production and innovation moving ahead.

Find a way to grow the business. What creates value? Growth does. From growth comes a cash flow over time. What will cause that cash flow to grow? A one-time cost reduction gives you a certain bang. The market quickly recognizes it, and your stock price is positively affected. But to reach the next quantum leap, you must experience growth. And that comes from the top line—sales. You can't count on price increases forever. There has to be a combination of volume and mix changes.

As you'll read in Chapter Nine, "Look Under 'M' for Marketing," we aggressively redesigned, relaunched, and remarketed the entire line of Scott Consumer and Scott Away-From-Home products. Where there were quality inconsistencies from region to region, such as in Viva paper towels, we brought the product up to snuff across the board. We upgraded Cottonelle from a small regional brand to an international star with multiple line extensions as part of a "personal hygiene system."

Equally important, we reduced the volume of products offered. We kept those that were actually profitable or had growth potential.

•••

Research and development is key for every manufacturing company. In consumer products, where something is always "New!" "Improved!" or "Better Than Ever!" product development plays a vital role.

But Scott had too many R&D fiefdoms that were only tangentially concerned with product development. Centralizing development and technology resulted in major cost savings and quickened innovation. At Scott, we decided which technologies we had confidence in and focused on them. We eliminated all independent development at our facilities outside the United States. We put all of our resources and power into centralized development and made the technologists and the R&D people accountable for producing results. Previously, R&D reported to the chairman; under me, they reported directly to the business heads for whom they were developing product.

The R&D group became more productive despite the restructuring. Like many big companies today, Scott's R&D people in the past wouldn't bring some things to fruition for five or even ten years. It was fun for them because they were experimenting all the time and didn't have to demonstrate concrete results.

"Oh, it's coming," they'd say. "It'll be here in five years."

I told them, "If you have something to show, show it now, not in five years."

Scott spent too much time working on process as opposed to

what it really needed—new products, different products—so we down-sized the process part of the labs. They were not paying any attention to product.

I told my executives I believe in awarding gold stars for finding some new technology outside of our four walls, if it keeps us from wasting years trying to invent it ourselves. Find a small entrepreneurial company and buy its nascent technology if we must. It's faster to market, and a small company often has better technologies than the big boys. You can't have a good business if you are not investing in product differentiation and innovation. At the same time, the scale of R&D must be manageable and productive.

We did that, and we shed a lot of unproductive guys sitting in R&D. Newt White said to me, "I've been here for twenty years and I never saw some of these guys till we fired them because they had hidden out over there."

As best I could see, they had no purpose at Scott Paper other than drawing a paycheck.

•••

Before I arrived at Scott, management and the board had laid some general groundwork, sounded the alarms, and hoped the organization could change. What the company lacked was an implementer with a doable plan.

Work done in 1993 educated staff to better understand their business in terms of what the shareholders, retailers, and customers were seeing and what they weren't seeing. And their vision of the company was acute: The shareholders were not making money and they were not happy. The customers were seeing a retail shift that altered their expectations, thanks to companies such as Wal-Mart, which had a computerized, satellite inventory system that allowed it to demand twenty-four-hour product availability, delivery, and replenishment. Scott could not deliver that way, and subsequently missed out on several marketing windfalls.

We educated employees to understand that the company didn't operate in a vacuum. It must be responsive and market-driven. If demand or the markets shift, companies must move accordingly.

The next step in that process was working with the cost side.

My team calculated to the penny where we stood compared with the competition, in every aspect of papermaking—labor, chemicals, and fiber. Our next step was to understand why we were at a disadvantage. We looked at the competition and found out which of our manufacturing practices were good and which were bad, so we could say, "Here are the things that we need to do to improve." We were particularly interested in things that increased productivity. The prep work was getting people to understand the need for change, getting them to begin planning for change.

I insisted that change be made quickly because substantial savings would come from the manufacturing side. The partial fundamental plans to reduce the cost of manufacturing were sitting on a shelf, but the previous management was so scared of implementation that they wanted to do it in three years. They were afraid the unions would strike and production levels would fall. They weren't prepared to take a risk; I didn't see how we could afford *not* to take the risk.

•••

If there was one overall theme that drove my vision for Scott as a consumer products company, it was *creating shareholder value.* Earlier chapters have covered the steps we took in wiping out debt and selling non-strategic assets such as S.D. Warren. Once we had our priorities straight in terms of what business we were in and had established a vision for the future, we prepared a growth-oriented allocation of capital.

My team didn't approve any substantial capital outlays until we assessed needs across the entire Scott universe. *That's* strategy. We spent money on our core business, investing millions to expand tissue manufacturing capacity and upgrade existing facilities.

The ways our team found to sustain and increase shareholder value never ceased to amaze me. One of the more unusual approaches was with our Mexican affiliate. In late 1995, the peso suffered a major devaluation. While other U.S.-based companies doing business south of the border used the devaluation as an excuse for poor results at home, or for getting out of the market entirely, we took a different tack.

Immediately following the devaluation, we put together an objective—to maintain the value our products had before the devaluation. No excuses, we told our in-country managers. "We must maintain the dollar value of what we promised our shareholders." How? For starters, we kept all expenses in pesos. If customers were paying 10,000 pesos before, the price was still 10,000 pesos after devaluation, although that meant the dollar equivalent went down. It wasn't that easy, of course. We looked at the expense of importing raw materials for manufacturing and did our best to replace imports with locally produced materials, which reduced the dollar/peso discrepancy. We maximized output from local paper mills and minimized imports.

We were among the first companies to petition the Mexican government for price relief. We didn't wait and study it; we went after it. Finally, we became much tougher in terms of collection and credit. We cut off sales to marginal customers.

The bottom line in Mexico: Devaluation or not, we had record earnings.

•••

A real strategy looks at short-term and at long-term results. You've got to know where you are going today *and* tomorrow, because the decisions you make today will influence you beyond today.

Executives must commit to a continuous, strategic process with plenty of room for change, because the business environment always changes. A proper strategy breathes new life every day. Still, you must have a direction that dictates what you do on a day-to-day basis. If your strategy is to have a global brand, what are you doing day-in and day-out to develop it?

Look ahead ten years but don't expect or demand precise adherence to such a long-term vision. That approach will bankrupt you. Instead, set new goals along the way, adjust annual plans so they dovetail into new strategic directions. Review action plans daily, weekly, monthly, and yearly, to assess whether conditions have changed and whether it's time for you to shift in a different direction.

Most companies are generally good in laying out a strategy.

They think through developing products and the competitive market. Where they fail is in implementation. Walk into most businesses and they can show you a thick strategic plan, attractively bound and labeled. But just putting the plan together doesn't make it happen. You have to have follow-through and the discipline to implement your plan or to change it if it is not working.

Most executives don't follow through enough. Or, they do it over such a long period of time that the competition beats them to the finish line.

Culture has a lot to do with it. A company's culture may create a process where getting something new into the marketplace requires a tremendous amount of internal consensus. You have to get manufacturing, technology, marketing, sales, leadership, and the board all to agree. Imagine coming up with an idea to create value that requires a $100 million investment, and then imagine the number of superfluous people who will insist on being involved in the process, whether they're necessary or not.

All it takes is one doubting Thomas to put a cog in the well-greased wheel and slam the process to a halt. A good idea can get lost in corporate bureaucracy—corpocracy—for months, even years in some cultures.

A corporation that can't reach a decision demonstrates the depths of the organization's and the leadership's aversion to risk. To get innovation, there must be risk. Find a manager who is right ten out of ten times and you've found a lousy manager. Find one who is right one out of ten times—no, you don't want that person, either. But if you can find one who is right six or seven times out of ten, that's your manager. Corporate culture and smart executives must allow people to make mistakes. You must get to the marketplace quickly and you must take risks.

Along the same line, the chief executive may give an order but, by the time it gets down a couple of levels into a corporate bureaucracy, everything is subject to debate. And maybe that's OK—for about ten minutes. The chairman should not be a dictator; every company should welcome a degree of open debate about any substantial action about to be taken. But at some point there must be a process for getting closure, for making decisions, and for going forward. That's when the questioning ends and implementation begins.

People are either prepared to be on the team or they are not. That doesn't mean they can't challenge management, but arguments should be considered, decisions made, and actions taken.

Let's say I go to my director of investor relations with an idea. The director should listen, but even better, he or she should be ten steps ahead of me. That director should come to me with ideas. If I go to the department head, it's safe to assume I've already made up my mind. The window for discussion is very narrow. My strategy is to have good people doing their jobs well. If they do their jobs well they should be ahead of me.

•••

I often hear this question from people frightened by large-scale restructurings: How do you keep your people and your organization innovative and creative when all hell is breaking loose around them?

That's the art form to leadership and management; that's how the good ones earn the big paychecks. We must take the people who remain and make them think of themselves as winners, make them understand they can play to win and cannot play not to lose. Take an aggressive stance and define the template for success. What can they do, proactively, to improve the business? What's the game plan? What are their individual roles in making the game plan succeed?

You can't inspire 90 percent of the remaining people when you start letting people go, when their friends leave the business, if you don't combine the cutback with a vision for the future.

Without a platform of strategy that makes sense, without a way to win, the whole thing is a sham and you can't build any energy around it.

How far ahead should a company look with its strategy? One year? Ten years? Your vision must be short- *and* long-sighted because if you don't get short-term results you will never survive into the long term.

A one-year plan should be a very detailed document, but it has to be done in the context of something else. Scott Paper focused on its primary business and unloaded noncore assets. Once it had a business that could generate cash, what then? It needed a contiguous plan for reinvesting the cash wisely while still providing a return on investment to shareholders. How do you create value with that asset base? If you expand, that doesn't take a year, it might take two or three years. From the time you commit to putting in a new machine until it starts making product, usually you've gone beyond a year. So a one-year plan has to be created in the context of a longer term.

Three years is very desirable for planning (as opposed to restructuring). You should know, for each product category, what you intend to do in the next three years. You should have a vision of the key things you intend to do to produce value.

A ten-year, detailed plan with lots of numbers, on the other hand, makes no sense to me. The world *changes*. What will you do with a bunch of numbers that project six years from now other than some basic financial planning that helps you understand the need for equity vs. debt?

If you are a $5 billion company today, will you be a $12 billion company seven years from now, or a $7 billion company? If you are in a cyclical business riding the upward curve now, it is important to understand what will happen during the next cycle. You can anticipate and plan for it, and allow for continuous earnings improvement.

A successful strategy includes planning what you will do with the new money generated. Are there other businesses you should be in, other businesses you should divest? Are there joint ventures that make sense? Are there business combinations— Scott Paper and Kimberly-Clark, for example—that make sense? All the answers are part of strategy.

PART III

WHO I AM AND WHERE I COME FROM

Chapter 7
"A NOTHING KID FROM HOBOKEN"

LESSON: THE ONLY BARRIERS IN YOUR CAREER ARE SELF-IMPOSED.

I was in London in 1989, at the center of Sir James Goldsmith's attempted $23 billion takeover of the British tobacco and retail giant, BAT Industries. Among Sir James's partners were Australian media mogul Kerry Packer and international financier Lord Jacob Rothschild.

Every day, I looked around the conference room in amazement at the cast of characters: Goldsmith, Rothschild, Packer—and me.

"This is amazing!" I said to myself, dazzled by my surroundings, as if I were Alice in Wonderland. Imagine me, a nothing kid from the slums of Hoboken, New Jersey, serving as chairman and chief executive officer to three of the richest, most powerful men in the world. How could this happen? Me, planning strategies for these three billionaires, and along the way becoming a multimillionaire myself.

It was a world away from where this son of a shipyard worker began his life.

•••

My success has everything to do with being a poor kid who was always being put down. Making my way in the world became a matter of self-respect for me, of a kid trying to prove he was worth something: you can't just brush me off because I'm poor. I can do anything, and I can be as good as anybody. It was always about achievement for me, about self-respect and living up to potential. The money I've made is wonderful, but secondary.

I remember going to a friend's house, a very nice house. We were playing a game when his mother said to him, "I don't want you to invite him again. He lives over in the *apartments.*" The way she said it made it sound like a four-letter word. I may have been a nothing kid from Hoboken, but I thought, "I'll show you what a boy from the *apartments* can be."

My father, Albert, spent his entire life working in Hoboken's Todd Shipyards. A very passionate union person, he rose up to become a union steward.

My father would be laid off from time to time, not because he didn't want to work but because there was no work. I saw him go to work on days he didn't feel well. But my family believed you *had* to go to work; that was it. You had to do your job. Dad always bought lottery tickets and believed one day his number would hit. Little did he know then that luck would skip a generation and visit his only son.

Money was always a cause of friction in our home and I was taught you shouldn't waste it. I had a healthy respect for cash because there was never enough. I remember my grandmother saying to me, "Al, you're a smart boy. If you really work hard, some day you'll make $10,000." That was fifty years ago. I thought, *That's really nice, Grandma, but there isn't $10,000 in this whole world.*

I was always intense and disciplined, even as a kid. Nobody had to tell me to study hard in school; I knew well what was expected of me if I was going to rise above the poverty into which I was born.

I grew up in a bedroom that was so small I was constantly bruising my knees, banging against the furniture. I knew I was poor because I could see other people were richer than me. But I didn't think I was poor in the sense of lacking opportunity. I was taught that you could work hard, make sacrifices, pay the price, and you would succeed. To this day, I feel I have to prove and reprove myself. If I don't continue to do well, then I don't deserve the wealth and success I've gained. That may sound screwy, but that's the way I feel.

My mother, Mildred, was a strong, disciplined woman who set tough goals and objectives for her kids, the same kind I later set for myself, my companies, and my employees. She said, "Here are the rules—follow them. You gotta do this and you gotta do that." She instilled in me the self-discipline it took to succeed. If! was expected home at a certain time, I'd be home. And if my grades weren't just right, I would hear about it. I was expected to do well in school and stay out of trouble.

My family offered constant encouragement and believed passionately in my future. My Aunt Bernice, my grandmother, my mother and father—all were my greatest fans. In their eyes, I could do no wrong. It didn't hurt that I was the only grandson, the only son, and the only nephew, so they all totally doted on me.

Physically, my father was a bigger man than I grew up to be, but people remarked that we walked and looked alike. My mother was very pretty; my wife Judy says I have my mother's eyes and nose.

For fun, I played city games such as stoopball and stickball, swinging a broom handle and using manhole covers as bases. For a while, I drew boxes on a factory wall to practice my pitching. That came to a crashing halt when I was ten. A window high above fell out of the factory and almost hit me.

When I was a teen, work was finally steady enough for my parents that we moved out of Hoboken and into a house in nearby Hasbrouck Heights.

At Hasbrouck Heights High School, I took a more serious interest in athletics—working out, lifting weights. I liked sports and excelled at football. I was named to the Bergen County All-Star football team and was a shot put champion as well. My football success thrilled my parents, and they came to every game and rooted us on.

After my parents, my high school football coach, Andrew Kmetz, probably was the next great influence on me. Many people may wonder how being sent out to get knocked on your ass qualifies as a great growth experience, but it was. Kmetz was a stern disciplinarian who demanded the maximum out of his players. Contact sports teach you about life. I also was struck by the coach's nothing-held-back commitment to his job and his boys.

Thanks to my performance on the football field, I was offered football scholarships to Ivy League schools such as Brown and Dartmouth. But the Ivy League wasn't for me. The school I wanted was more mesmerizing: the U.S. Military Academy at West Point.

I was the first person in my family to go to college and, almost equally significant, I was the first person ever appointed to West Point from tiny Hasbrouck Heights. I also was the first person in my family to serve in the military. Working in the shipyards, the men in our family were always considered critical industry personnel and exempt from the draft. My parents were enormously proud of my appointment.

I knew by reputation that West Point offered a great education and that military life could be very difficult. But I had no idea how difficult until my first days as a cadet. It seemed as if the instructors spoke a foreign language. They were constantly chewing us out. I was ill prepared for the military life. The two biggest drawbacks for me at the Point were that I couldn't march worth a damn and that I never wanted to be an engineer, the primary career for which cadets at the Academy were trained. Frankly, I hated engineering. I wanted to be a lawyer, actually. I was drawn to its competitive, adversarial nature and saw the law as a way of putting my verbal skills to effective use.

The Point was extraordinarily difficult. It looked glamorous on the outside, but inside there was nothing but hard work. My class started with 998 cadets and we graduated with 560. Of the eleven in my original barracks, only four of us survived. I was one of them because when I committed to something I committed for the full term. I would do anything to succeed, no matter what the task. Even back *then—especially* back then—I was enormously competitive. I said, "Whatever it takes, I will graduate. It is the right thing—the smart thing—to do."

My parents were so proud when they came to visit. I decided surviving West Point was not just a matter of meeting a single challenge. If I was ever going to be somebody in life, I had to get through this first.

West Point is a great place to be from but a very difficult place to be. Through my whole life, it has raised my stature. The end product of West Point is character. It builds men and women who take responsibility. That's why West Point is the best business school in the world. On the same page as West Point, Wharton and the other leading business schools are but a footnote. West Point teaches you how to lead, how to think, how to deal with adversity, how to take responsibility, how to detail your actions. It teaches you for military purposes, but its lessons can easily be applied to business.

Wharton teaches business. I wonder how much it teaches about how to be a businessperson. There is a world of difference. The typical MBA doesn't understand how to deal with people at all. When I've interviewed newly minted MBAs and discussed their need to learn manufacturing or marketing, they have little interest. They don't want to do the lowly jobs and learn their way to the top. They make it clear they've been trained to be chairman, and they don't want to wait. It just doesn't work that way. Too many MBAs are arrogant and have a superiority complex. Some don't live up to their potential because they've skipped the rudimentary lessons gained from working with and managing people.

By contrast, I've interviewed West Pointers just out of the service and they say, "Give me a chance. Let me learn manufacturing by working shifts." They want to succeed, aren't afraid of dirt under their fingernails and are willing to prove it.

One institution, West Point, teaches its graduates to work like hell; the other, Wharton, says, "You're anointed, you *deserve* it." I'll take the former every time. And I look for the same motivation in everyone else I hire—no matter where they come from.

The most important job in the world to people in business is the job they are doing now, at this point in time. If they do the job better than anybody else, they will be discovered. If they focus on doing the next job and not doing the job they are in, they will ultimately fail and never reach their full potential.

•••

After graduating from West Point, I earned my paratrooper wings at Fort Benning and became executive officer of a nuclear missile installation on the Eastern Shore of Maryland. When my three years of active duty were up, I was ready to try the business world.

There was only one problem: I knew how to manage and motivate people, but I didn't know anything about business.

Fortunately, Kimberly-Clark had a management training program; it hired one person a year and put him or her through all the work shifts. I applied for the junior executive position and was hired. It turned out to be a job that nobody else with a college education wanted because it literally started you at the dirty, grimy bottom of the labor pool. It was not at all glamorous, but I thought I might actually learn something valuable. Which I did.

I started in a nonunion, New Milford, Connecticut, mill so I could do every job. Besides learning about manufacturing products, I noticed more than expected, especially laziness, waste, and management ineptitude.

My next job was a promotion to the Kimberly-Clark paper factory in Neenah, Wisconsin. I became a superintendent, responsible for all the paper and converting machines during my shift, including manufacturing, scheduling, and handling raw materials. And because of my experience working on the shop floor, I could be of great help to workers when process problems arose.

My very first day, I walked up to the plant's general superintendent, Ben Nobbe, and introduced myself.

"Hi," I said, putting out my hand, "my name is Al Dunlap." Looking down through his bifocals, Nobbe eyed my outstretched hand and looked me over, up and down.

"So what?" he sniffed, and walked away.

But he ultimately liked me, even though he really didn't care for college guys and none had done terribly well with him. Nobbe, who was in his 60s, was a stern disciplinarian and a tough guy who didn't take crap from anyone. He was always chewing me out. If he didn't like the way something went during one of my shifts, he would wait till I got home and was probably about to fall asleep. Then he'd call saying I screwed up something.

I remember going into a bank in Neenah and a woman behind the counter looked at my paycheck and said, "Oh, so *you're* Al Dunlap! I've heard my father chews you out all the time."

Still, Nobbe rapidly won my undying respect and admiration because he wore his bastardness like a well-earned badge of honor. He had done everything on his own and became the first strong influence in shaping my business life. Nobbe set high standards, always demanded the best, and made employees realize their potential.

One day, Nobbe took me fishing. I'm an inner-city kid from Jersey. What did I know about fishing? But there I was in a boat on the Fox River with my curmudgeonly boss. At one point he said, "Throw out the anchor," so I threw out the anchor—without tying it to the boat.

"There!" he exclaimed with great pleasure. "I knew all you college guys were dumb as hell."

I worked blue-collar shifts for a couple years in Neenah, learning every position—machine tender, back tender, beaterman, fourth hand, fifth hand, third hand. I learned a lot, and not just about making paper products. I learned about life in a factory on shift. It's very different than most people think. I saw the inefficiencies, the management bureaucracy. I learned why products get made right and why they get made wrong. I saw some really good leadership and I saw terrible management. The good came from Nobbe. He would walk through the mills and talk to workers. He knew them by their first names. He was tough, but he knew and respected his people. He'd get his hands dirty. Like me, he was a guy who came up through the ranks. He'd give you hell but he'd stick by you, too.

There were things that even Nobbe couldn't control or didn't see, however, such as the people who came in too tired to work on the second or third shifts, who would sleep some place while someone covered for them. Once I saw a tired man drive a forklift backward down some stairs.

Bad management stemmed in most cases from "ivory-tower" disease: layers of managers sending and shuffling memos, never actually answering questions or solving problems, and always making life more difficult for workers on the shop floor. (Years later, I saw the worst example of ivory-tower disease. One of the top Scott managers in England didn't know how to get to our local plant from the airport.

Literally, he couldn't find his way to his own production facility. Not a good way to impress the boss.)

During my four years at the Neenah plant, I rose from superintendent to project leader, first in R&D, then in paper machine startup and installation. As a result, I received a hands-on education in the entire pulp to tissue to converting to finished product process. When I was in R&D, I learned how to blend my practical knowledge with our scientists' research and innovate better products and processes.

I took my experiences along with me to every higher rung of the ladder. Nothing was unimportant: every bit of data and experience made the next challenge—whether in tissue, cups, timber, oil, land, or media—easier to conquer.

Kimberly-Clark had a need for some extra production capacity, so we bought it from nearby Sterling Pulp & Paper in Eau Claire, Wisconsin. Nobbe and I set up the deal. But they had all kinds of problems with a new pulp mill and paper machine, as well as labor and operational problems. By this time, I had become knowledgeable and experienced in every facet of plant operation. What didn't come naturally, Nobbe taught me. I was making great strides in confidence and savvy. He was the kind of mentor everyone needs but few are lucky enough to meet.

Ely Meyer, owner of Sterling, took Nobbe and me to dinner a few times, and we got on well. One time it was just the two of them and Mr. Meyer said, "I have too many problems here. I need someone who can properly run this company." To which Nobbe replied, "You need Dunlap."

At Kimberly-Clark I *learned* about managing. Working for Mr. Meyer at Sterling, I *became* a manager and put my training to work. He gave me my first big break and even introduced me to the woman who would become my wife.

Sterling, which made private-label/store-brand tissue paper and had about 1,000 employees, had gigantic problems. Mr. Meyer had borrowed a great deal of money to put in a new tissue paper machine and a new pulp machine. He picked up a lot of debt, and the equipment wasn't performing. There were problems upon problems.

The banks were uncomfortable with the equipment loans. Roth Schleck, president of First Wisconsin Bank, said to me, "I sure hope you fix this because the last thing this bank wants to own is a paper machine."

Sterling had purchased equipment that was more sophisticated than anything they'd ever had before. It put them into competition with much bigger companies; it was like going from triple-A ball to the major leagues. But because of my experience at Kimberly-Clark, I was able to get Sterling back up and rolling.

My view has always been that you should start work with one of the large corporations. They give the best training and have a variety of facilities. Moving to a smaller operation then gives you the opportunity to be a big fish in a small pool. You can really prove yourself, gain management experience, and then move on to a larger company where you can continue building expertise and management ability. That's a faster, smarter path than spending a career in the same corporation and waiting for your turn. It's also the way the business world is moving. Fewer and fewer people are lifetime employees. The smart person takes on a series of challenging experiences at different companies and builds a valuable portfolio of skills.

That's exactly the reason Mr. Meyer, who was seventy-five at the time, asked me to run Sterling. My work at Kimberly-Clark gave me valuable experience. I broke away from the herd and raced past my contemporaries.

Although I had moved on from Kimberly-Clark's Wisconsin plant to another one in Memphis, Mr. Meyer invited me to visit him at his winter home in Tampa, Florida. I knew he wanted me to work for him, but I didn't want to go back to bitterly cold Wisconsin.

But that first weekend, he didn't offer the job after all. He did ask me to come back the following weekend. I agreed and the same thing happened. By the third weekend, I didn't know what he was up to, but I sure liked Florida in the winter! My strategy for avoiding another subzero winter and thereby turning down the job—if it was ever offered—was to ask for what I thought was an outrageous salary.

So when he did, in fact, finally ask me to run his company, I was ready.

"Well," I said, asking for the moon, "I'd have to make $20,000." Mr. Meyer looked at me for a moment and thought about it.

"I'm not going to pay you that," he said, and I was relieved. Then he said, "I'm going to give you *$25,000.*"

So I took the job.

Whatever could go wrong did go wrong. In my first sixteen weeks, we had a flood, a fire, an explosion, and a strike.

The flood. . . occurred because the Sterling plant was located at the confluence of the Chippewa and Eau Claire rivers. One winter, there was a big runoff from melting snow and a heavy rain. The road to the plant flooded, and we had to take a rowboat to get in. There were pumps in the basement that we raised off the floor so they wouldn't short out. And sand was coming in with the water, covering the paper machines. It was a true disaster.

The explosion. . . happened about a month later, when an air cap over the paper dryer exploded. It blew the roof off the building and shut down half the plant for a week. We sent our people out on planes to find and bring back new replacement equipment.

The fire. . . took place in one of our warehouses a few weeks after the explosion, damaging product and shutting us down for a day.

The strike. . . hit between the flood and the explosion, a result of poor communication between management and labor. Sterling was not very skilled in listening to its employees or getting across company goals and strategies. As a result, strikes were almost a part of the way they did business. In fact, employees there would go out any time there was any kind of disagreement. A change in the manufacturing process or a scheduling snafu was enough to instigate a wildcat strike. The union tried to leverage the company's financial woes by constantly being in a state of labor chaos. It wasn't limited to Sterling, however; the whole town was a union nightmare. Uniroyal once had a giant plant in the city. They had so many labor problems, ultimately they shut down local operations completely.

I told the union leaders, "This is nuts! You can't keep going on strike—nobody benefits from this. The next time you go on strike you can stay out forever."

"When will you talk to us about our grievances?" the union leader asked.

"As long as you are out on an illegal strike, I'll never talk to you," I said and we were at an impasse for several days.

Finally, I called the union leader and gave him an ultimatum.

"If you want to bust this company, that's it; it's over. I am not going to operate a business like this. We will not continue in this atmosphere of constant blackmailing. I will not allow you to hold this company hostage.

"Look," I said, "we can sit on each other's lap in the electric chair, but what does that accomplish? Let's get this place running right and we will be able to pay you more money. But if we go bust, we are both out of a job—you *and* me."

The union wanted respect and I wanted to give it. But it wasn't easy on either side.

When I started at Sterling, people there didn't respect me because I was an outsider and a very young one at that. I remember a reporter got my age wrong and wrote that I was 30 instead of 29. Someone said, "Doesn't that upset you?" "No," I said with a laugh. "If it makes me seem older and more mature, maybe people here will finally pay attention to me!"

From then on, I had a pretty good relationship with the workers. We talked out various issues through the appropriate grievance committees. Sterling is now the only major company from 29 years ago still operating in Eau Claire. None of the others recognized their bloated payrolls and high costs until it was too late.

But in 1967, I was brand-new on the job. I knew when I started that there were problems, but a flood, an explosion, a fire, and a strike were beyond my wildest imagination. I addressed each disaster head-on. None of them panicked me, which I attribute to my West Point training. It was the hand I was dealt, so I played it and put into place corrective measures so that problems that could be controlled wouldn't happen again. (Floods I couldn't do anything about.)

I remember going home on a Sunday night to get some clean clothes after working straight through the weekend, and discovering that my car, a Ford Mustang, had a flat tire. Dead tired, I thought, "God is trying to tell me something."

But I patched up myself, my car, and the company. I put the right people in the right jobs, I fired the people who weren't performing, and Sterling once again became a great success with increased market share, greater profitability, and new product innovations.

Mr. Meyer treated me like a son from day one. He was very good to me but nevertheless expected me to get the job done. I was only 29 years old when I started there as general superintendent, but he handed me the keys to his manufacturing plant and all the responsibility that entailed.

Sterling was my first real chance to turn something around, even though I didn't realize that was what I was doing. To be honest, I was just there doing a job instinctively, cutting costs, hiring better people. Intuitively, I knew the business was manageable as long as I kept operations simple and profitable. Under my watch, Sterling entered the diaper business, producing the first private label disposable diaper, "Pee Wees." We also converted pulp mills to secondary fiber, using waste paper instead of virgin pulp, which resulted in drastically reduced costs.

Even though I didn't realize it at the time, I was beginning to formulate the four simple rules covered here in Chapters 3 through 6: getting a good management team; attacking cost; focusing the business; and getting a real strategy.

•••

Sterling Pulp & Paper was an important step in my personal development, too.

Mr. Meyer threw himself a big birthday party each year, inviting about 200 people. The first year I went, I found myself assigned a plum seat next to the boss.

"You're here by yourself?" he said unhappily, shaking his head. "Al, I want you to like it in Eau Claire and make a home here. Tell you what, I'll find you a nice girl."

"No," I said, somewhat flustered. *"I'll* find me a nice girl."

But he wasn't a man who took "No" for an answer.

By the end of the evening, he said he had checked around, pulled in a few social favors. "Come to my house tomorrow evening for dinner," Mr. Meyer said. "I've got a nice girl for you to meet."

He wasn't kidding—that girl was Judy Stringer, 26, whom I married less than a year later. Eau Claire was a small town in those days; everybody knew everybody. So when Mr. Meyer made inquiries on my behalf, he didn't have to wait long. Judy worked in a local bank, some of whose directors were friends of Mr. Meyer.

When I saw her for the first time, she struck me immediately as a beautiful, intelligent woman who initially didn't seem that affected by me. Indeed, Judy's first impressions of me were not inspiring. She thought I was handsome, but also aggressive and brash. I came on like a locomotive—not like the restrained Midwest fellas to whom she was accustomed.

But she must have seen something she liked because we became a regular item over the next six months. We got engaged and I told her it was my intention to get married before the end of the year—for a tax deduction. Six hundred dollars seemed like a lot of money.

"No, no, no," she said, "things are moving too fast."

I didn't give up easily, even going so far as to recruit her boss, the president of the bank, to try and talk some sense into her. But in the end, she made me wait until March of the following year.

Sterling was a company in huge financial trouble, which is why Mr. Meyer hired me. He needed an outsider to do all the unpleasant things that a restructuring called for. It was just a job to me, but it was tough on my fiancée and her parents. Judy, the second of three children, comes from a working-class background similar to mine. Her folks, Joe and Virginia, instilled in her the same basic values and sense of humor that mine gave me. That's why it hurt when people would say terrible things to them about what a cruel, cold person I was, or that I must have had no feelings to have laid off all those people.

There were also physical threats of violence. We received anonymous calls and letters from nuts who said they were going to blow up my car or shoot me in the parking lot.

Years later there was a happy ending to my Sterling Pulp & Paper experience. Judy wanted to attend her twenty-fifth high school reunion, but because I had been responsible for so many layoffs, she thought it would be awkward (and maybe dangerous) for me, and she tried to talk me out of going with her. She thought it could be unpleasant, but I went anyway.

We went to a cocktail party and then dinner. After dinner, I went to the men's room. As soon as I was gone, old friends who wanted to talk to Judy alone converged on her. Some time passed and, when I hadn't returned, Judy grew worried that somebody had taken me outside for a get-even thrashing.

Then she looked over and saw me at the end of the bar, surrounded by guys who had worked at the paper mill. Much to both our surprise, they were buying me drinks, congratulating and thanking me for saving their jobs. They were grateful for what I had done 20 years earlier.

•••

After I had been with him for almost seven years, Mr. Meyer, now in his eighties, entered a hospital and never came out. Every night, on the way home, I would visit him and discuss the day's business. No matter how ill, he would always shake hands when it was time for me to go. We both knew his days were numbered when his grip was completely gone. Even then, the expression in his eyes made me feel special when I entered his room. It was like losing a parent.

Mr. Meyer's family sold the plant to Gulf+Western after his death (it is now owned by Pope & Talbot), and I moved on to take a role in group strategic planning at American Can Company's Greenwich, Connecticut, headquarters in 1977. I got the job following a chance encounter with the vice chairman, Harry Howard, at a business meeting. He suggested I interview at American Can.

After restructuring and rightsizing Sterling, American Can's responsibility-free matrix management made no sense to me. Under matrix management, I reported to several different people, some for hands-on issues, some for administrative things. In the matrix, no single person could fire me, nor was any one boss responsible for my work. It's the direct opposite of the military, which has a very clear chain of command.

As head of special projects, I coordinated an American Can group that studied the matrix system and convinced management to return to more traditional business units where ultimate responsibility rests with the head of the division. Most businesses have chucked the matrix in the years since, returning to a direct system of responsibility.

As another result of the same study, American Can itself became a business comprised of four basic business units. I was handed one of them, the Performance Plastics division. It made plastic wraps for meat, cheese, cream cheese, potato chips, and Kool-Aid.

The chairman said to me, "Take this thing for a year and see what you can do."

Everyone thought the division should have been a great success, although it had always been a disaster. Promoted to the level of senior vice president and group executive, my task was to either turn it around or dispose of it.

Performance Plastics had never amounted to much. Management in the division was brain dead, but I changed that. Instead of letting them daydream about decisions and strategic moves, I made things happen in rapid succession and tossed overboard anyone who couldn't keep up. My method was simple: "Do it, dammit!" which employees referred to as "D-I squared."

I took us out of a multitude of money-losing businesses such as bread wrap, which produced the plastic bags in which loaves of bread are stored. The manufacturing process for making these bags was too expensive for us, compared to what it cost our competitors. Instead, we moved into the high-end and far more profitable meat wrap.

Then we cut the heck out of costs and came up with numerous new products, such as the retort pouch, a reheatable food package used by the military for food rations; microwave trays used by manufacturers of TV dinners; and the glaminate tube for toothpaste, a polyfoil tube that could be rolled like metal to squeeze out the last blob of toothpaste. It had a "dead-fold" characteristic; that is, it could be folded and would stay folded. We also developed the tubular water-quench process, which brought together seven different types of plastic all at once.

American Can's philosophy at that time was to pursue specialty niche markets. Under my leadership, Performance Plastics established itself as the leader in the higher-profit plastic and laminated tube markets, in the sophisticated photographic and medical packaging areas. We also expanded our position in the growth segments of the high-performance food film business.

As our business evolved, I shut down a large American Can plant in Scranton, Pennsylvania. It had produced a commodity resin product that our competitors made for less cost. The plant was losing money and was just too expensive to continue operating. Naturally, this didn't go over well with some people, especially Lieutenant Governor William W. Scranton III. He didn't like the idea of anyone closing down a plant in the town bearing his family's name. Scranton wrote a letter to American Can's chairman of the board that said, "You've got this terrible young executive who did this and he should be fired!"

But the chairman admired my steadfastness in facing down a lieutenant governor and, after I laid out the fiscal reasons behind my decision, reiterated his support for me. My letter to him somehow circulated throughout the company giving me a sort of folk-hero status with some and attracting flak from others.

Despite joining the management executive committee in 1981, I never quite fit the mold of the prototypical American Can executive. It was a traditional conglomerate, complete with an innovation-stifling bureaucracy, a stodgy, out-of-touch management, and a cost structure that was out of control. I was truly a maverick there, making decisions on the spot instead of shuffling responsibility off to some faceless committee. If a change needed to be made today, I made it today instead of putting it off into the far-flung future. I was always challenging the way things were done, saying what I thought, and making my share of enemies in the corporate hierarchy.

My next project at American Can was "The Gamma Project," the code name for development of a plastic ketchup bottle. I use ketchup all the time and never understood why it had to come in a heavy glass bottle. The bottles broke all the time and weren't functional. We reckoned that a plastic ketchup bottle would be lighter for shipping and would bounce, not break, if dropped.

While it sounds simple, manufacturing a plastic ketchup bottle wasn't easy. The original designs broke or cracked. Some left a funny taste. Ketchup spoiled. Or the lids didn't close. In fact, the project was almost killed when the chairman of the company took home a prototype one-gallon container and put it in his refrigerator. His wife took it out and accidentally dropped it, splattering plastic and tomato sauce everywhere. It looked like hell. But in the end, we overcame the manufacturing snafus by developing a new resin process, and the bottle's successful development and rollout pushed us into the very high end of plastics packaging.

By this time, I pretty well knew what I was doing as a turnaround specialist, but I still wasn't doing it as consciously as I would at my next job. I was focusing on good managers and marketers, cutting the hell out of costs, and selling assets. I didn't have a philosophy then; I was doing everything on automatic pilot, based on what felt right and what delivered the most value to the shareholder. But out of this madness, a method was beginning to take shape—one I employed in my next job as CEO of Lily-Tulip.

Chapter 8

RAMBO IN PINSTRIPES

LESSON: DON'T TAKE THE EASY WAY OUT.
IT'S ALWAYS EASIER TO TAKE THE EASY
WRONG THAN THE HARDER RIGHT.

Few people at Lily-Tulip Company in Toledo, Ohio, the U.S.'s second largest supplier of disposable cups to the food service industry, had ever heard of me when I was hired as the new CEO in 1983. All they knew was that somebody was coming in from Kohlberg Kravis Roberts & Company (KKR), the Wall Street investment banking firm which pioneered the leveraged buyout (LBO) in the 1970s and had purchased Lily-Tulip for $180 million in a well-publicized, highly leveraged buyout the year before.

There was great trepidation about what the new CEO might do. The perception was that I was a KKR person, but that wasn't true; I had no prior association with KKR. I was recommended for the job by turnaround consultant L. Eugene Clayton. But all that Lily-Tulip's staff knew for certain was that it was getting a tough business manager.

The press follows my every move today, but in the early days at Lily-Tulip, my ideas and management methods weren't widely known. The executives had my resume and knew I was a take no BS.... West Point graduate, but that was it.

They expected KKR would bring in a tough manager to change the company and turn it around. Even so, I don't think anybody anticipated things were going to change to the extent or as rapidly as they did.

Morale was horrendous. People told me there were probably more resumes on the street from Lily-Tulip employees than from any other company in the city. Everyone was figuring how to bail out; it was a sinking ship.

How bad was it? The debt-to-equity ratio was 9:1, meaning we had nine times more debt than we had equity. To put the ratio in perspective: Most companies have a debt that is equal to or less than their equity. Lily-Tulip's debt was outsized; there were leveraged buyouts and then there were overleveraged buyouts. Our situation was over the top. A 9:1 ratio at a company making money was no problem; a company that had a 9:1 ratio and was losing money hand over fist was terrible. At the time, however, this type of crushing debt arrangement was not uncommon; today, most acquiring firms are fortunate to get 1:1 ratios.

Lily-Tulip was financed at prime rate plus 2 percent at a time when the prime hovered between 16 and 18 percent. That's big money in any deal, but especially in a leveraged buyout. It was choking the company, and the banks were going nuts.

KKR was losing its ass, $11 million lost on sales of $275 million in just the first year, representing one-third of KKR's equity investment. Pretty sad, especially considering KKR had given the old management an equity stake in running Lily-Tulip.

The problem was not in Lily-Tulip's products—disposable paper, plastic and foam cups, plates, bowls, lids, foam labels, and plastic carriers for the bottling and beverage markets. It wasn't even the debt from the LBO. No, the fundamental crisis at Lily-Tulip was that management's way of running the company was lousy. And it wasn't as if no one knew. As *Forbes* magazine reporter Allan Sloan put it, "Too many people involved in the deal were contemplating their paper millions instead of making paper cups." The banks were screaming at KKR because it was straining loan covenants to keep Lily-Tulip afloat. The company was so badly managed it couldn't even scrape together enough money to pay its monthly debt service.

Bankers Trust and Continental Illinois threatened to pull the plug during my first month.

Lily-Tulip was a $300 million business run by people who had been spun off by Owens-Illinois, a $3 billion business. They sustained a large-company mentality that was no longer appropriate. The reason the company had no money was that management had staffed up at the administrative level, imitating the Owens-Illinois model, rather than designing a new, more modest model to fit the much smaller Lily-Tulip. Everyone had a secretary and it was not uncommon to find spouses or adult children on the payroll as well. A $300 million company didn't warrant its own plane or limousine, but the previous management didn't understand that, and KKR, which granted tremendous latitude to its managers, didn't care about those things as long as the company made money.

The mood around Lily-Tulip when I arrived was fatalistic. Managers hoped the company could survive, but didn't have a clue how to do it and really didn't believe it could be done.

In Lily-Tulip's case, the problems were primarily concentrated at the headquarters level. Out in the field, our products were still selling. Lily-Tulip's customers included McDonald's, 7-Eleven, Dairy Queen, Hardee's, Kentucky Fried Chicken, Taco Bell, Wendy's, White Castle, Coca-Cola, 7-Up, and Pepsi. Because the company was private, few people knew how really bad the situation was. Executives in a private company are more insulated against adversity because they don't have to report details in documents such as annual reports to stockholders.

My first day on the job, I called a short meeting of the senior management. The company was in terrible trouble, and most of these managers were to blame. Looking around the room, I kept my remarks simple and pointed my index finger at the people I wanted to remain. "You two stay—the rest of you are fired. Good-bye."

How did I know who stayed and who went? As the Scott Paper board of directors would do many years later, I was briefed by KKR on who was deadwood and who had the potential to grow the company, such as the newly installed CEO, Art Witt. I took this information and used my own instincts. There was nothing random about who got the ax.

People perform in the future the way they did in the past. Most

LBOs, if they fail, do so because management was poor in the first place. If lousy management hasn't changed following the LBO, how likely is it to be any brighter now? Lily-Tulip's senior executives didn't recognize themselves as the company's problem and they didn't express any interest in change. I needed people willing to do whatever it took to make money for the shareholders—KKR.

The financial record of what occurred at Lily-Tulip in the absence of those executives—as documented in *Forbes* and reported by CNN—would indicate my intelligence dossier on prior management was well informed:

- 1982: Lily-Tulip lost $11 million the year before I was hired; debt was at a record $165 million.
- 1984: Lily-Tulip *earned* $23 million after my first full year; debt dipped to $43 million.
- 1985: Lily-Tulip went public, earning KKR a $120 million stock profit on its $30 million equity investment.

Furthermore, on the day I arrived, Lily-Tulip's stock was $1.77 unlisted. We ultimately sold it at $18.55, a 1,100 percent increase in two and a half years.

In those same two and a half years, shareholder equity rose from $19 million to $108 million—all as a result of drastic cost-cutting, selective investment, and common sense. Headquarters staff was cut in half. Salaried staff was cut by 20 percent. The Toledo headquarters was closed and moved closer to our plants in Georgia, where we paid just $10 per square foot for office space. We grounded and sold the corporate jet. We unloaded unproductive manufacturing plants in New Jersey and Maine. Waste product was cut by 15 percent.

We increased our budget for research and development, and we spent capital on making manufacturing less labor-intensive and more efficient. And we launched a fabulously successful new product, the co-extruded Trophy® XL cup, the first two-ply foam-and-plastic disposable for either hot or cold liquids.

Lily-Tulip became a great success. It demonstrated that when KKR gave great freedom to talented executives, it got great results. It also betrayed the firm's weakness, of course: When KKR had bad executives, the results were horrendous. A very supportive parent company, KKR was dependent on its operators because the KKR people were financiers, not managers. Their success or failure was predicated on their ability to get top-flight managers. Unfortunately, they tended to support bad managers too long. But as history has shown, they have more often chosen quality people and been rewarded. They are the most successful leveraged buyout firm in American history, buying and or selling companies such as RJR Nabisco, Duracell, Borden, and Safeway.

A cover story in *Georgia Trend* magazine, reflecting on the speed with which we changed Lily-Tulip and my personal style in doing it, called me "Georgia's Toughest Boss." It didn't matter what they called me, really; at the end of the day, everyone knew I got the job done.

Seven months into my tour of duty at Lily-Tulip, things were really going well, and KKR partner George Roberts threw a little dinner for me at the Huntington Hotel in San Francisco. He toasted me and said, "I always thought that if you were twice as good as I thought you were, you would have a 50 percent chance of pulling this thing off."

"George," I said, "that is not what you said when you hired me. You said it would be a slam dunk for me."

"I lied," he said.

That night, they made me chairman of Lily-Tulip.

•••

In December 1985, an executive headhunter for the search firm of Heidrick and Struggles passed my name on to Sir James Goldsmith. Goldsmith, a European billionaire who had just acquired a failing San Francisco-based timberlands company, Crown-Zellerbach, needed someone who could save it from itself.

Goldsmith was an Anglo-French financier turned statesman whose net worth was $1 billion when I met him in 1986. He was reportedly a multibillionaire upon his death in 1997. When our paths first crossed, he was an internationally renowned hostile-takeover specialist who had been knighted by British Labour Prime Minister, Harold Wilson. Until the early 1990s, when he devoted all his energies to politics and environmental issues, he ran a business empire with operations in Britain, France, the United States, Mexico, and Guatemala. His best-known company was the Grand Union supermarket chain, which he acquired in 1973 for $62 million.

A London journalist once said of him, "He was not the inventor of the hostile takeover, but he took it across the Atlantic and perfected it into a work of art."

In 1986, he called my boss, KKR partner George Roberts, who described me as "the best operator KKR knew of." That was enough for Goldsmith, who asked me to his home in New York City for an interview.

Afterward, Judy asked me how it went.

"I don't know," I said. "He's very smart and he talked about a lot of things."

"Did you like him?" she asked.

"I think so, but he's different than anybody I've ever met." I also doubted that anything would come of it.

But three days later I got a call from Sir James, inviting us to London for Christmas week.

There were many parallels between what I had done at Lily-Tulip and what needed doing at Crown-Zellerbach, and over dinner at Aspinall's, Goldsmith's London gaming club, I detailed the turnaround of Lily-Tulip.

That was all Sir James needed to hear.

"We will work out a deal," he said.

I said, "Yes, Sir James."

"Call me James," he said, then changed his mind. "No, no—Jimmy. You must call me Jimmy because that is what my friends call me."

•••

One on one, Sir James Goldsmith was not your typical predator engaged in hostile takeovers. Elegant, gracious to a fault, he was ever the sophisticated European. But in reality, he came up through great hardships in his time, including war and hard times. He climbed life's rungs one step at a time—just like me.

Goldsmith's father once managed hotels in Europe, giving Jimmy great connections, but no money. Then came World War II; his family fled Europe and emigrated to England. Whatever they had had before was lost, and Jimmy's father enlisted in the British army, rising to the rank of major.

Despite the hardships that beset his family, Jimmy entered

adulthood as a roguish playboy. It wasn't until later in life that he became a billionaire. He made his money the old-fashioned way, as they say: He earned it.

He often remarked to me, "My dear boy, you and I have an enormous respect for money because we had to make it. We had to live by our wits."

Sir James was a larger than life influence on me, an absolutely brilliant, dynamic, and gregarious man who fished me out of the corporate stream and made me what I am today.

He backed me in everything I did. He encouraged me and introduced me to another world, a world of enormous wealth and power. He was a brilliant financier, and I became financially sophisticated working for him. For six years, I ran all of his business activities.

His impact on me was all the more significant because, considering my modest starting point in life, I already thought I was on top of the world. I'd just done a high-profile turnaround at Lily-Tulip for KKR and was a millionaire several times over.

Until I met Sir James, all my experiences had been in the United States. I'd been a good generalist up until then, but I learned from him that there is far more business to be gained outside our borders than within. Working with him, I found myself at the center of enormous power. I learned how to do international deals, buying and selling assets, and how to deal more effectively with investment and commercial bankers. It broadened my horizons tremendously.

In every deal I ever did with Sir James, when it came time to settle, he was always more generous with me than he had to be. He had a special aura about him and was fun to be with.

He once said to me, "It's amazing how we always come to the same conclusions." Jimmy never second-guessed me, was always supportive. He never came out and ordered me to do anything. His manner was more, "I would appreciate it if you would look at this." He was subtle, and I was more like a sledgehammer. Jimmy had a charming, aristocratic personality except when provoked.

He entered politics before his death. I miss him. I think we were an absolutely unbeatable combination.

•••

Sir James was the first to call me "Rambo in Pinstripes." It was something he said offhandedly to a reporter and meant to be a great compliment. He explained it to me this way, "You're like Rambo. You go into a situation that's totally chaotic and you clean it up, fight the good fight, and when you leave, you've won the war."

During my days in Australia, restructuring companies for Kerry Packer, the press there picked up on the nickname "Chainsaw," which I never liked, but it stuck. "Chainsaw" was given to me by John Aspinall, the famed British naturalist and gambler. He once said, "Al is like a chainsaw. He goes in and cuts away all the fat and leaves a great sculpture." It, too, was meant to be a great compliment, but over the years it sounded like I was some kind of serial killer. That one's always been a bit of a thorn in my side.

I love the Rambo movies. Here's a guy who has zero chance of success and he always wins. Rambo goes into situations against all odds, expecting to get his brains blown out. But he doesn't. At the end of the day, he succeeds, he gets rids of the bad guys. He creates peace out of war.

That's what I do, too. It's always easier to justify why you *didn't* make a decision. I set myself apart by taking on the most difficult turnarounds, like Scott. The lost causes. I don't worry about taking a lot of prisoners. I don't get bogged down with the social baggage. I do the right things and I do them on a consistent basis.

How do you get to be a "Rambo in Pinstripes"? By having strong convictions. By making the tough decisions that other people walk away from. By taking criticism. By knowing when to say "That's enough," ending debate and beginning implementation.

People want a leader they can look up to. They may not like him or what he's doing, but at least they know he's getting things done. If you're going to be in public life, you must have a strong personality. It inspires people.

The outside world thinks, "This guy is tough." And I am tough. Damn tough. But, for good employees, I'm the best boss they could have. For bad employees, I'm the worst. I appreciate people who make the effort; I appreciate a good job and I reward people.

The business establishment either likes me or they abhor me. There's no in-between. Those whose nice, comfortable bureaucratic worlds I've upset, hate me. Those CEOs who've been asked, "Dunlap did it, why can't you?"—they loathe me.

Employees never know what to expect from me, which keeps them on their toes. I'll join them at lunch, or wander through production facilities in casual clothes and without a contingent of senior VPs in tow.

Once I went on a fact-finding trip to one of Lily-Tulip's mills. The crew there thought they would entertain me with flip-charts and a slide show, and then I'd leave. That's the way they always did it before, at least. I kept them locked in a conference room all day, answering tough questions. One of the managers later said, "We'll do anything you ask. Just don't send Al back."

•••

My last assignment leading up to Scott Paper was in Australia, running Kerry Packer's far-flung media empire, Consolidated Press Holdings.

When Packer asked me to work for him, he said, "I want you to do two things. I want you to run this company and I want you to train my son, James."

At that point in Kerry's life, he was already a very wealthy man. He had worked his whole adult life in this family media business, most of it in his legendary father's shadow, then as very much his own man. Kerry had taken a successful company worth a few hundred million and pumped its value up into the billions. But his health was poor. He had lost a kidney, survived a cancer scare, and, in October 1990, actually "died" for several minutes following a heart attack. For the rest of his life, he wanted to do what pleased him. That meant getting his business affairs in order and preparing the fourth generation of Packer men for the owner's chair.

James was a complex young man who idolized his father and who will one day be the richest man in Australia. He has a quick mind and is highly intelligent—despite never going to college. I found him to be a good student with a burning desire to learn.

I was a very tough taskmaster with him. Then in his early

20s, James was too young to take over Consolidated Press Holdings, but the hard-living Packer men had all gone to their graves as relatively young men. Kerry—who had learned the ways of business the hard way, without any direct tutelage by his father—wanted James made ready for any eventuality. He loved his son and didn't want him to be a lamb among wolves as he had been when his father died.

•••

I ran Packer's companies as if every last penny flowed from me personally.

One of the reason Kerry needed me in the first place was that, over the years, his payroll had collected a multitude of hangers-on—political or sports friends of Kerry's who were being paid by the company but offering no return on his investment. There was no one else with fortitude and backbone enough to make decisions on Kerry's behalf. He'd hired people in the past to clean up, but whenever there was a confrontation, the manager would either get fired or acquiesce because he needed the job. I didn't need the job and I wasn't intimidated by Kerry.

Kerry is a very big, strong willed, demanding person. I was specifically hired to go in and fix his companies. But when you change something that has been family-owned, you are messing with things that the family itself put in place. Even though I vastly enhanced Packer's wealth, the family tie always created an awkward situation. Assume for a moment it is your business. You want it to be successful, you want it to make money. But you will also tend to be sensitive because somebody is changing your creation; you feel as if it is an attack on you. It should be viewed as a dynamic business correction, but it's not that easy for some families.

Kerry didn't have anyone on his payroll like me. I could afford to walk away from his operation anytime, and I wasn't afraid of telling the boss when he was full of crap. Nobody else told Packer that, but we both agreed that that was the way it had to be when I was hired.

I fired many people who had been close to the family. I changed relationships and sold family businesses that had lasted for years and years.

Kerry encouraged me to toughen his son up and expose him to the ways in which business is done. I took him under my wing like he was my own son. He is going to be worth billions of dollars, but I treated him like an employee. He was my assistant. I included him in everything and asked his advice on many things, but the final decisions were mine. I was running the companies on a day-to-day basis.

Focusing, pruning, and reducing debt in the Packer businesses meant layoffs and hard, unpopular choices. It was a difficult time for James to be introduced to his father's world.

"Life is not easy, business is not easy," I told James. "Sometimes you will make difficult decisions and know that those decisions are going to perhaps hurt other people. But you must know in your heart that they are still the right decisions to make."

I sometimes got upset with him. "James," I'd say, "you have to make a decision. You have to determine whether you are James or 'Jamie.' If you want to play polo and take out a different model every night and go skiing, you can continue to be Jamie. But if you want to learn how to run a business you have to become James. And James, I believe you can be a world class executive if you want."

James told *Australian Business* that he had never seen anybody as tenacious as me—including his father—but that I was also the least political person he ever met. He saw me do things that he didn't think could be done. Sometimes he told me that I pushed someone or something too far. But he learned the lessons of how hard and how far you could push. When the Packers talked, most people automatically said "Yes" to whatever they asked and told them what they wanted to hear. It was a new experience for James when I thought he or his father was wrong and I would take them on.

Kerry and I were such strong personalities, there was bound to be friction. We fought and argued on occasion. There were times we would have pounded each other into the ground except he was a hell of a lot bigger than me. One reporter wrote that Australia wasn't big enough to hold both of our egos.

We did have our calmer moments, however. I remember

playing tennis at his 70,000-acre ranch at Ellerston. I heard a little tendon or something snap and I suddenly fell down. Kerry immediately rushed over, picked me up, and put me on a lounge chair. This was not only a wealthy man and a man who had political power, this was a physically powerful man.

In the end, Kerry and I split because we were just too similar. We were like two strong-willed, dominant animals who hunted together and brought down the biggest prey, but, when not hunting, fought each other.

Nonetheless, James and I became very attached. For eighteen months, he had an office adjacent to mine with an open door between us. We spent an enormous amount of time together. He was a friend to me in a place where the work could be quite lonely and I had few friends.

James once said to me, "I can't understand how somebody like you, born with no contacts and no money, how you could succeed the way you did."

I saw myself in him at that age, despite his wealth. He had a burning desire to do good. If I thought he was just another spoiled rich kid, I would have had nothing to do with him. One day, he'll be a great businessman on the world stage, and I'm proud that I had a hand in his development.

PART IV

DUNLAPPING THE CORPORATION

Chapter 9
LOOK UNDER "M" FOR MARKETING

LESSON: DON'T BE AFRAID TO REPLACE THE WAY THINGS WERE WITH THE WAY THEY SHOULD BE.

I knew I was in trouble at Scott Paper when I started talking about marketing and everybody ran back to their offices and looked in the dictionary under "M."

Early on, when I held meetings with the marketing committee. I'd say, "What are our plans?" This would be greeted by blank stares and long silences. Here was a company that apparently forgot that its business was marketing products. When I talked about marketing, they talked about tons. Everything was tons. "Oh, we produce this many tons and we sell them at the best price we can."

As I visited our international plants and operations around the world, whenever I brought up profits, somebody inevitably would say, "Well, we sold this many tons."

"What's our margin?" I'd ask.

"Can I get back to you on that?" somebody would say. But they never did. We didn't even speak the same business language. And they didn't think in terms of Scott brands—improving or growing one or the other. They were trying to wheel and deal the price of a ton of paper as opposed to viewing the tons as an intermediary step to finished, branded products that command a greater markup.

Their other insanity was a preferential attitude toward private labels over our own brands. Scott sold a third of its manufacturing output to private labels or store brands.

Why? We had capital in place that required a gross return on capital of at least 20 percent. But instead of selling Scott products, which provided double the margins of private labels, they settled for half that return, from no-name generic store brands.

They bragged to me about selling all this product, but that was crap because they sold it all for nothing! They were throwing away a third of Scott's capital assets for no good return.

The challenge we faced was not only to sell all the production but to sell it in a universal branded form around the world. And to do it at reasonable margins that generated an adequate rate of return for the company and its shareholders.

As Scott's branded products went down in sales, the old management moved more production into private label products, in order to sell the tons. So not only did the sales dollars go down, the margin dollars fell, too. It was a never-ending spiral because we weren't increasing sales of the branded product.

We had *engineers* doing marketing, a mismatch if ever there was one, and it was reflected in lousy advertising, miserably packaged products, and no new product innovations. Is it any wonder that we rebuilt the marketing department from scratch?

One of our greatest challenges in marketing was the conversion of Scott's industrial culture from that of a paper producer to one of a consumer products company. Instead of seeing ourselves as manufacturers of generic paper products, we had to recreate our image as the proud proprietors of branded household names such as Scotties, Scot-Towels, Viva, and Cottonelle. The previous management had obviously lost sight of this image; there hadn't been a substantial advertising campaign for any brand, except Andrex in the United Kingdom, for more than a decade. In fact, our brands were declining worldwide, and our profit margins were eroding. The old Scott consumer business was well on the way to extinction.

That's where Dick Nicolosi, whom I hired as senior vice president of Scott's Worldwide Consumer Products Business, became so important. The veteran Procter & Gamble executive analyzed our products and technology, in search of the pearls of value: profitability leverages and growth opportunities. They were there, but they were hidden within a mindset and a prevailing belief that Scott just sold tons; tons was the name of the business. Looking at the business category by category around the world, Nicolosi recognized that we had to take immediate action to staunch heavy bleeding.

I'm real good at doing the nuts and bolts of running a corporation; Nicolosi's talent is conceptualizing and implementing marketing strategies and business plans. Working together at Scott, we were an example of how 1 + 1 can equal 3 or even 4.

Nicolosi put in place a product strategy that focused on three core product lines: bath tissue, towels, and wet wipes. Every product would be fine-tuned or overhauled and then repackaged and relaunched under his direction. He had to start from scratch because Scott did not have a marketing strategy.

When you play a sport, you have a game plan. I play tennis. I always know what I am going to try and do during the course of a match. I may have to adjust as the game goes on and I learn things about my opponent's strengths and weaknesses. That new knowledge requires changing the game plan. But I always have a plan to win.

The same is true of winners in business. Call it a strategy, an operating plan, or even a recipe; regardless of the name, it's a roadmap for success based on knowing what you do best versus the competition, and recognizing customer needs. Scott had no strategy. Not on an individual brand basis, not on a collective brand basis, not on a global basis. Nicolosi's first job was to construct global strategies for the consumer business. Absent that, we might as well have locked the doors and walked away.

Scott had twenty-seven brand names in America—but that wasn't a reason for bragging. The company actually had created a vexing problem: Many similar Scott products were known by different names. Consumers could buy Viva paper towels in Connecticut and in Washington State, but the name might be slightly or completely different—and the quality radically different. A total hodgepodge. Same problem in Europe and Asia. Logically, everything should have been the same name; if nothing else, it was cheaper to advertise and manage one name.

Viva was a crap product in the Eastern United States and a good product in the Midwest and part of the West, but it didn't exist in the Southwest. And its quality was inconsistent from market to market. One version would be softer, one more absorbent. A consumer who picked up the product in New York would try it and say, "This is terrible! I'll never buy it again!" It would be like buying a Coke on the east coast and it's caramel colored, and buying one on the west coast and it looks and tastes like watered-down iced tea. Someone who had the watered-down iced tea once would never buy it again. It would poison the predisposition of the consumer forever. And every consumer is going to tell his or her share of people, so this quality problem spreads like wildfire.

Viva paper towels in the Western United States were made with the best technology available in America, and it was the highest quality product of its kind. With proper marketing know-how, Nicolosi said, Viva should have been No. 1 in its category. Scott had the technology for decades but didn't have the brains to get word out to consumers. It was truly remarkable how blind and nonproactive this company was. Nicolosi consolidated Job Squad towels into Viva and added a highly effective scrub cloth from the Away-From-Home business.

•••

Our new strategy became "Scott the World Over." We established a new consistency in bath tissue, towels, and facials, instead of a multiplicity of names and qualities throughout the world. Coke has that strategy. You can buy a Coke in Zimbabwe or Duluth and it's always Coca-Cola. We believed Scott had a great franchise name and our products should be Scott the world over.

The worldwide branding issue should have been dealt with years earlier, but the previous management was too bogged down needlessly expending capital and seeking executive consensus on all issues. No one was manager in charge of breaking the logjams or ties. They were all in endless détente. Because of that, the same product was marketed and sold in different ways in different places. That fragmentation around the world prevented Scott from truly becoming a global brand. It was not positioned; it was not marketed or advertised as one brand. These people—more than a dozen people were making these decisions—did whatever they wanted. And whenever any one of them was questioned, a finger got pointed at somebody else.

This is a fundamental problem in many companies that have brands throughout the world: They don't have a worldwide, coherent plan and positioning for their product. In one area of the world, it may be viewed as junk; in another area of the world, it may be viewed as a premium product. But what does it stand for? That's the beauty of Coca-Cola—you know what it stands for, worldwide.

In late 1995, Pepsico Foods apparently came to the same conclusion we did. Its dominant soft drink, Pepsi, is known the world over, but its potato chips went by different names. In Britain, it was Walkers Crisps; in Mexico, Papas Sabritas; and in Spain, Matutano. Like us, it repackaged and relaunched its product under one label—Lay's chips.

Scott, a company with operations in twenty-two countries and product sales in eighty countries, had lost the benefit of being a big global operation in an evolving world economy.

•••

While we were repositioning products and adding new ones, we also made significant decisions about eliminating products.

We dropped tissue product lines such as Family Scott, a regional brand in the West and Southwest that had no distinctive identity and actually competed with the Scott line. We also discontinued Chelsea, in the West; the brand was sold mostly in select trade channels, such as warehouse clubs.

You won't find our moisturizing cream, 24 Hours, on the shelves anymore. Gone, too, is Scott toilet bowl cleaner. Also missing in action: Scott training pants for small children, and Promise, our adult diapers. All were poor-selling, ill-marketed efforts.

We saw no advantage in each of our paper brands—Scott, Viva, and Cottonelle—being in the dinner napkins business. It was a low-margin category that drew valuable capital resources away from other things. We retooled it to one product, Scott napkins.

In western Canada, just across the U.S. border, we had Purex, a Canadian toilet tissue brand that existed nowhere else. In eastern Canada, we didn't produce Purex; our brand there was Cottonelle. For some stupid reason, we didn't produce Scott in Canada at all. Purex became Scott Purex, then Scott by Purex.

Being so spread out kept Scott from maximizing its business and marketing investment. Redundancy and duplicity flourished across the board. Plus, we had a confusing plethora of different stock keeping units, or SKUs, because we had different products with different packages and different market positions for each. It was a fragmented global business that would reinvent the wheel 100 times without getting any economies of scale or leverage in the global marketplace.

In all, we eliminated 31 percent of the consumer product items we had offered, while creating, reformulating, or repackaging 107 products that sold better and were more profitable. In total, our worldwide finished product inventory levels actually went down by almost 25 percent.

Reducing the volume of different products cut our total sales, but the remaining product mix went on to sell over half a billion dollars more than they ever had before—at twice the profit margin.

Combined market shares of Scott Tissue and Cottonelle grew to roughly 20 percent; Scotties grew to 7 percent; and once we solved its consistency problems and made Viva a high-quality towel across the United States, the brand rose almost two share points, up over 30 percent in less than a year's time. Meanwhile, our Away-From-Home products for commercial and industrial markets showed sweeping increases in product variety, geography, and sales.

The one product that still worked hard for the company was Scott Tissue, which we renamed Scott 1000s (referring to the number of sheets in each roll of toilet tissue). Despite years of neglect and great efforts to tank that business, it had held up and was a substantial, ongoing profit center. It became a cornerstone from which we could build a healthy product as opposed to yet another patient in intensive care or on its deathbed. We broadened the architecture of Scott toilet tissue products through line extensions: Scott 1500s; Scott Moist Cloths; and Scott Extra.

Cottonelle was another tissue brand that refused to die, a regional as opposed to a national brand. The brand had two different formulas, one that was positively and enthusiastically accepted by consumers and another that was not. So we had a brand that had a neat name, decent positioning in limited markets, and a real viability to be nurtured and expanded. We restaged the Cottonelle brand around the concept of advanced personal hygiene—a breakthrough new concept for bath tissue. While other products talked "squeezable" and "angel" softness, we were the first to bring a new benefit to the category. We introduced a series of brand extensions, including a hypoallergenic product and another that contained baking soda. We also laid out plans for an antibacterial Cottonelle product.

The relaunch worked. Retailers gobbled up every case of Cottonelle we could make—product often never even made it to the warehouse. It was sent straight to trucks and on to the stores. Our warehouses collected no dust once we revitalized these products. We took Cottonelle from being a regional, multiproduct, unfocused brand to one that was national and at the head of its class in terms of growth.

Some people asked why we didn't put the Scott name on Cottonelle when we took it national. That was a judgment call. Nicolosi and I felt that Scott stood for a different set of values and had a different character than Cottonelle. Scott was what we'd call an "honest American value." It had the tradition of something long-standing and trustworthy, a utilitarian product that had achieved credibility by enduring for decades. Cottonelle, by contrast, cost a little more and attracted a more upscale consumer who had much more sophisticated needs.

As we did our market segmentation work, we concluded that there was a role for a no-frills brand—Scott 1000s—as well as Cottonelle, which represented added values all driven by chemistry.

The two products were distinctive in personality and character, distinctive in positioning and consumer appeal. That convinced us to support both brands.

On products we continued producing, Scott achieved sales growth of 24.5 percent and tissue margins of 20.4 percent in less than two years.

•••

Our goal in marketing was to build not only a sense of competitiveness but of winners. As soon as our marketing department felt some self-esteem and developed some courage, it would succeed big-time.

Momentum was key for rebuilding this part of the organization. That's why we hired fourteen experienced marketing directors with history at Kimberly-Clark, Procter & Gamble, Colgate-Palmolive, and Coca-Cola.

We reorganized the marketing hierarchy by category of business. For the first time, we had a person in each category responsible for profit and loss, volume, share, dollar sales, margins, inventory, and so on. It was as if he or she owned a small paper towel or bath tissue business. Each person made decisions and was accountable to improve P&L, volume, share, and margin. The second thing they were accountable for was working with their colleagues in Europe and Asia to make sure that the best ideas overseas were being used in the United States, and, conversely, that the best ideas in the United States were being applied in Europe and Asia. A good idea would be a bang heard 'round the world, as opposed to a cap pistol shot that barely made a sound.

We got higher productivity out of those who remained on the team because we assigned personal accountability for product development by group and by category. Before, a group of people had sat around indulging themselves with scientific curiosity, posing questions like, "Wouldn't it be neat to see if this could be done with paper?" They lacked a vision for how the consumer would benefit, or how the product could be translated into something the consumer would want. They never worried about whether the market was big enough to justify developing the product, either. So we had situations where they had created nifty little inventions that only ten people in all the world wanted.

As I mentioned earlier, the consumer business at the old Scott was at war with the Away-From-Home business. New products in the Away-From-Home business would be ignored by the consumer side out of pride—or maybe jealousy. They just couldn't condescend to use Away-From-Home inventions.

We said, "A good idea is a good idea. Who cares where it's from? All we're counting is the total number of dollars we make in the marketplace." All of a sudden, new ideas were like low-hanging fruit.

The breakthrough idea was this: Away-From-Home industrial products were often superior-performing consumer products because they had to do double duty. They had to succeed in stressful, torturous situations. Interestingly enough, that made them all the more successful as consumer products, because a meaningful percentage of consumers always want the Mercedes-Benz of performance. So we had a lot of product development that was already done but Scott wasn't using it.

Those two factors made an enormous opportunity for us in the first eighteen months.

Nicolosi also looked at our Baby Fresh product, a premoistened hygienic tissue for wiping babies. It was a technologically advanced product that released a microencapsulated lotion as the baby was cleansed, leaving a protective layer on the baby's behind to prevent diaper rash. No other competitor had this product but consumers didn't even know it existed! We closed this gap with advertising, and Baby Fresh regained category leadership in the U.S. market.

For nine years, Scott had been sitting on advanced technology for manufacturing moistened toilet tissue, but never marketed it. Nicolosi supervised its release as Cottonelle Moist in the United States and Andrex Moist in the United Kingdom. (Andrex was a particularly strong brand name in the United Kingdom and we stood by it.)

We estimated the potential market for moist tissue was at least $1 billion. Why? Traditional dry toilet tissue doesn't clean, it wipes. We believed most households would stock both, once they understood the advantages of moist toilet tissue. It will be years before anyone knows if we were right.

One problem in exploiting the potential of moist tissue was inventing a dispenser that handled both dry and moist toilet tissue but fit into a traditional dry-only toilet paper dispenser. I told my marketing and R&D people that when they figured that out, the home marketplace would be at our feet.

They agreed and immediately created prototypes and began consumer testing.

The bigger problem was that Scott couldn't afford to effectively market new products such as these as long as it was pouring hundreds of millions of dollars into capital projects such as S.D. Warren and the Mobile, Alabama, co-generation energy plant. *(See Chapter Five, "Rule 3: Know What Business You're In" for more detail.)*

Scott had reached a point where it couldn't afford to invest and improve its branded products, which exacerbated their decline. It was like having an artery cut on your arm. You bleed and bleed, getting weaker and weaker. All of a sudden you can't run anymore, then you can't walk anymore, then you die.

While I worked on unloading costly assets and redirecting capital toward value-added endeavors such as product exploitation, Nicolosi reapplied core competencies in the areas of leadership, marketing, business strategy, and analysis. He also recognized that we were spending way too much in trade or co-op funds and rechanneled about $100 million into advertising and consumer promotion efforts without spending an extra dime in total. Instead of giving money directly to retailers in the hope that they might market our product (a common retail practice), we did the advertising and drove the demand ourselves. Then it was up to retailers to either meet consumer needs or lose business to stores that did. We took moneys we were already spending and spent them more wisely and more strategically.

•••

Some things, like developing advertising for a brand, or new package designs and market positioning, take more time than others. Even before we had a strategy, we appointed new global advertising agencies and assigned our brands to packaging-design houses so that we could get that work under way. Operating concurrently, we avoided the dead time of doing these things sequentially. Part of the challenge was thinking through all that stuff: Which decisions could be implemented simultaneously and which ones had to be sequenced?

Part of the reason Scott was so disparate in Europe was that the company's original strategy had been to partner with local companies rather than build facilities and products from scratch. This made the company a 50/50 owner in many existing brands. In the late 1980s, Scott management maximized its investments and bought the other 50 percent of most of its European companies. Where it fell short, until I came along, was in establishing the Scott brand across all these product universes. Even when 100 percent Scott ownership went into effect, every country's producer was left to its own devices.

Also complicating Nicolosi's task: Each country has its own needs when it comes to products such as toilet paper. The Dutch want plain white paper, but in Belgium, the only product that sells is imprinted with designs. In France, there are five different colors that sell, and each has a different perfume. Meanwhile, German consumers insist on four-ply paper.

The width of a toilet paper roll also varies from the one we use in North America. Some countries use a model that is 1/8" smaller; in others it's ¼" smaller. That requires different machines. So wherever we could consolidate to one size, we saved a ton of money.

Scott was a strong brand in countries such as Italy, Spain, and Belgium. In the past, there had been also a halfhearted introduction of the Cottonelle brand without a distinctive marketing and advertising campaign—the company's first move to have a worldwide brand name.

The thing that surprised almost everyone, in the company and out, was how little consumer resistance there was to pushing the Scott name above regional brands.

Even more fascinating, as old borders to Eastern Europe broke down, we found that English-language brand names such as Scott were eagerly scooped up because the name immediately suggested quality in places where standards in the past were not as high.

As one part of the "Scott the World Over" campaign we plotted to make Scott facial and toilet tissue and paper towels as ubiquitous around the globe as McDonald's or Coke. Just as Scott put out different toilet paper brands within the United States, we owned an entire roster of names around the world. We produced Andrex bath tissue in the United Kingdom, Servus in Germany, Page in the Netherlands, Popla in Belgium and Luxembourg, Scottex in continental Europe and in parts of Asia, and Sujee in

Taiwan.

As in Canada, our first step with these various brands was to put the name "Scott" before them and gradually have the Scott name grow and the regional brand shrink until it disappeared altogether.

Every single package was changed. Every single brand was repositioned.

Each regional and international brand required unique advertising and marketing campaigns. Many of these brands were started by Scott companies; some were acquired but the previous management never moved to consolidate them. In the United States alone, we had the same brands with different products in different parts of the country. We had brands that weren't national so we couldn't effectively sell them in the national accounts, the Wal-Marts, the Kmarts. This hodge-podge prevented us from maximizing the business in any way, shape, or form.

The amount of money being spent as a result of this scattershot approach was criminal. At one point, we had eleven different ad agencies around the world. When we cut to three proven worldwide agencies, we saved millions in agency fees. And whereas the previous management had spent $14 million annually in worldwide market research, we reduced that amount to less than $3 million a year and got results.

Marketing Scott across Europe was pretty easy, as long as we stuck with universal themes such as kids, dogs, and cats. They can sell anything around the world.

It was terribly important that the entire organization know there was only one strategy for the brands and only one set of products around the world, and that there would be no equivocation on that approach. This actually made our worldwide job easier and allowed us to operate even more effectively with fewer personnel.

•••

The marketing lessons from Scott Paper were:

1. Define what the problem is.
2. Define alternative solutions to the problem.
3. Evaluate the possible solutions.

4. Pick the best solution you are going to lock and load on, and execute it right away.

5. Quickly develop a winning cadre of people who will play ball with you and your organization; encourage a winning attitude, strong self-esteem, and the courage to take risks.

6. Establish goals that stretch traditional expectations.

7. Hold the marketing staff accountable for achieving these goals without equivocation; teach them to live by the following ten two-letter words: "If it is to be, it is up to me."

8. Establish a strong monitoring and control system so you know what is happening, when, and where; if there is a problem you will then know about it quickly and can take action before it becomes bigger or gets out of control.

Chapter 10
FIRE ALL THE CONSULTANTS

LESSON: BUT IF YOU ABSOLUTELY *MUST* WORK WITH ONE, HERE'S WHAT TO DO.

The opportunities to save money across the corporate world are phenomenal. Cutting back on consultant expenditures is a good place to start.

Scott spent $30 million on consultants before I arrived. $30 million! And look at the mess they were in.

All consultants do is tell you what you want to hear. Scott had stacks of consultants' handsomely bound ten-year strategic reports. If you're surrounded by similar reports, do what I did: Get a firm grip on the stack with both hands, and throw them out. Then fire the consultant who wrote them.

You must have goals and objectives, but they must be your own and they must be ladder rungs that you can climb. Your managers and employees must be able to understand what you're talking about and what they're doing. If people were so clever that they could predict the economy ten years ahead and could tell what products will be hot in a decade, I'd hire them. But these people don't exist.

No-account CEOs hire consultants so they don't have to be

responsible and so they'll have someone else to blame when things go badly. Some CEOs lack the strength of their convictions or don't feel they have the clout to sell an idea. In those situations, the consultant is a source of much-needed credibility.

In the lower levels of an organization that has trouble making decisions, talented managers will bring in consultants to simply reinforce ideas they have been pushing for a long time—ideas that upper management will not otherwise accept. Remote executives won't accept the recommendations of their own people in the field, but when a consultant says the same things, they anoint them with meaning and substance.

Consultants generate ten-year plans for CEOs to take to their boards. That way, the CEOs and the consultants buy themselves a credibility policy for ten years, a kind of cover-your-ass pension plan. When none of the plans or predictions has worked out ten years later, "unanticipated developments" can be blamed, and some of those can get pretty creative.

A real chief executive says, "Here's what we're gonna do, here's how were gonna do it, here's when we're gonna do it. And *I'm* accountable."

One of the first things I do when I run a company is take a hard look at all of the previous management's consulting contracts. I wipe out most of them.

The worst example of consultant excess at Scott Paper was the $2.8 million it spent developing a compensation system that made no sense. And that was just one-tenth of the $30 million the company spent on consultants *in one year* before I arrived.

What was Scott spending $30 million to learn about?

Scott used consultants in human resources, marketing, manufacturing, training, research and development, delivering process changes, and compensation and benefits. The previous management also relied on outsiders who specialized in helping people make decisions. How do you get a large group to reach a consensus? Every consultant has a different pitch, and the old Scott paid to hear them all—never reaching a consensus on any one solution.

Some consultants help a company understand how it stacks up against the competition by asking: What are your relative strengths and weaknesses? What is your cost position?

Before I arrived, the work Andersen Consulting did to lower costs on the manufacturing side justified the expenditures. Scott subsequently developed strategies that dealt with a culture resistant to change. The Andersen consultants armed us with facts, and we used them as levers to force change. Those expenditures on consultants didn't cost very much, maybe $1 million. So the previous management could have cut consultant expense by $29 million and not missed the results.

The most ridiculous consultant expenditure under Scott's previous management was related to an individual who came in and tried to make employees think differently about their business. He had this notion that the most valuable commodity in the business is not cash, paper machines, or people—it is *time.* And the ultimate competitive advantage, under his scheme, came from reducing the time it takes to do any particular task. It sounded like a brilliant concept at the outset: If you reduced the time it takes to innovate, to develop products, and to get them into the marketplace, you would be very successful.

This consultant had executives and managers look at the whole process of researching, developing, financing, manufacturing, and selling a product. He said, "If you look at it as one process and shorten it, you will make even more money."

His approach fell apart and lost credibility with Scott's hierarchy when it became touchy-feely. To make his point, he would have people stand in a circle and designated himself as a thrower, someone else as a catcher, and a third person as an inspector. The idea was that the catcher was across the circle from the thrower and the inspector was somewhere else across the circle. The thrower threw an orange to the catcher, who then threw it to the inspector, who inspected it and put it on the ground. Got the idea? That would have been enough for most people, but this consultant lined up thirty people, in teams, to measure the time it took for the whole process to be completed. His point was, "What would you do to shorten that time?" And sure enough, you could reduce the amount of time.

What if the guy who is catching is also doing the inspecting? The idea was good but, thanks to the wacky way it was presented, the message got lost in the laughter and orange pulp.

•••

Coopers & Lybrand partner C. Don Burnett is the only consultant I have ever trusted in fifteen years as a chief executive. I have great respect for Burnett, one of the few outsiders who can influence my thoughts and decisions.

Burnett is a down-to-earth guy. He knows I hold him to a very tough standard. He knows I will execute based on his recommendations. He gives me extra eyes, extra ears. He'll take his team out to talk to everybody. They'll come back with a plan and help me master the specifics. They're the only consultants I ever thought were worth a damn.

Look, don't get me wrong: I obviously use a consultant. And I know he represents a firm of over 30,000 people around the world. But the reason our relationship works and I go back to Burnett over and over again is that he gets the job done. If I want to improve efficiency and cut costs, I want to hire a consultant who is just that: efficient and cost-sensitive. Other chief executives go wrong by randomly hiring consultants who don't give them confidence enough to implement their recommendations. That's a double cost for shareholders: their CEO isn't doing the job he was paid to do and neither is the consultant he hired to bail him out.

Not everyone can use Burnett personally—then he'd have no time for me. The point is: Develop a long-term relationship with one multi-faceted consultant, but no more.

Coopers & Lybrand helps me organize a plan of action, providing an opportunity to jump-start a company. I don't rely on them to make decisions or give me a scapegoat for a corporation's past misdeeds. They get me up and running, identify opportunities, feed me invaluable information, and then formalize a plan that's been shaped and influenced by me.

I think one of the most significant things I've learned from twenty years of working with Burnett is that the consultant must work for and report directly to the chairman of the board and/or the CEO, not a division head. Why? Because whatever the results of the consultant's study, the recommendations will need the driving force of the person atop the organization chart if something is going to be changed.

Because I hire Burnett every time out, most people probably

think that by now he gets a sweetheart deal with fat payoffs. Those people haven't been paying attention. I cut as good a deal with Burnett as I would with any supplier. If he says something is a $2 million job, I'll negotiate that down as far as I can go. However, I do know that the $30 million Scott spent could have bought eighteen separate studies from Coopers & Lybrand, and I bet they would have launched eighteen companies to greatly improved profitability.

How does Coopers & Lybrand feel about me? Well, their auditors always complain about the deals I cut with them, but that hasn't stopped them from taking my money. They don't lose money on my business, but they're not getting rich on it, either. And it has earned them a degree of notoriety that hasn't been bad. Recently, Burnett did a review of business relationships at Coopers & Lybrand. He created a tree-chart, of all the work he had gotten, and he traced, directly or indirectly, $25 million worth of work back to me—all because Burnett and I once had a good laugh at a friend's expense.

•••

Don Burnett and I met socially in 1977. I was an executive at American Can at the time, and he had just joined Coopers & Lybrand after four years as CFO of a Chicago-based paint company. A mutual friend of ours, American Can comptroller Walt Scott, threw a party at which everyone turned and teased him in jest. In the midst of double-teaming poor Walt, Burnett and I hit it off.

Fate threw us together again shortly thereafter, when I hired Coopers & Lybrand to help me downsize American Can's Performance Plastics division and Burnett was assigned the job.

The division was losing a ton of money. Everybody thought plastics was dead; it was a dog job. American Can threw me in there because I was the kind of mutt who might yet save their investment.

Performance Plastics oversaw maybe a dozen plants. In the course of restructuring, Coopers & Lybrand worked with my plant managers to plot out what they could fix. What Coopers does not do, however, is make in-house presentations on behalf of their clients, so the plant managers themselves had to understand, participate in, endorse, and present the consultant's recommendation, not just hide behind it.

I remember the day the manager of plastics' biggest plant got up at a meeting to make the first restructuring presentation.

"We are going to let people go," he said.

"How many and when?" I asked.

"Thirty this month," he said confidently, "40 next month, and 50 the month after that."

"Wait just one minute," I said, "that is not the question. The question is, when *this month* are all those people going to go?"

That was not just my manager's first indoctrination to my methods and need for speed, but Burnett's as well. He coached future managers of mine to prepare much faster action plans, and I never had to confront another manager who intended to stretch out painful layoffs.

Burnett's philosophy is that while he can tell me what positions I don't need in what departments and how to efficiently implement staff reductions, I'm management. I make the decisions. The speed at which I implement is mine to determine.

Many of Burnett's clients are uneasy when it comes to actually firing people, so he would many times give them an out. If he thought they should eliminate 100 people, he'd say, "I think you can get by with cutting 120 jobs." Then he helped them add back the 20 people they thought essential. With me, he quickly learned, if he said 120 were expendable, 120 were gone.

Later in my career, I was between assignments and Burnett, a true friend, brought me to New York. He put me up in his own home for a time, gave me an office in which to work and access to his own secretary and introduced me to several executive headhunters, a process that led me to KKR and the CEO position at Lily-Tulip.

Burnett wasted no time in joining me at Lily-Tulip. He packed a bag and arrived in Toledo, Ohio, on my second day on the job.

Together we toured the company's headquarters and facilities, looking at everything. By day's end I said, "Don, why the hell are we in Toledo? There is nothing here except the corporate headquarters. Why are we not down at one of our plants?"

When you locate a corporate office at a plant, you don't need duplicate finance, duplicate human resources, and so on. Don agreed and, before long, I moved Lily-Tulip's headquarters to

Augusta, Georgia, the location of one of our best plants.

Most companies don't need a big corporate headquarters. We often repeated, almost as a mantra, Sir James Goldsmith's comment that when he sees a beautiful headquarters edifice, he knows the people inside are very happy, but he also knows that he can make a lot of money. I am not sure Burnett always believed that, but we believe now that a corporate headquarters belongs at a plant or a mill, not standing alone somewhere. We also believe that we can out-source many more things than we thought possible. And we are getting back to the basics where the men and women in the plants really make the product and earn the money.

Burnett and his team of engineering and manufacturing consultants went through all of Lily-Tulip's plants, discovering numerous things that were not being done effectively or efficiently. They even tested the types of glue being applied to certain products. Their manufacturing study led to our investment in what became the revolutionary Trophy cup, which held hot or cold liquid. Based on Burnett's observations, we closed plants, laid off unnecessary workers, and relocated facilities such as the underutilized Holmdel, New Jersey, plant.

The working relationship between Burnett and me at Lily-Tulip was pretty simple, really, and always productive. When I decided something had to be done, I'd give Burnett a theme, such as, "Waste is high, spoilage is high," and then I'd always add, "Go fix it." He'd assemble a team who knew the machinery, the glue, the workflow, how to stop spoilage and reduce waste, how many people were needed, and what skills were needed to operate efficiently.

Hands-on work in the plants is difficult, and paper-shuffling consultants rarely know what the machines do. Any factory worker can spot a phony a mile away. A smart consultant has knowledgeable people who know how fast the equipment can really run and what it takes to make it run faster. They recognize that an increase in waste paper can be caused by a number of things—running the machines at the wrong speed, poor maintenance, using incorrectly sized sheets, laying out the sheets wrong, or just plain inattention on the part of the operator. They also know the difference between spoilage and waste. When you hire consultants, their only valuable skill is experience—not filling a conference room with hot air and a bookshelf with paper.

Burnett brings in the right people—those with industry experience. He puts manufacturing people on manufacturing issues, engineers on engineering issues, and sales and marketing people to look at sales and marketing.

Burnett organized teams that examined all the overhead, finance, human resources, legal, administration, and so on. It was much the same procedure we later went through at Scott.

•••

Business leaders must decide for themselves whether they need consultants. If the issue is one of implementation and the business leader can't do it, then maybe the company has the wrong business leader.

If a company pays its executives big salaries *and* hires all these consultants, what the hell is it paying the executives for?

And hiring consultants works only when they're given a specific timetable and a targeted outcome. The process should not be too fluffy or open-ended. I initially hired Coopers & Lybrand to do something very specific at Scott: reduce costs. That included looking at people, purchasing, controllable costs, assets—anything that wasn't adding value to the business.

Consultants, even the good ones, can fail because they only *recommend* a course of action; they still need somebody motivated and in a position to implement their recommendations. If somebody doesn't implement, the consultant's job is no more than an expensive academic exercise. I implement because the final consultant's report reflects something in which I am deeply involved.

•••

Consultants who haven't run a company or faced a payroll create academic, esoteric reports that sit on desks and shelves forever but most of these reports never amount to anything—they can't even get their recommendations implemented. Burnett once told me that probably up to 70 percent of all consulting studies may never be implemented.

Burnett understands what I want in a report: a true executive summary. Work out the nuts and bolts with the appropriate department manager or senior vice president, then bring me three pages that spell out my action plan. If my managers have participated in the plan's preparation and approved it, that's often all I need to know.

Burnett's team generates data on who is responsible and when things should be done. That becomes the company's plan of action. Each department gets the portion of the total report that's appropriate to its own function. The accounts receivable group, for example, knows in excruciating detail what it must do. It knows what systems must change. There is a hell of a lot of detail.

If some group in the company tells Burnett's team they can't do something that the consultants say they can do, we will walk over the people standing in the path of progress and assign somebody who can accomplish our goals. If you believe you cannot do something you are not going to do it. Under me— or Burnett, for that matter—you'd better have a can-do attitude. If something couldn't be done, Burnett's team wouldn't have recommended it.

I go back to the well with Burnett over and over again because there is no learning process between us, no courting ritual and no kissing ass. He knows precisely what I want and I know he has the horses to deliver the goods.

I most often credit Burnett personally for our many successes, but I recognize that he, like myself, leads a talented team of go-getters. One of his partners is Andrew Molenaar, an engineer who has been on every one of my jobs. While Burnett keeps me happy, Molenaar gets into the trenches and determines what is needed.

Burnett knows that I like to see a little age and grey hair on the team. I won't trust my billion-dollar corporations to a bunch of wet-behind-the-ears kids just out of Harvard Business School. That's why the youngest men and women Burnett puts on my account are at least thirty-five to forty years old.

He almost snuck a kid past me at Scott, however.

During an early meeting with Burnett's team at Scott Plaza in Philadelphia, we were talking about the kinds of waste that could be eliminated at headquarters.

"Why do we have a medical staff at corporate headquarters?

Get rid of them!" I thundered. "And while you're doing that, get rid of the nursery school!"

"I hadn't seen a nursery school," Burnett said, startled that he had missed something. "But I will be glad to get rid of it."

Then he caught the twinkle in my eye, followed my gaze around the room, and realized I meant the young kids on Burnett's staff. When I left the room, he compiled a dossier of his team's age and experience to convince me they were right for the job.

Age aside, over the years, some of Burnett's people haven't had the right personality for working with me. I like tough people. Age isn't really the issue, it's competence and toughness.

One summer, Burnett brought in a kid who was in his second year at Harvard Business School and interning with Coopers & Lybrand. My usual attitude toward such kids made me leery until Burnett told me that the young man, Wesley Mukai, had just lost in the NCAA Karate championships. That impressed me because here was a kid who had excelled in something. (Wesley later told Burnett that I reminded him of his father.) He subsequently was on hand at all of Burnett's meetings. And any time somebody—whether it was one of my guys or Burnett's—made a silly comment, I'd laugh and say, "Wesley—take care of them!"

•••

I brought Burnett along when Sir James Goldsmith hired me in the late 1980s to turn around his U.S. ventures. We raised many of the same questions as we had at Lily-Tulip, including: Why is the headquarters for Crown-Zellerbach's forest products division in San Francisco when all of its operations are in Oregon and Louisiana? Portland was cheaper, labor costs were lower and everyone who lived there raved about the wonderful lifestyle. All it lacked were decision makers.

During the Crown-Zellerbach restructuring, Burnett had a top-notch management information systems (MIS) guy named Pete Solano. Solano was dispatched to Crown-Zellerbach's MIS facility in Redwood, California, and in a couple of days he convinced us that we could close the whole facility and combine it with MIS operations in Portland without any disruption. And we did!

But what I remember best about Solano, a Bronx native who was about thirty-five at the time, was the day he flew with a group of us to Eau Claire, Wisconsin, my wife's hometown. We were staying overnight in Eau Claire so we went out for dinner and a sunset drive in the country. As we drove by a cornfield, Solano said, "What's that?" As a city-bred guy, he had never seen corn growing!

Burnett and his team accompanied me on my first tour of Crown-Zellerbach's facilities in Bogalusa, Louisiana. Our accommodations there left a lot to be desired. In fact, one of Burnett's guys refused to sleep underneath his bed sheets because the joint was so infested. Somebody else put his valuables in the bathroom sink and covered them with a towel. Another guy blocked his door with a chair. It was filthy, hot. The next morning I decided we were all leaving. Not long after that, I closed the headquarters and transferred its operations to Portland.

The Coopers & Lybrand team spent just six weeks working with us on the Crown-Zellerbach turnaround. It didn't require a lot of thought: All the world knew it was poorly run. They recommended closing certain mills and outsourcing a multitude of functions. When I examined Crown-Zellerbach's habit of cutting timber when the prices were low, Burnett backed me up on paper with research confirming that that was an ass-backward way of doing business. From a cash point of view, it was stupid; from an environmental perspective, it was unnecessarily destructive. We changed the policy. When the price went up, we cut trees. When the price went down, we laid people off and cut fewer trees. That decision alone played a significant role in boosting cash flow from $15 million a year to $180 million a year.

On another occasion, when Burnett looked at our troubled industrial products company, he recommended combining its twenty-two warehouses located throughout the United States into just four strategic locations, to continue to assure twenty-four-hour deliveries. We accomplished the consolidation itself lightning-quick, in a matter of days. We closed the warehouses on Friday, emptied eighteen of them into long-haul trucks, and reopened fully stocked the following Tuesday morning.

With that company, perhaps the only time in twenty years, Burnett said he could do something but he failed. He assured me that by year's end, December 31, the company, which was losing over $1 million a month, would break even. But it didn't. It registered a $14,000 loss for the month. The new president of the company called Burnett to discuss the situation.

"We have a presentation tomorrow in our offices and we are going to have to tell Al we didn't make break-even," the man said. "I don't want to surprise him tomorrow: Can you call him tonight and tell him we are going to lose $14,000 this month?"

Unfortunately for him, Burnett delivered the message. I didn't take it well. The next day, I gave him an earful at the meeting. Too much, perhaps, because we didn't speak again for eighteen months.

Russ Kersh finally broke the ice between Burnett and me by organizing a dinner at the Harvard Club in New York City. I said to Burnett, "We have been friends too long to let a little thing like this come between us," and he agreed.

•••

Here's an example of one of the more unusual ways I use Burnett. Jack Dailey, my senior purchasing executive at Lily-Tulip, had spent the years since then working for a computer company in Silicon Valley. And although we had not worked together for seven years, I knew Dailey was the right guy for the Scott restructuring. I put a call in to him, we became reacquainted, and I turned the rest over to Burnett.

The very next day, Burnett called Dailey and said, nonchalantly, "I am going to be in San Francisco later this week. I'd like to stop out at the house, but I can only stay less than an hour."

"Well, shit, I'll meet you in the city," Dailey said.

"No, no," Burnett said, "I'd rather come out to the house."

That very Friday night, Burnett was driven to Dailey's home by someone from Coopers & Lybrand's San Francisco office. Dailey, his wife, Beth, Burnett, and his driver walked to the backyard, shared a bottle of wine, and socialized for a few minutes before Burnett asked if Dailey would go to work for me again. Dailey was surprised, but said yes, of course he would.

They chatted a few more minutes, then Burnett got up and left. "What the hell was that all about?" Beth asked her husband.

Dailey scratched his head and laughed.

"Al dispatched Don to come out here and make sure we had not become Californians, that we weren't stark raving idiots or drunks," he said—correctly, I might add. Burnett was my insurance that nothing had happened to Jack during the intervening years that would be an embarrassment to me or to Scott.

The next day, I offered Dailey the job of vice president of procurement, distribution, and logistics for Scott Paper.

•••

When Burnett is on a job for me, he is typically in our offices two or three days a week. He synthesizes functions with my executives and becomes a part of our corporate machine for that period. If he were filing memos from Manhattan, it just wouldn't work. And when he's not physically on the premises, I enjoy carte blanche in terms of calling him whenever the necessity arises. The odd late night or weekend call is usually forgiven by our personal relationship—we play tennis together several times a year and socialize more often than that with our wives. (Burnett's wife, Jara, is one of the most liberal people on earth. I am one of the most conservative. Out of respect for our friendship, we have an agreement never to discuss politics.) When Burnett is on the job, he gives himself 110 percent. I will call him when I have an issue with his auditors or when somebody screws up. Even if it's an issue outside Burnett's immediate realm at Coopers & Lybrand, he'll get the answers or action we need.

At Scott, Burnett spent many of his long hours with Dick Nicolosi, senior vice president of worldwide consumer products. That was particularly true when we reorganized Scott in Europe. He worked side-by-side on that reorganization with Nicolosi and Newt White, senior vice president of Away-From-Home products. Burnett was at every major presentation; his people stayed in Europe for stretches of six weeks or more. Burnett himself saw all of our European installations, flying in from New York every week or every other week, overseeing his staff.

Even when he's not officially working for me, Burnett and I talk every couple of weeks or so. He keeps current on issues facing my company and will call unbidden if he has an idea or suggestion.

I know he and his team will be there when I need them.

If Burnett assigns nine Coopers & Lybrand people to work on my company, he expects nine of my people to work directly with them because he wants them to know exactly what his people are thinking and to act as implementers when the time comes. And my people will also know how to do it the next time.

Burnett knows I don't go in for fads. "Business Process Re-engineering" (BPR) is just consultantspeak, as is "Total Quality Management" (TQM) or "Just in Time" (JIT). *People* fix companies, buzzwords don't.

We have learned from each other over the years, and we've formed a strong and firm platform about what works and what doesn't in a corporate restructuring.

Burnett told me recently that he and his team are tougher than they were twenty years ago. They cut deeper and know what a company can bare-bones get by with today, more so than twenty years ago. Together we have redefined what has to be done to restructure a corporate headquarters and what should be done out at the plants and mills.

Chapter 11
REAL JOBS, REAL CUTS

LESSON: COMMUNICATE, COMMUNICATE, COMMUNICATE.

Scott Paper issued *three* three-year plans in the four years before I arrived. They kept shuffling the plans but not the company. After looking at them, it was hard to find a coherent theme.

In the back of my Scott office in Philadelphia was a bookcase. The shelves were filled with restructuring plans. When I arrived at the company, I wanted to see what they laid out. Among other things, they announced to the world a three-year plan to lay off 8,300 people over three years. I thought I could use this as a basis, so I read the plan.

But it was fiction. I hate fiction.

That three-year plan just threw out numbers. It was not grounded in reality. It was an idea that hadn't been quantified; the company never identified the 8,300 people it planned to cut. They were phantoms. No one ever defined where those job cuts were going to come from. The board was under the impression that they were already being cut when I was hired, but I was forced to report that the jobs weren't cut, or some were cut but the same employees had mysteriously reappeared on the payroll.

The last three-year restructuring plan was hopeless, not just because it lacked specifics but because the man who should have implemented it, my predecessor, was retiring. Changes were coming but they wouldn't be *his* changes.

I told my managers, "This is so bad, it's going to pollute my thinking. Shred all these reports and take out the bookcase." I replaced it with Aboriginal paintings I had acquired in Australia because, to me, the paintings made a lot more sense. They showed people who had to survive by their wits, people who couldn't call out for room service.

Three years is a lifetime. Who remembers what you said even three weeks ago? It's like economists and weather forecasters. Has anybody ever held one of them accountable? I'm reminded of the disc jockey who once recommended that every time a weather forecaster was wrong he or she should lose a finger. That's extreme, but would you trust any fingerless forecasters?

What is the result of a three-year restructuring plan? Paralysis of the corporation. Paranoia. How do employees respond? "I'm going to be very cautious," they think, "I don't want to take any risks. I don't want to draw attention to myself, I don't want to leave my office, this will probably be the day they get me."

People don't know what their status will be. "What do you hear?" will become the most frequent conversation opener around the office as weeks turn into months of waiting for the restructuring to happen. It is far better to make a change and make it quickly. Slow death is terrible.

The smart employees say, "This is nonsense, I'm leaving. My future is being totally undermined." They can see right through a phony plan. That's what makes them the smart employees.

If you say that you will cut 11,200 people over the next three years, your employees will polarize. They'll say, "He won't do it." But in my twelve-month plan, people expect change, they're ready for it, they crave it. And they're not going to fight you.

Beyond twelve months, human nature says, "We've had enough of this," and people will fight you and you will lose.

A three-year restructuring plan is the addle-brained notion of woefully weak executives who cannot face up to putting themselves in a twelve-month time frame. If you tell your employees that the bloodletting will be done in twelve months, you have committed to a time frame. You have set yourself a goal and promised to achieve it. You have put yourself under scrutiny.

I tied the restructuring at Scott to my birthday, July 26. I told analysts and shareholders at my first annual meeting, on June 3, 1994, that I was going to give myself a birthday present by announcing the restructuring. They were looking for something to happen pretty rapidly; an eight-week time frame was extraordinary. And when we announced the restructuring details, I said I would execute our plan within six months, as my Christmas present to our investors.

The financial community and the media greeted the restructuring announcement and the speed with which I promised its delivery with a big dollop of skepticism. I was, as had become their habit, roiled by the Philadelphia newspapers. Analysts doubted it could be done; reporters and editorial writers feared it not only could be but would be done.

•••

I made the first announcement that job cuts were coming to Scott Paper during a thirty-minute meeting for 1,600 general headquarters staff in the largest of our two cafeterias. I said, "We can't continue running this corporation the way it's been run in the past," and I laid out the problems.

I expected these people would be deeply concerned and they were. But when I got done, they clapped! When I got back to my office, I said to Basil Anderson, "That was amazing!"

"These people," he said, "are desperately looking for leadership."

How does an outsider wrest control of a resistant organization?

It's like building a wall. I don't start with the old foundation, which is cracked and crumbling. I tear the whole thing down and start over. I rarely see any good in what came before. If it was any good, they wouldn't need me.

I want executives and managers to see things my way. I will paint a picture for them of the way the outside world sees them. The picture is dark, very dark, so I give them the motivation to change.

Next, I'll start working on finding a core of people who can initiate those changes. Are the existing executives and managers tough enough? Do they have the spirit and the will to do what needs to be done? At Scott, I released 70 percent of the management team. Everyone else knew immediately: "This guy is dead serious."

I think it takes great courage to do all this. Not just on my part but from the directors, executives, managers, and salaried employees who must all contribute to an atmosphere of change. At Scott, we looked at the balance sheet and found a way to eliminate $2.5 billion in debt and quickly convert an incredible magnitude of assets to cash.

In a publicly held company especially, none of this occurs in a vacuum. The financial and local communities are all casting a wary, if not disapproving, eye on a landmark institution undergoing radical surgery to remove a cancerous and potentially lethal growth.

When people read stories about Scott Paper in the Philadelphia papers before I was hired, the company appeared at war with itself, playing the blame game. That could have continued as a fight to the death in which they all would have died.

In 1993, work was already being done to get Scott Paper ready for change. Establishing what it called "jointness" committees, management put people in classrooms where they heard from marketing, manufacturing, finance, and sales representatives. They would show fellow employees in different disciplines how to look at their business through others' eyes, through customers' eyes, through cost position.

I followed up and used the jointness committees to keep all levels of the company informed of the changes being unleashed. I involved the unions at every step. I talked to them directly, spending time on the shop floors.

The days of the pitched labor battle are gone. Look at the 1995 strikes at Caterpillar or the Detroit newspapers and find me a winner. Everybody loses in those things. In this day and age, you have to communicate.

In a massive restructuring, you can't deal with the unions by saying we will fire your people, change your jobs, and take our profits out of your wallets. Start at the top! Get rid of the corporate toys, squeeze the corporate headquarters, shrink high-priced management. The last thing you do is deal with the unions, so they know you went after real waste first. That gives you credibility in their eyes.

I can imagine the doubt on your face. You're thinking: First or last, unions are unions; they won't give in quietly. Right?

Wrong. Scott released thousands of people without losing even a single day to work stoppages or wildcat strikes.

Scott had been moving for years toward granting its unions and the men and women on the shop floors more say-so about the conduct and productivity of plant operations. I'm not against that. But it had escalated into such chumminess that Scott actually invited a union into a plant instead of asking people in the plant if they wanted to be unionized.

I set the standard right at the beginning, in a Philadelphia hotel meeting with union leaders. One of them was incensed about the announced layoffs. He tested me; he wanted to see if I might close a specific plant in its entirety.

"Every plant is subject to being closed," I told him plainly, looking him in the eyes. "We won't keep operations in place just to create a busy-work environment but, rather, if you can provide a cost-basis that allows us to compete in the marketplace and make money, *that* is the way to keep plants open."

I also told him Scott would no longer battle with its unions— as long as Scott shareholders were being taken care of. If that happened, the unions would also be taken care of and be respected.

I positioned it right up front that we were not there to preserve employment but rather to take care of customers and produce profit for shareholders. If Scott didn't cut back its workforce, everybody would soon be out of work. We were going to get our cost-basis right again. Scott had too many people producing too little. We had already done research that told us what kind of labor density we needed to be competitive again.

We also made it clear to the people on the shop floors that our first targets were management and bureaucracy. Those jobs would be the first to go, and the proportion of job losses in their ranks was guaranteed to be higher than those of the union staff.

My position with the unions was simple: Don't hurt me and I won't hurt you. I am not anti-union and I wasn't going to de-unionize Scott.

In the back of our minds, we knew how delicate our approach had to be. We could have been hit by crippling strikes.

The thing that I am proudest of is what happened instead in our labor relations. We had production and maintenance people, most of them organized, in paper mills all over the United States. About 22 percent of that workforce was eliminated. We worked very hard with the unions and took what in 1989, was a bombastic, acrimonious labor/management relationship, in which Scott was coming off the worst strike record in the industry, and turned it into probably the best big labor/management relationship in the paper industry. The incredible thing was that we eliminated 7,000 union jobs, one in every five, yet had no strikes and, to the best of my knowledge, no grievances. Not one.

Other companies could avoid conflict, too, if they first laid the groundwork for creating a nontraditional labor/management environment and then stayed the course, working with labor through the restructuring period. The unions at Scott provided leadership because they were tutored at understanding Scott as a business. Most companies would never allow that to happen. Educate the enemy? Never! They would never put themselves in a position where they would tolerate that kind of partnership with the union. But we took the time to educate our unions about *what* was coming and *why,* no holds barred. In the end, they believed we were doing what had to be done, not committing some heinous or arbitrary act of greed.

This educational campaign had been started three years earlier; we merely stepped up the process and prepared the troops for implementing real change, long overdue.

Scott had traditionally organized mills that had been around a long time. We needed to eliminate the barriers and boundaries that get in the way of motivating these work organizations and initiate an approach that was nontraditional and would bring new thinking to how work should be organized. Otherwise, those same mills would soon be completely uncompetitive. That was our tack. And the workers not only understood, they appreciated our candor.

Finally, while no one was happy with the impending cutbacks, the bulk of the remaining employees trusted us to do the right thing—there were no pay cuts—and to treat those who would be let go with respectful separation packages. The unions participated in determining where the jobs would be eliminated. We negotiated what I think was a very fair and caring package with the United Paper Workers International Union's seven union locals across seven different production facilities. You don't get to that kind of relationship without first dealing with issues of trust.

If I tell a union leader that our company has 1,000 people and we need, for all of these reasons, to get it down to 900 and he or she resists, then the message is that this person doesn't really care if this place survives. In this day and age, union people know that can't be their role.

We went through a major effort with the leadership, both at the international level and at the local-union level, showing them around and spelling out our specific problems. We brought in reports and we talked through what our cost structure was, what the benchmarks looked like, what the competition was doing, and what was happening to our margins.

We started with why these things had to happen. We never blamed the unions for Scott's turmoil. We looked to them as reasonable people. If they weren't, they could never be part of any solution.

We did this in a systematic fashion across our sites in the United States, bringing in the union leaders and spending time answering all their questions. "Understand what we have to do to be competitive and save ourselves," was the message.

By the time we actually got to the bargaining table, the hardest part had been done. They could resist, but we didn't have to threaten them. It was pretty clear what was going to happen with or without their cooperation.

Unlike many modern chief executives, I relate to working people. That's genuine, something you can't fake.

There wasn't a conscious effort to market my working-class roots in the midst of all this. That's just a natural part of who I am. I don't have any problem talking to the people who fidget over every minute on their weekly timecards. I went to every plant and talked about what was going to have to happen. I got to the right people, both management and labor, at the plants.

It was expensive, but I was willing to support the cost of helping people leave with dignity and have a few dollars to tide them over until they could find something else. Cut that out and you destroy the unions' ability to help you.

We respected the union leaders' dilemma. After working with us in structuring the cuts, they had to stand in front of their membership and say, "Look, it could be much worse."

•••

Let me anticipate the question you've been dying to ask since page one: How do I, as a human being, justify putting that many people out of work?

When I fire people, *of course* I feel for them! But what I keep uppermost in my mind is that if I don't release them today, I'm going to have to cut more of them in six months or a year anyway. Doing it piecemeal is a fraud upon everybody—the employees, management, and the shareholders. No one's job, my own included, will be safe until I execute my responsibilities, thoroughly and completely.

I say to myself, in the cool of the night, that if I don't do this, *all* these people will lose their jobs. I may fire 35 percent of the workforce, but the remaining 65 percent have a more secure future than they ever before had in their lives.

If I didn't have the guts to do it, if I wasn't willing to take the intense criticism and take the personal and emotional anguish, I would be like almost any other CEO. They look for the easy way out. But that would be dishonest.

•••

My philosophy is to err on the side of too much. Too many asset sales, too many layoffs. I am a less-is-more guy. I told my managers at Scott, "Let's do this one time and do it right, as deep as necessary, and we can always add back."

Coopers & Lybrand did the critical analyses that designated which facilities and systems worked, what was core and necessary, and what had to be done in the future. Their formulas and rules of thumb about how many people had to do different tasks enabled us to quickly get down to what was appropriate for the work and size of our business.

The average cost per person laid off was about $60,000 or $450 million.

With every person that you have on the payroll, phone bills go up, electric bills go up, office supplies go up, there is wear and tear on everything. The cost factor involves more than one person's salary. Cut back the payroll and everything goes down proportionately.

Numbers like that only make sense if you cut permanently. Firing people and then rehiring them as temps or contract workers accomplishes nothing. If you lay them off and then bring them back in, it doesn't work. In our restructuring, we spent $60,000 on each dismissed employee one time rather than spending $60,000 per person in perpetuity.

If you do a restructuring right, you take a fat one-time hit to save an amount that would soon be much greater than the hit you took. And you create a long-term impact on the business. Your short-term hit gets you a long-term gain.

Chapter 12
THE BEST BARGAIN IS AN EXPENSIVE CEO

LESSON: TIE EXECUTIVE PAY TO
SHAREHOLDER VALUE.

Many times during the years I worked for Sir James Goldsmith, he would say to me, "My dear boy, I'm a very clever fellow. You do 95 percent of the work and get 5 percent of the return. I do 5 percent of the work and I get 95 percent of the return. Aren't I a clever fellow for hiring you?"

Very clever.

And while Sir James, Kerry Packer, and Scott Paper grew richer as a result of my ideas, decisions, and innovations, I profited right alongside them and their shareholders, commensurate with the returns I produced on their behalf.

Sir James knew it all came down to this: You cannot overpay a good CEO and you can't underpay a bad one. The bargain CEO is one who is unbelievably well compensated because he's creating wealth for the shareholders. If his compensation is not tied to the shareholders' returns, everyone's playing a fool's game.

Even though I walked away from Scott more than $100

million richer than when I arrived, I was still the biggest bargain in Corporate America. I created $6.5 billion in value; the shareholders made billions. The company was worth $2.9 billion when I arrived, more than $9 billion when I left. I received less than 2 percent of the value I created at Scott, but at $100 million, I was still the biggest bargain in the corporate world.

Negotiating my deal at Scott, I had strenuously insisted my compensation be tied to shareholder value. That was an eye-opener and almost a deal-breaker. The board, which had negotiated multimillion-dollar contracts before—my predecessor was certainly well paid by contrast with his results in recent years—had little experience and some reticence directly linking compensation with performance.

The board brought in a consultant to cut a deal with me. He came to my home in Boca Raton, Florida, but he just didn't get it, and I told Scott director Gary Roubos that I would not continue the negotiations. Salary was not the issue; incentive was. Roubos and another board member, Bill Andres—two men with CEO credentials themselves—stepped in, grasped what I was after, and took a leap of faith that I was the right man for the job. We quickly closed the deal.

"I would rather see you guaranteed a piece of the action at that level," Roubos told me, "because it is just too easy to take the money and underperform. I'd rather see *you* be at risk than the employees, who have much less control of what is going on in the company."

To this day, I doubt either Roubos or Andres ever guessed I'd be so handsomely rewarded in so little time, but neither had room for complaint. They thought it conceivable I might pick up $100 million for five years' work. I'm sure they never dreamed it would happen in eighteen months, but that's the result of being properly motivated. Besides, my success was theirs and that of every person who invested in Scott Paper.

Scott could have disappeared down a sinkhole. The board could have bet on someone who would have cost less, but would another person have gotten the same job done? Somebody else could have been hired, laid off all these people, sold assets less advantageously, and been paid a huge amount of guaranteed money no matter what the results. That would have created a tremendous amount of resentment and negative attention for the company and its shareholders. The fact that I was successful beyond their wildest dreams made me a bargain. My payoff came from 750,000 shares in options that would have been valueless if the company did worse, not better. It was obviously the right incentive model for Scott at the time.

The best bargain is a CEO who has a competitive compensation package with an opportunity for a big stock equity payoff. Such a deal must be shareholder-friendly and justifiable, not just a board throwing piles of money at the chief executive. The board must be competitive on the cash guarantee side, but I don't think it must be tradition-bound on the equity side. In special situations, a board should provide incentive above and beyond what it has ever done before, either to accomplish a Herculean task or to attract an extraordinary executive.

I believe passionately in motivation. I believe corporations should reward successful people. When you're in school, you get a report card. In business, money is our measurement; money is a CEO's report card.

So many CEOs and other executives have nothing at risk and yet one study showed that 73 percent of companies that lost money still incentivized their CEOs. Why? They're all living well with nothing but disdain for their shareholders. They view shareholders as a nuisance, a necessary evil. They won't speak to them unless push comes to shove. When shareholders call me, I pick up the phone and talk to them. They own the company. They take all the risks. When they go to bed at night, if I'm not doing a good job, they are screwed. If I don't care about them, they don't have a chance. They're dead.

That's why executive compensation must be tied to shareholder return. If boards always align it with shareholder gains—shareholders gaining ahead of the CEO or along with the CEO—the boards need no further justification. But if you reward failing executives who have no stock, what do they have at risk? Nothing. In many corporations, chief executives are paid scads of money, they get huge bonuses, and, by the way, results are secondary. This applies to all executives and managers, and it's this behavior we sought to answer with the performance-based compensation system we put into place at Scott.

Newsweek once described me as being critical of executive pay. Not at all. At one company where I was the CEO, I was not the highest paid person in the organization. That honor went to the sales manager. And if you are lucky and smart, that is what you want because that person makes money on commissions. Likewise, the board of directors should want the CEO to make money only when he or she makes money for everybody else.

There are some who would say nobody is worth $1 million, $5 million, or $10 million a year. But if compensation is tied directly to results, the executive doesn't get a dime extra if the stock price doesn't go up and options can't be exercised.

Scott shareholders saw their shares multiply in value. These were not just rich people who owned millions of shares of stock, but pension and mutual funds, the investments of everyday moms and dads who put their hard-earned money into Scott and were rewarded.

If you do the job, you should be well paid. If you don't do the job, you should not only lose your incentives, you should lose your job.

Why don't more boards fire their nonperforming CEOs? The No. 1 reason is that the CEO probably chose all the people on the board. There are relationships all around. If the CEO goes, the directors know they will be next to walk the plank. In other cases, the board may feel that the individual had worked assiduously and, due to temporary, mitigating circumstances, it was impossible to produce results. In those situations, keeping the CEO on is understandable; rewarding him or her when the company loses money isn't.

Was I worth $100 million to Scott Paper? My answer is: Go ask the shareholders. They should be very happy with the return they earned. In terms of the gain they got, what I picked up was not a very large figure.

We are very inconsistent about pay in America. When was the last time you heard somebody say Microsoft's Bill Gates makes too much money?

•••

Before I started at Scott, senior management executives received 2,000 options a year, every year, regardless of performance. They normally received salary increases, regardless of performance. The incentives they received were outrageous. And their performance stunk! The year before I got there, Scott lost $277 million, but the senior executives all picked up their options, their benefit programs, and their perks.

Their options were worthless at that time, of course, because the stock was worth less than the value of their options. But nobody was going broke working for the company, either.

My plan was to recast Scott Paper as an entrepreneurial company. How? By example. On my first day on the job in April, 1 bought $2 million worth of stock. The stock price stood at $38. That investment was made with no Scott loans or guarantees. It was paid in cash, out of my pocket, the same as any other shareholder. A few months later, the stock rose to $50 and I bought another $2 million worth. That particularly impressed stock analysts following the company. "He must be pretty confident the price will go up," they said.

In September, I called in my top executives for a meeting. By then, our stock was selling for around $63.

"If you believe in this company," I said, "I want you to buy stock."

Most were instantly amenable. But it wasn't easy for all of them. Our chief financial officer, Basil Anderson, for example, was at Scott for twenty years before I got there. He was a father of two, divorced, and didn't have a lot of money. But he went to the bank like the other guys and took out a loan because he believed in what we were doing.

Our top ten executives soon owned $10 million in stock. They took a risk and it was up to them, and only them, not to fail. If the team did the job for the shareholders, they would be richly rewarded. If they failed, they really failed. We worked very long hours—days, nights, and weekends. Many of us traveled for weeks at a time. But in the end, we produced significant results and were well rewarded in the increased value of our stock. My team made its money on stock.

Many people get options and/or restricted stock. That's nice. Options—heads you win, tails you don't lose. Restricted stock, that's a gift.

A restricted stock grant is different from a stock option, in which the CEO is granted options to buy a stock at today's market price. An option only has value if the stock goes up. A restricted stock grant, in effect, is a gift of stock to the executive. It's restricted in the sense that there is a limited time to exercise the grant. If the CEO is given restricted stock grants for 100,000 shares and the price of the stock today is $30 a share, it has a current value of $3 million. That is real money.

Some packages will be more subject to criticism than others if the rewards are not related to significant accomplishments. One example of this might be restricted stock grants.

Such grants often vest over five years at 20 percent per year, so the executive would get 20,000 shares per year free and clear at whatever the price of the stock. There are rules for restricted stock grants, but they have the equivalent of cash once the restriction is lifted.

I have always received options and restricted stock at the companies I've run. I could have avoided taking chances with my own money. Those deals have no risk and lots of upside. But that's no comfort to the people who invest in the company. If they think it's a good investment, then if I'm going to run it, I'd better think so, too.

The critics said that I was showboating at Scott with these big stock purchases, but all I was doing was investing in my belief in myself. I did it first when I went to Lily-Tulip in 1983. KKR gave me options for 200,000 shares and I bought 200,000 more out of pocket. The privately held stock had a $1.77 book value. Lily-Tulip had lost more than one-third of its equity and was headed toward bankruptcy. But the banks wouldn't let KKR sell it for less than $2.50. My lawyer said "Al, this is nuts even for you! How can you pay $2.50 for a stock that's worth $1.77 in a company that looks like it's going to go bust?" I said, "I believe in the future." He said, "You're nuts."

He wasn't just referring to the price being too high; he also knew I didn't have any money in the bank. I borrowed $500,000 by pledging the stock as collateral. If that thing went sour, I was broke.

But only a hypocrite takes over a major corporation and is gun-shy about putting any of his own money at risk.

The long and short of it? I sold out my Lily-Tulip stock after two and a half years at $18.55, and nobody had sympathy for me. I didn't have money when I started, but I was willing to put my butt on the line for a loan. I've been willing to take that kind of risk again and again. I'll always invest in me and my determination to win.

Scott employees, who, before I came, were too smart to invest their retirement funds in Scott stock, also got our entrepreneurial religion and bought $250 million worth of stock through their 401K plans. And believe me, they didn't do it because I called them into my office and demanded it. They did it because they were working harder and increasing productivity, and they wanted a piece of the payoff.

An Australian television crew came to Philadelphia to do a story on the Scott turnaround, and it captured a few candid moments that showed how our employees felt about their Scott stock. In one, I was talking to the reporter and two guys leaving the plant shouted, "Keep that stock price going up, Al! We love it!" Then there was a woman packaging product, who, before the cameras were rolling, said, "Thank you, Mr. Dunlap. My children will go to college on my pension plan because I invested in Scott stock."

•••

Money is very important as motivation. Not long before I was hired, Scott paid consultants $2.8 million to design a compensation program. I had run seven companies before Scott but I couldn't understand this plan. Sometimes the financial goals weren't set at the start of the fiscal year. Managers didn't know what their targets would be until months had passed, so they didn't start right off chasing the rabbit. It was like somebody who doesn't understand golf and thinks he won a round because he shot 110 and the other player shot an 80.

I believed Scott needed a more appropriate and *just* system of rewarding performance. Scott's consultant, a very highly recognized and regarded compensation expert, wrote a mind-numbing plan. In it, Scott's annual incentive plan had double and triple thresholds and some other things based on subjective criteria that I just didn't understand. It wasn't that I was unable to understand the detail; I just didn't understand the philosophy.

The consultant came in and gave us a presentation. Basil Anderson, Newt White, vice president of corporate human resources John Nee, attorney Chris Sues and I were in the room looking at graphs and other visual aids that purported to show how people got paid. Even Sues found it too complicated. After twenty minutes, I said to the consultant, "Don't give me all this bullshit. Show me what my people have to do, what they have to produce, in the form of a business plan, to get a bonus. I don't want to see the graphs, I don't want to see all this fancy stuff, I don't want anything subjective."

The consultant was startled, as if no one had ever dared ask him to spell it all out in English before.

Not long after, I asked the two best people at Scott, Anderson and Newt White, if they would come to my office and explain the compensation plan to me. They sat very quiet and sheepish before Basil took a shot at it. When he was done, there was a long silence.

"You guys really don't understand it, do you?" I said, laughing.

"No, not really," they said, looking worried.

I told them to relax.

"I thought I was a total idiot," I said. "But you're the smartest guys I've got. If you don't understand it, I feel vindicated. Let's trash it and get a system that works."

One of the most significant steps we took was in shaking up our restricted stock rules. Managers would no longer receive a share of restricted stock unless they hit certain targets. In most other companies, it's a gift. You just get it. Those days were over at Scott Paper.

All of our incentive programs were based on performance. We set high goals. If you hit the goals, you received a high bonus. And the company as a whole had to achieve a certain goal or there was no pool. Within that pool, there was a formula. But even if you were doing a good job, if the company didn't do well, there was no pool. I don't care how hard somebody works; if the company is not doing well, if the shareholders are not doing well, no one deserves a bonus. Period.

The communities in which we choose to stay will prosper as we expand our business and invest in our plants instead of constantly shutting them down. The customers will, of course, be delighted as we offer improved products at a competitive price, with improved service levels. Suppliers, lenders, and bankers will be better off as we create a revitalized company with a stronger balance sheet.

How did Scott reform bonus compensation to make it merit-oriented?

Probably the most substantial change was in making better and more important use of stock options and restricted shares. Instead of arbitrary in-house goals, we let the stock market measure performance. At the end of the day, if we've done well but the price of the stock doesn't reflect it, what have we really accomplished?

When I arrived, Scott was granting stock options based on subjective criteria, as a function of hierarchy. Everybody at a certain level received 4,000 options, everybody at the next level got 3,000. They were not performance-related grants for the most part. Even though the company was losing money, the fact that, in time, those options could be worth something was being ignored. Executives and managers were earning options in years when Scott was losing money. It wasn't right. It made no sense. The long-term, subjective plan I inherited provided for wads of restricted stock. I didn't mind having restricted stock awards. But if my key managers wanted them, they had to buy in, out of pocket, first. Then I was more than willing to award three shares of restricted stock on a vesting schedule for every share that they bought, up to a maximum number.

Before this, management didn't have to make an investment in the company to be rewarded under a bonus plan.

We wanted everybody on the same team working in the same direction to accomplish the same things because now they had a personal investment in the company.

Under our leadership, many more people at Scott than ever before were given restricted shares, so their focus on the company's performance became acute. Before I arrived, few had that kind of vested interest. The level of awareness changed immediately.

We took the options deeper into the organization and gave key people more of them. We also changed how they were granted. Rather than a few shares once a year, with each batch vesting over two years, we gave a large number of shares one time that would vest over five years. And we provided greater opportunity because our mega-grant that vested over five years had a single strike price. (The strike price of the shares is their value on the day they were granted.)

At a certain level of the organization, an employee might get 2,000 shares under the old scheme. Those shares would be granted at $44, with 1,000 vesting after one year and the other 1,000 vesting after the second year. When the stock was at $44, they were worth nothing. If the stock went up $1, the options were worth $2,000; if the stock went up $2, the package was worth $4,000, and so forth. The value was the difference between the strike price ($44) and what they were now worth. The problem with stock options under the former Scott regime was that the company never performed long enough to have them mean anything. Before I arrived, Scott had thousands of shares that were granted at $44, $42, and $41, but with the stock selling at $37, they were worthless.

When we granted shares under our new vestment plan in 1994, we granted them for five years at a strike price of $63.75. This was almost a 50 percent higher strike price than under the previous management.

In effect, we said: "Here is a much larger number of shares, and 20 percent will vest to you every year. But the strike price will always be the same." If the price went down, we were not going to reissue at a lower price. So our employees had the advantage of the continuing growth of the stock. If the price went up, they were rewarded handsomely. If it went down, they got nothing. We didn't re-price the shares as many corporations do, increasing the strike price the next year.

Before the Kimberly-Clark merger arose, we planned to go even further into the Scott hierarchy, including more people globally in the stock option plan than the company had ever included before. If you believed in this philosophy, you'd go deep into middle management. We fundamentally offered stock down through senior management and included a significant percentage (but not all) of senior management on a global basis. What we were talking about doing next was taking it even further into middle management and including more people worldwide, because we were acting and thinking like a global company.

Roughly 8 to 10 percent of Scott's salaried employees received stock options. We would have expanded that to 15 percent had we continued. It was fairly generous; other companies are less generous, but I really believed in engaging people with these stock options.

For those who were already granted options, the timetable was accelerated by the merger and the options were fully vested from a single strike price.

In the end, the five years' worth of options we granted at $63.75 were worth $120.00 (based on Scott's presplit price) at the time of the merger. That was no gift; our people worked hard and made enormous sacrifices to achieve that payoff. They, like me, earned every penny because our shareholders made money, too. When you are tied to the idea that the fundamental, essential responsibility of the corporation is shareholder equity value, your focus changes. Newt White's pre-Dunlap options weren't worth squat. After working with me, he was worth approximately $23 million.

•••

People working in a company are looking for a sense of security. In exchange, the company needs ways of perpetually motivating its employees. That's why we must hold them accountable. We must have goals and accountability, whether in the form of a bonus or a promotion, or their name in the paper or on a reserved parking space.

What executives lose track of is that people *want* to be held accountable for their actions. If they are not held accountable, we'll have the corporate equivalent of social anarchy: bankruptcy.

How do we hold people accountable at different levels? There must be a consequence to any action. And it must be something that they can control. It doesn't do management any good to say, "You will be rewarded for something Joe does," if the person is not held accountable for his or her own actions.

Accountability can be as simple as, "You will not get a raise."

On the other hand, if you set up a system whereby everybody gets the same raise regardless of performance, mediocrity sets in. But if employees know they did a great job and they will be rewarded for it, they will consistently improve on their performance. I believe people want to do a good job.

Financial incentives can be kept very simple. Tie rewards to the company's overall performance. How did a given department do vs. budget? I tell my managers to give me four key goals for the year. What are you going to do this year? Tell me when you are going to do them, tell me why I should keep you. A year later, I'll ask, "Did you achieve all these goals?" and if not, why not? We can work out a reward system that way.

It doesn't have to be huge. It has to be *something.*

Everybody's coming to work 52 weeks a year, 40 hours a week. That's what their base pay and benefits cover. Performance rewards cover what employees will accomplish beyond the basics.

The next question must be: How do we reward people without creating a new bureaucratic and paperwork nightmare?

Even with the best of intentions, it is a constant battle. We must be vigilant. Beat back corpocracy at every turn! Outside bureaucratic influences will require you to do certain things just by their nature. Establish an internal environment in which excess paperwork is not tolerated and is discouraged.

At Scott, our managers understood we were not interested in drowning in a sea of memos. There wasn't much handwritten stuff. Memos are just reinforcements of a behavior we wanted curbed. "We will not have a rule book this *big,"* we said. "We will have a rule book this *small."* Hold people accountable and much of that paper trail will go away.

Bigness by itself can cause bureaucracy. If everybody has to approve everything, then that system becomes bureaucracy.

•••

No discussion of incentives would be complete without an examination of executive and employee benefits.

Attorney Chris Sues handled employee benefit matters for Sir James Goldsmith's American companies dating back to 1981.

We met when I was hired to turn around Crown-Zellerbach—he helped design my own benefits package—and have worked together often since then.

When I met him, Sues was with the New York law firm of Shea & Gould, best known for founding partner Bill Shea, for whom the New York Mets baseball home, Shea Stadium, was named. The firm often represented New York-area sports franchises, including the Mets and Yankees, the football Giants, and Madison Square Garden.

Sues's individual practice was focused on corporate benefits, including work for Hanson Industries and Grand Union. When he went into companies, he studied packages and questioned expenditures and largesse that nobody had properly questioned before.

Sir James wasn't sure what he was getting into when he first hired Shea & Gould. But after Sues did an in-depth examination of Diamond International and documented millions of dollars in corporate losses due to benefits, Sir James was sold. "That guy is my benefits lawyer," he announced.

I relied on Sues during the Goldsmith years to reconceive the benefits and compensation packages at the many companies we took over or considered taking over.

During takeovers, we encountered all sorts of benefits—often called poison pills—established by sitting management teams to entrench themselves. Sues was typically assigned to look at costs associated with those benefits and to assess whether they were ironclad or were so disadvantageous to shareholders that they could be renounced. It was an intellectually challenging area because we were always uncovering arcane compensation twists that were established for a company's officers but were extremely disadvantageous to shareholders.

These included every form of compensation known to man: stock options, termination bonuses, stay bonuses, merit bonuses, and annual incentive plans with triggers so that if a hostile takeover were to occur it might double or triple a payout. Various forms of compensation, severance pay, and employment contracts would pay three to five times a person's annual salary, and some were automatically renewed annually for a five-year period.

At both St. Regis Paper Company, which Sir James attempted to take over, and later at Crown-Zellerbach, which he did take control of, his arrival had been preceded by significant contracts that were put in place before the companies were acquired. The same approach was used at Continental Group, another company Sir James bid on, but ultimately did not win.

Let me put into perspective why executives set up such sweet deals for themselves. Certain companies became takeover targets in the mid-1980s because management was no longer doing the job for the shareholders. Management was lazy and sleepy—but fat and happy, thanks to salaries and bonuses that had no basis in reality. They knew if they were ever caught in this lie, they'd lose their heads, so they wrote golden parachutes as protection. The parachutes provided a final, undeserved pot o' gold in the event the no-accounts were ever ousted.

In May 1994, I hired Sues and turned him loose on Scott Paper. He tackled two jobs simultaneously: (1) generating reasonable separation packages for the 11,200 workers laid off in our restructuring, and (2) reconfiguring compensation and benefits packages for employees who remained, based on performance and tied to shareholder gains.

Bonus compensation aside, companies overcompensate many people and make labor much too costly to the company. We must provide for people exactly what they need and not more than that, and work much harder at making them understand the benefits that the company provides. You might think of that as a way of giving less, but I don't think that is true. It comes from not providing benefits that have no real value or from providing fewer options around what you get.

For example, when I came to Scott in April 1994, the company ran an unbelievable sixty-one different medical plans! In a matter of months, we whittled it down to six.

How could a company even *administer* sixty-one medical plans? Bureaucracy had clearly run amuck. Someone needed a new plan here and another one there; two options weren't enough, let's offer four.

In the late 1980s and early '90s, U.S. businesses shifted from first-dollar indemnity coverage to managed care, health maintenance organizations (HMOs) and comprehensive plans. Rather than making clear, decisive shifts from one strategy to another, Scott commingled plans. Big bureaucracies prevent companies from decisively and nimbly adjusting plans, and I found Scott in a period of transition, introducing new plans without ending others.

It's not that big companies aren't trying to do the right things, but bureaucracies make these changes more slowly than they should.

Scott also had an array of different kinds of leaves our managers and executives could take: executive sabbatical, personal, educational, and so on. There were multiple long-term disability benefits, which we reduced to two options. It's this stuff that complicates people's lives and costs more in administration than the actual benefits provided.

Corporations regularly review their compensation benefit programs. When one company adds a benefit, others feel compelled to do the same; they talk themselves into doing it for reasons of being fair. In the 1960s, enough companies had pension plans so everybody had to have a pension plan. In the 1980s, everyone added 401K savings plans. That's easy to follow. But what happens inside those plans is not quite as clear-cut because they keep getting bigger and more out of control in the same way Corporate America annually and routinely increases executive salaries without tying them to shareholder returns. The same attitude draws them into saying, "We have 11 paid holidays, and the average is tending toward 11-1/2—maybe we should have another holiday."

Scott Paper did not cut, in a significant way, any important benefits. We did not reduce holidays or any of the better medical plans. We made a shift to what I would argue was a better pension plan. Nobody lost a thing. The 401K was left intact.

I believe that, under the circumstances, employees laid off by Scott were dealt with very fairly. Every individual and every executive received a nice separation package based on the employment time with the company, and it included pension protection and medical continuation protection. Scott's termination policy was a week of severance pay for every year of service, plus one additional week of pay for every year of service beyond 15 years, and an additional week of pay for every year of service beyond 40 years, to a maximum of 52 weeks. A great many people left us with a year's severance pay. We negotiated similar benefits with our unions, which was really extraordinary. It wasn't a perfect match, but it was unusually close. For the hourly folks, we were truly generous. I know of at least one company that laid off workers in 1996 and gave them four weeks of severance pay no matter how much service time they had with the company.

Scott's existing labor agreements, for the most part, provided no more than four weeks of severance. But the company nonetheless negotiated severance benefits similar to those received by salaried employees, ignoring and *exceeding* what was in our legal agreements.

And at headquarters, where the job cuts were the most severe, we also provided pension enhancements that included a factor of five; five years of service or five years of age were granted to senior employees who had the ability, with that additional service or age, to retire. For example, quite a few employees in the 60-64 age bracket would have had to wait until they turned 65 for pensions to kick in. But the factor-of-five plan kept them from waiting.

Finally, people who moved to Boca Raton, Florida, with Scott and subsequently lost their jobs as a result of our merger with Kimberly-Clark, received 52 weeks of severance pay, regardless of prior service.

The final cost of employee restructuring at Scott was about $60,000 per person. That figure included severance pay, pensions, and the present-value cost of retiree medical insurance, which today is a tremendous benefit. Quite a number of our employees might have been in a category where they were not age 65, when Medicare would kick in; so people in that 60-64 age group probably found the continuation of medical insurance a very valuable benefit.

Compare that with situations where people are let go, effectively, with a couple of weeks' pay, and I think our managers did a fair job of balancing the needs of people who were not going to continue with those of the people who were. Many of our separation policies were actually in place when I arrived. We had the opportunity to change them and go cheaper, but chose not to. Being let go is tough enough; being slapped in the face was not necessary. We were not looking to hurt anybody; we just wanted to get the company back on its feet.

Chapter 13
WHOSE COMPANY IS IT, ANYHOW?

LESSON: THE PEOPLE WHO INVEST IN A
COMPANY OWN IT—NOT THE EMPLOYEES,
NOT THE SUPPLIERS, AND NOT THE
COMMUNITY.

In corporate circles, the world's most abused minority is the shareholder. Barely tolerated, not respected.

All you need to know about a company when it comes to its treatment of shareholders is the answer to this question: Have the CEO, the senior executive team, and the board of directors made significant investments of their own money in the company? If they have, the rest of the shareholders can sleep easier, because everyone's in it together.

Who are our shareholders? By and large, they're not a bunch of rich people on Wall Street. Shareholders are our parents, who've invested their pensions and 401K plans in our companies. Shareholders are the people working in our factories. They're the police, the firefighters, the teachers. They entrust people like me with their safekeeping. If their money gets invested and a company does poorly, they will be penalized up to and including the loss of their life savings.

That's why a company's No. 1 responsibility is not to the customer but to the shareholder. It doesn't mean that the customer is not of the utmost importance. But when you adopt the attitude of shareholder value first, then the way you spend the corporation's money becomes a function of how you spend money on behalf of the shareholder.

If a shareholder calls me and says, "I want to talk to you," I have an obligation to talk to him or her. And call me they did. When we announced plans to revamp all of our product packages, shareholders called. Many agreed but were worried. "Isn't that an awfully big risk?" I told them, "The important thing is that when consumers walk down that supermarket aisle, Scott products must stand out from the competition!"

Others wondered about the wisdom of entering the Asian marketplace. "There are 2 billion people in China," I'd reassure them. "If we could enjoy the percentage growth there that we have elsewhere, we could double our business every four years."

I find people want to be personally reassured about strategy. And sometimes they want a peek behind the scenes at how their money is being spent and the logic of the decision-making process. It's their money—I think they're entitled to answers.

Some companies just don't see it that way—especially when their performance is lousy. They will go to great extremes to make it as difficult as possible for shareholders to be heard, even moving their annual meetings to an unusual and distant location where it's inconvenient or too expensive for many shareholders to attend. Some have even been known to take their meetings out of the country, to escape shareholders. That kind of behavior is reprehensible.

Another sign of disrespect for shareholders that really burns me up is hearing about chief executives being given raises or being paid huge bonuses even as their ships are sinking. The stock drops 60 percent but the board gives the CEO a 40 percent raise. Why? "It was a tough year," the directors will say. Exactly! It *was* a tough year... *for the shareholders!* They're the ones who lost money! The *CEO* had a great year! The *CEO's* salary was guaranteed, the *CEO* flew around the world at company expense, the *CEO* led the good life and used the shareholders' diminished returns to refurbish the corner office.

It's the shareholders' company, not the CEO's. If the shareholders lose value, the CEO doesn't deserve to gain! Talk about mixed-up priorities.

The risk of buying a share of stock is enormous. It's not like buying a U.S. Treasury certificate, which is guaranteed. When someone buys a share of stock, he or she may lose some or all of that money. That's why executives of a company must respect that investment and treat it as an awesome responsibility.

Who gives the shareholders their money back when the company screws up? Nobody.

Most companies don't put the shareholders first. If they happen to create some shareholder value along the way, while pursuing their own objectives, fine; but it is unfortunately not the sort of thing that they are out there championing.

Shareholders own the companies in which they invest. That means the employees—executives included—work for the shareholders. Let me put it in perspective. If you own a house, do you let the gardener tell you when you should sell your house? Does your auto mechanic say, "Oh, no, you can't sell your car!" Stock ownership is the only situation where someone who doesn't own the asset usually gets away with telling the owner what to do.

It is very easy to spend money when it belongs to someone else. However, when a person invests in a company, the list of things he or she wants the company to do does not include pissing away the investment on exquisite perks and poison-pill takeover defenses. If shareholders wanted their money spent on Paris apartments, hunting lodges, yachts, and airplanes, they'd buy them and enjoy such toys themselves. That is *not* why they gave their money to stockbrokers or mutual funds. They want the company to build new factories, innovate products and services, and enhance research and development. Most of all, they expect the company to make money.

If a company is not delivering shareholder results, it should be making changes. But many companies don't. Why did Scott Paper's board of directors and management sit on the sidelines year after year and idly watch the value of Scott's stock deteriorate? Who lost money as the company blithely spent billions in capital and still lost market share? Not the directors or the managers—it was the shareholders who took the beating.

If you are shareholder-friendly, you will have the best management, the best products, the best facilities. That's your obligation to the shareholders. You serve at their pleasure. Don't forget it!

Despite the logic of this perspective, you can count on one hand the number of CEOs who are shareholder friendly, as evidenced by the billions they have created in shareholder value. Among them: Jack Welch at GE, Coca-Cola's Roberto Goizueta, Bill Gates at Microsoft, and Disney's Michael Eisner.

•••

The worst kind of CEO for shareholders is the corporate elitist who utterly and disdainfully rejects suggestions and pleas made by shareholders. That's a huge mistake. Even if that shareholder is only in the company for one hour, he or she is still a shareholder.

It was Scott shareholders who, when our stock began its dizzying ascent in mid-1994, first suggested a stock split to make our price more affordable. And it was the shareholders who stated the case for what I found so obvious: Scott is a consumer products company. Why is it in health care services and energy production?

They were asking the same questions we were asking ourselves internally. They reinforced our thinking, confirming that we were on the right course. Our opinion wasn't just developed in isolation—our owners were thinking the same way.

At Scott, I endeavored to be the most shareholder-friendly CEO in America. It was something I took great pride in.

How does a CEO become shareholder-friendly? For starters, he or she must be a shareholder. Read a proxy. You'll find it's full of astonishingly creative writing that attempts to demonstrate how many shares of stock a company's executives hold. But they're usually just grants of restricted stock and options that they exercised when they were so far in the money they couldn't lose. Usually, the only executives who buy stock in their companies anymore are the founders.

•••

The most ridiculous term heard in boardrooms these days

is "stakeholders."

Who or what are stakeholders? They're the company's employees, the community where a business operates, even the company's suppliers. They're people or institutions that have a stake in the company's well-being and continuity because they rely on it for a paycheck, supply or service contracts, taxes, or, in the case of a community, general economic development.

CEOs who bow to multiple constituencies are shirking their duties. I know it has been fashionable in some communities for management to seek tax breaks or community support by emphasizing stakeholders over shareholders, but that moment has come and gone. We can do more good for our communities by doing right by our shareholders.

Stakeholders! Every time I hear the word, I ask, "How much did they pay for their stake?"

I object to the whole concept of stakeholders—who are differentiated from the shareholders, who literally buy and hold stock. Stakeholders don't pay a penny for their stake. There is only one constituency I am concerned about and that is the shareholders.

If you see an annual report with the term "stakeholders," put it down and *run,* don't walk, away from the company. It means the company has its priorities upside down. Which companies am I talking about? Well, *CFO* magazine and the Walker Group, an Indianapolis research firm, published a study in 1995 that singled out Harris Corporation and Eastman Chemical Company as businesses going out of their way to profess their devotion to stakeholders.

Companies such as these make major decisions that are more in tune with employees and the community than with shareholders. They give away to charity millions of dollars that rightfully belong to the shareholders. They keep thousands of people on their payrolls even when they clearly cannot afford such largesse and are putting the entire operation at risk.

I think they're making a huge mistake. Shareholders take all the risks; they own the company. Everyone else—employees, contractors, and the community—justly profit when the company and the shareholders do.

I am not unmindful of interests other than shareholders.

However, managing for the interests of stakeholders runs contrary to our fiduciary duty and destroys accountability. It also blurs management's concept of whose interests it serves. You can't measure success by the interests of multiple stakeholders. You *can* measure success by how the shareholder fares.

Stakeholders benefit when the shareholders benefit. If a company performs well and its shareholders make money, then the community benefits because it taxes people, and employees benefit because the company is successful.

Too often, the notion of other interests and other constituencies becomes an excuse for flaccid management and poor results. Management at businesses such as these may spread assets around for purposes other than the core business of the company itself. Then when it doesn't produce profits, management points a collective middle finger and virtually says, "But we do all these other things, so it's OK not to make money." I don't buy that for a second. The mission of a company is to protect the interests of its investors. They stand front and center for the gravy train, not at the rear of the line.

A side issue is that, for the shareholders to do well we need employees who care about the company, work hard, and feel they are being treated right. It is important to treat employees well, and we do it because it's good business. That's another way to create shareholder value. That's the right way to run a business.

Employees are stakeholders but they don't deserve rights the way shareholders do, unless they've invested some money in the company they're working for. We have gone way overboard in creating rights for everybody, and companies have been pulled into that mess. It makes management fuzzy and harder than ever to focus.

As a result of stakeholder pressure, Scott gave away large sums of money to the community instead of improving its facilities and directly improving the lives and welfare of its employees. Being stakeholder friendly was nothing but a smokescreen to keep the management from being held accountable to a measurable standard.

Scott Paper, a company that lost $277 million in 1993, still had $3 million earmarked for charitable contributions for 1994 when I was hired. I can't see the justification of such a giveaway in a *profitable* corporation, so this certainly made no sense at all. I put an end to it.

Scott's giving was not done blindly. It was a very conscious decision based on the previous management's philosophy that if you are part of a community you have to contribute directly to that community.

When charities came around knocking at Scott's door for contributions, we told them that our No. I objective was creating shareholder value. That was the policy, strictly upheld. It allowed very little discussion. Once a corporation establishes clarity around an issue, whether it be charitable giving or anything else, employees can deal with it.

Our mill managers, who dealt with such giving on a more face-to-face, local basis than did corporate headquarters, had to say, "I know we used to contribute, but company policy has changed and I have to adhere to it." But there was nothing stopping our managers or employees from reaching into their own pockets or volunteering their own time to help. These were steps we encouraged.

I knew I would be severely criticized for ending Scott's enormous reputation as a corporate benefactor. I was. Combined with our business cutbacks, taking this step did nothing for my personal popularity in the company's hometown of Philadelphia. But I did it because it was the right thing to do.

•••

If you're in business, you're in business for one thing—to make money. You must do everything fiducial, legal, and moral to achieve that goal. And making excellent products that are expertly marketed is the primary way of making money.

Executives who run their businesses to support social causes—such as Ben & Jerry's or The Body Shop—would never get my investment dollars. They funnel a portion of profits into things like saving the whales or Greenpeace. That is not the essence of business. If you want to support a social cause, if you have these other agendas, join Rotary International.

I have no problem with giving. I've left in my estate the largest gift ever to be presented to my alma mater, West Point. And Judy and I give money regularly to hospitals and animal shelters. But it's *our* money, *we* earned it.

Corporate charity exists so that CEOs can collect awards, plaques, and honors, so they can sit on a dais and be adored. But that is not what the shareholder is paying them a million bucks a year—plus stock options and bonuses—to do!

Show me a chief executive who's on five boards and who lends his or her name, prestige, and time to fifteen community activities, and I'll show you a company that's underperforming. A chief executive is paid to run the company. *That's* the CEO's job. Corporations become woefully inadequate when CEOs think they are great social messiahs.

My distaste for corporate giving began as I worked my way up the ladder at American Can in the 1970s. American Can gave away scads of shareholder money. As a representative of the Connecticut-based company, an executive such as myself could have gone to a charity event every night of the week in New York City. It was totally part of the corporate culture.

One day it occurred to me how wasteful this was, and not just from a financial angle. If you went into the city midweek and had to be at work the next morning, you couldn't help but be tired and unproductive—two big fat strikes against the shareholders.

Let's assume that a corporation creates $5 billion worth of value and that its shareholders all sell their stock. If the tax on that increased capital is 30 percent, that's $1.5 billion the shareholders would give to government. Much of that money will go to social causes. Isn't it better for $1.5 billion to go to social causes in that manner than for a corporation to waste its time and resources trying to duplicate the purpose of other agencies?

This policy is no different from the one I enforced with the publicly held companies Sir James Goldsmith and Kerry Packer ran.

Goldsmith, for example, was a most generous benefactor who gave large sums of money to his favorite charities through a foundation. He earned his knighthood for his steadfast devotion to ecology and the environment. But it was his personal money to give, not the investment of his shareholders. He would say to me, "My dear boy, I am going to make a donation of $500,000, but it's my money."

I know people look at me and say, "He's against corporations giving to charity? What a cheap SOB!" But that money is not mine to give. I have no right to give away a shareholder's money, but I have every right to give away my own money.

Whether the United Way or the Red Cross should be supported is a decision that should be made by individuals. Why should the chairman of a company make a decision about the worthiness of a charity on behalf of shareholders? It would be like saying, "We, the company, know which causes are worth supporting better than you do, so we will make that decision for you."

•••

In 1989, Sir James brought me and my chief financial officer, Russ Kersh, to London, where he was searching for new and bigger fish to fry. Our new assignment was to identify U.K. companies in which management had neglected its shareholders, causing the companies to be severely undervalued. We would be shareholder-friendly, buying assets and quickly turning around their value.

Jimmy bought a 37.4 percent stake in Anglo Group PLC, a British leasing company controlled by the Rothschilds, and we used that as our acquisition vehicle to buy more companies.

One of the similarities Sir James and I immediately discovered that we shared was an unassailable commitment to a company's shareholders. It didn't matter to either of us whether the business was publicly or privately held, the best interests of the shareholders came first.

I would look at the boards of these companies and discover that few directors, if any, owned any stock bought out of their own pockets. Then they would fight us using the corporate treasury to keep their own legitimate shareholders from getting what they were entitled to for taking risk.

If most directors and executives bought stock, like we did at Scott Paper, fewer of them would be fighting unwelcome takeovers. They would have worked smarter and better and created value. Then the company would have been so attractive they would have been happy to sell at full value.

We came up with about fifty companies in all that fit our depressed shareholder-value criteria. But no matter how we reshuffled the deck, No. 1 on our list was always BAT Industries, one of the largest companies in Britain, a tobacco manufacturer that had diversified into retail (it owned the Saks Fifth Avenue and Marshall Field chains in the United States), Appleton Paper, and Farmers Insurance. But it was a conglomerate that had historically underperformed. Russ discovered that in 1972, BAT and an American tobacco giant, Philip Morris, had the same operating income, although BAT was actually bigger than Philip Morris at the time. It still is, in terms of the sheer volume of tobacco sold. Fifteen years later, the difference in value between the companies was far starker. Philip Morris's tobacco division *alone* made more in 1987 than all of BAT's diverse operations combined.

I recommended to Jimmy that we look into it, and he was intrigued. At the time, he was contemplating a run at Britain's General Electric Company (GEC), which itself was eyeing another defense company, Plessy, in a hope of combining them. One day, about ten of us—Jimmy, Lord Jacob Rothschild, Kerry Packer, Russ, myself, and several outside advisers—gathered in a conference room to decide which route to take.

"We've got these two things," Jimmy said. "We've got GEC and we've got BAT. GEC, I think we can get, but it's a single. BAT—I don't know if we can get it but if we can, it's a home run. And if we can't get BAT, I'm not sure if we will ever be able to do anything in Europe. What do the rest of you want to do?"

There was very little doubt in anyone's mind. Everyone in the room said, "Let's go for BAT. Go for it, and if we blow it, we blow it."

That's how the Anglo Group's $23 billion bid for BAT was launched on July 11, 1989. It was the biggest attempt of its kind ever in the United Kingdom. The numbers rivaled the Kohlberg Kravis and Roberts takeover of RJR Nabisco in terms of sheer size.

Today, I may be best known for my work at Scott, Consolidated Press Holdings, and Lily-Tulip, but BAT was just as important in my development. It demanded every bit of knowledge, strategy, and invention of which I was capable. And while Jimmy was on the frontlines, guys like Russ and me were intimately involved in the details and fine print. It was the ride of a lifetime.

BAT was doing things that kept its shareholders from getting adequate value, which made an indelible impression on me. Its tactic of using shareholder money to prevent shareholders from getting value was abhorrent to me.

The BAT bid brought together many of Sir James's best and brightest associates, including Packer and his son, James; Rothschild, a brilliant intellectual and well-respected financier from one of the best known families in Europe; Kersh and myself; attorney Fin Fogg; former Goldsmith European chief executive Madame Gilberte E. Beaux; a dozen U.K. merchant bankers and lawyers; and U.S. investment bankers. It was quite a show.

Weeks before the bid was announced, Sir James convened us all into what he called his "takeover panel." It was a great occasion, and the atmosphere was charged with power. We met daily in a beautiful old house that Sir James had leased in London's St. James Square. He and I ran the show from a huge converted dining room on the second floor where all of our strategies were devised.

Sir James's place wasn't air conditioned, however, and it was one of the hottest summers in English history. One day, every window in the place was open and there were at least thirty of us working in the conference room. Outside, in the Square, men were doing construction work with jackhammers. Jimmy, who rarely lost his temper, couldn't take it any longer. He whipped out 100 pounds from his wallet and instructed one of his assistants to tell the workers the money was theirs if they'd only be quiet for an hour. The noise stopped. But here's the twist: Jimmy's assistant came bounding back into the meeting and returned the money.

"I got 'em to quit for free," he said.

"You idiot," someone cracked, "you could have pocketed that money and nobody would have ever known!"

We all fell over laughing.

The Anglo Group was nothing if not well organized, but meetings would still last all day sometimes, break for dinner, and then come back for more. Jimmy was a forceful, dominant personality in those meetings. He had particular advantage over me and my fellow Americans because he knew how things were done there. We knew how to do acquisitions and hostile tender offers, but Jimmy knew how and where the rules were different.

We had a very powerful case setting out the underperformance of BAT's sitting management versus its competitors, as I mentioned earlier. Management lacked a commitment to shareholder value. Our view was that to save BAT, we would "unbundle it," as Jimmy put it, and concentrate on the core tobacco business. Everything else would be sold or spun off. Besides, we didn't think that the merchants of death (tobacco) and the merchants of health (insurance) should be in the same company. On top of everything else, it was a hypocritical conglomerate. How could anyone justify such an ungodly marriage?

BAT would have been the biggest takeover in the world. And we would have gone to $29 billion!

The next nine months were marked by a series of overlapping negotiations, legal and public relations battles, the likes of which U.K. business had never seen before or probably since. BAT management fought us tooth-and-nail during those months. They finally divested some of the very noncore assets we had targeted, in an effort to raise support among wavering shareholders.

I was unrelenting in protecting Jimmy on the BAT deal when it came to legal and public relations fees. I didn't change my modus operandi just because it was a big deal; I would not allow our hirees just to bill him for hours. They had to justify their fees in detail.

For example, the public relations firm we hired submitted a bill for nearly $750,000. Through negotiations, we got it cut to $300,000, mostly by suggesting their fees be audited. We saved more than $5 million on legal fees the same way. Instead of just accepting bills, we asked for time sheets.

I did chafe a bit—as did other Americans in the panel—because the United Kingdom businesspeople seemed so clubby and class-conscious in their resistance to outsiders. But they have a takeover code that everybody observes. To get an approval, applicants go through something like a stock exchange club. The Americans were not invited to those meetings and neither were the British lawyers. Only the merchant bankers took part.

In a sense, we were at their mercy. But Jimmy knew their game and prevailed on many points of preference. For example, on one problem, the takeover code said we couldn't do something that Jimmy said we should be able to do. The Americans suggested presenting a written proposal to the exchange, and they let us do it.

Once the bid was launched in earnest and everything was off and running, we realized that we would have problems with U.S. state insurance regulators. In order to acquire an insurance company, you must be approved in each state where it does business. Normally, if a tough, large state such as Illinois or New York approves a deal, other states follow its lead. It's hard for one state to say you're unfit if another says you're fit. An outside law firm we hired for its insurance expertise didn't dent the regulators' resistance, which should have tipped us off that a storm was brewing out of control, but we still tried to manage it. The problem was that the Illinois insurance regulators would not let us acquire Farmers Insurance.

I grew frustrated by the insurance roadblocks. Gilberte Beaux introduced Jimmy to an enormous French insurance company called Axa-Midi and we cut a deal intended to assuage the Illinois regulators. If and when Jimmy took over BAT, Axa-Midi would have immediately taken over the Farmers Insurance operation.

During the ten months of Sir James's run on BAT, the government bureaucracy we faced was stifling. On one proceeding alone, there were sixty-eight depositions that consumed eighty business days, including two each for Sir James and myself. Eleven more depositions were taken in London. In the end, for just one proceeding, 177 pages of motions were filed, resulting in 132,000 pages of legal documents.

Illinois still turned thumbs down on the deal. The irony is that several years later, the same insurance commissioners—joined by the New York insurance commissioner—let Axa-Midi in effect buy control of The Equitable in a friendly deal.

The failure of the deal was a big disappointment to all of us because it should have been done. We did everything that should have alleviated the Illinois insurance regulators' concerns, making it clear we had no intentions of running the insurance company. We did nothing illegal or immoral, there was no hidden agenda.

It was expensive, too, a battle royal that cost the group $2 million a week.

The whole thing ground to a quiet end on April 22, 1990. It wasn't a happy result, but Jimmy and his partners actually had bought enough BAT stock that they at least covered expenses. The company's value rose significantly during the takeover run as management sold off assets such as Saks and Marshall Field—exactly the kinds of thing we said we would do. They were forced—by our takeover attempt—to create shareholder value that otherwise would not have been accomplished.

Why companies like that don't always see shareholder value as their entire reason for being, I'll never know. How can anyone in business miss such an obvious concept?

Chapter 14
BOARDS OF DIRECTORS,
GOD FORGIVE THEM

LESSON: BOARDS OF DIRECTORS PERFORM
BEST WHEN THEY ARE ALIGNED WITH
SHAREHOLDERS.

Scott Paper's board included one director best described as Mr. X, a man who gave me night sweats. He had served on the Scott Paper board for several years. This man apparently had no problem with management's taste for luxurious appointments, judging by the conspicuous excess he lavished on himself at the company's expense.

My wife, Judy, and I had been invited to a private dinner with the board in Philadelphia, to celebrate my hiring. After a series of interviews with individual members of the executive search committee, this was the entire board's first chance to meet and greet me.

It was the only time I met Mr. X face-to-face, and he used the occasion to needle me about the importance of the board and how I had to heed the board's instructions on how the company should be run. His message was simple: it was *their* company to run; not mine, not the shareholders'. That didn't go over real well with me and it didn't reflect reality. The board hired me to tell *them* what management needed to do, not vice versa. They hired me to protect the shareholders' interests and enhance everyone's investment.

I answered him in the only way I knew how: with brutal honesty.

"I will fix this company," I said. "I will get it right. But rest assured *you're* going to go through enormous changes. If you don't want change, I'm the wrong man for you. I'll do it, and I'll do it my way. The changes will be dramatic and swift; there will be an enormous amount of criticism."

Those—like Mr. X—who weren't on the search committee and hadn't met me before that night bridled at my razor's-edge retort but offered no reply. In Scott's case, it was either me or Dr. Kevorkian, the assisted-suicide guy. I'm more fun, and at least they stood a chance of living through the experience with me at the helm.

Mr. X's problem was that he saw himself as a member of a different class than the rest of us, the corporate elite, or "corpocracy," as Sir James Goldsmith and I described their ilk.

I come from a different culture—and I don't mean the difference between a brash fella from New Jersey and a refined gentleman member of the corporate elite. The real difference: I believe in shareholder value. Mr. X did not.

People who blend the most stultifying elements of corporations and bureaucracies—corpocrats—are bureaucrats who run corporations for their own well-being and not that of the shareholders. I do not believe in management being cast as a new aristocracy, an elitist group who put themselves above the shareholders.

(I remember one board that Sir James had in London. It was full of the Right Honorable This or Lord That. One day I had some cards made up that said, "King Albert J. Dunlap." No one thought that was funny but me.)

In the days that followed my confrontation with Mr. X, I heard from friendlies on the Scott Paper board who said there was a great deal of discussion about who was in charge, and who would be in charge, the corpocrats or me. It would obviously be tough for some to accept the cultural changes that I would prescribe. Director John F. Fort III, former chairman, president, and CEO of Tyco International, warned me, "I've never seen a board get into so much nit! There are so many major, overall philosophical issues that are never discussed."

The next time I heard from Mr. X was when he was making travel arrangements in anticipation of attending the company's June 3, 1994, annual shareholders' meeting, my first as chairman and CEO.

At that time, Scott was not reimbursing its directors' specific travel expenses but was, instead, providing a generous expense allowance. Generous? I'd call it outrageous. The company policy was to pay first-class air fare from wherever the director was based, to the meeting and back, plus room and board—never mind what the actual costs were, because the directors didn't have to submit receipts. If they flew coach, they still got first-class money and could pocket the difference. If two directors carpooled to a meeting, each still received mileage money. Whether or not they stayed in a hotel, they still received hotel reimbursement. The most extreme example was a director who spent a night at Scott Plaza, *our office complex,* and still put in for his hotel allowance.

In Mr. X's case, he informed us that he would fly the Concorde from Paris to New York, then the Scott corporate jet would pick him up in New York and fly him to Philadelphia, then back. He wasn't *asking* for the jet, he was *telling us* it would be there. That jet cost $3,000 an hour to operate.

I looked at his expenses and concluded they were just more than Scott could afford to pay. He would take the Concorde where others would travel via less expensive commercial jets. He stayed at first-class hotels instead of business hotels.

When I replied to Mr. X via fax that the company could no longer afford to provide the jet for his personal use, he replied that, in that case, he would have to reconsider coming to the meeting.

I shot him back a letter saying, "1 accept your resignation."

"I didn't resign!" he protested.

"Funny," I said. "I thought you did."

In England, where I lived for three years, they have real royalty. In America, we have corporate elitists. Both are self-inflated windbags; they don't believe they're accountable to anyone. They enrich themselves at the expense of hardworking men and women who have actually invested in our companies. It's time they were accountable to someone.

The last thing struggling Scott Paper needed was an imperial director. We'd never get along. The board agreed with me and cut ties to Mr. X right then and there, neat and clean. Mr. X, who, I'm told, was the first to help my predecessor out the door, was no doubt surprised by our action, as were outsiders. Still, no one raised a serious challenge when we accepted his resignation.

•••

It's not just the corpocrats we have to beware of. Professional directors, who earn their living from doing nothing but serving on boards, are just as dangerous. Less damaging but equally undesirable on boards are men and women whose sole qualifications are based on sex or color.

Too many of these directors—corpocrats, professional directors, and symbols of diversity—are just not looking after the shareholders. That's because many boards simply don't consist of the best possible people.

A top-flight board should be comprised of outsiders, except for the CEO and perhaps one other inside executive. You need a brilliant investment banker and a skilled lawyer, preferably one who understands securities. You need people who have demonstrated themselves on the job as great CEOs, not the token failed CEO who needs a job or a second pension. You need people who have global experience, in Europe, in Asia. And you need people with real marketing skills. These are the people who will be resources to the CEO, people who add value.

Too many boards skimp on these essentials and include directors who are there just because somebody said they need a token African American or a woman or some other minority. To me, a board of directors is like a sports team. Give me the best damn players—male or female, black or white—and I'll deliver the best results.

I want the best people on my board, period. All that matters to me is what you bring to the table, not what part of the rainbow you represent. I'm not against diversity on the board. I just don't want diversity for diversity's sake.

And I don't believe in affirmative action. Hell, I was born a dirt-poor, inner-city kid. I believe if you work hard, you will be rewarded.

I never wanted to be anybody's token. Today's minorities, today's women, are as good as anybody and they don't want to be somebody's token. They want to get where they're going because they're just damned good.

I don't see men, I don't see women. And I don't see race. I see qualified people. I see talent. I look at a board and ask myself, "How many qualified people do I see?"

Forget about being politically correct. When you put any adjective in front of correct, it's no longer correct. Correct is correct. By itself, the word speaks volumes.

•••

Perhaps the only thing worse than putting people on a board for diversity's sake is the professional director, the man or woman who serves on a multiplicity of boards. What profession is a professional director? What class do you take at school to become a professional director?

The only profession that parallels professional directors is the *oldest* profession. Both do it for the money, and neither is very selective about the clientele.

Directors should only serve on a few boards at most, with term limits and under carefully regulated conflict-of-interest rules.

People who serve on multiple boards go to the meeting. They get the check. Then they get the little briefing book. They thumb through it. The meeting's over. They wait until the next time. They get another check, another briefing. Show me the person who is on a multiplicity of boards, and I will show you the person who isn't doing the job. They never attack the true issues facing the company, such as firing lousy managers, cutting costs, and keeping the business focused on whatever it does best. Instead, they spout off how "The new director manual for this month says we should be doing this," or "The new director manual says diversity is important." Or, "Community giving is important."

If you sit on many boards, it's probably a sign that you're not a very good director. And yet the reputations and marketability of directors who have served on multiple failed boards do not seem affected. Amazing. Let's hope that will change as activist shareholders cast a more wary eye on the credentials and past performance of directors.

I favor term limits for politicians and corporate directors. Five years and you're out. I don't care if you walk on water, or even if you know where the rocks are. Nobody can justify a spot on the board of a publicly held company for more than five years. After five years, go do a great job on somebody else's board. You start thinking of management as your friends, and the company's interests are no longer No. 1; your friends are.

•••

Scott needed change from the top down, starting with the board. Guiding me through it was the chairman of the search committee that found me, Gary L. Roubos, chairman and CEO of Dover Corporation, a New York-based $2 billion manufacturing consortium. Together, we studied the board and made quick but informed assessments based on length of service (too many years was a negative), overall contributions (we wanted to move forward, not back or stand still, as the professional directors would have had us), skill (marketing background was a plus), and attitude (who was going to exacerbate problems and who was going to contribute to solutions).

We also trimmed the board from thirteen members to nine, and cut back the frequency of board meetings from monthly to every other month. And we changed the content of these meetings, from rote recitations of the things everybody already knew to hard details, strategic planning, and vision.

I changed the reporting structure. Instead of bringing in a roomful of executives to drone on endlessly, I handed out printed versions of the same information so directors could study it at their leisure.

Scott's finance group used to take three hours of the board's time to go through its report. I cut that to thirty minutes, reviewing only the highlights. Someone who needed to know more could have it in writing the next day. But the three-hour meetings buried the directors in so much detail they couldn't find the important stuff if they wanted it.

When we were getting together the first plans for restructuring Scott, the board wanted to know how long it was going to take my guys to make a presentation. My own staff thought it would take three days.

I said, "You've got one hour."

How much work would they have done to make enough charts for three days? Think about that. But that's how Scott's business was conducted. Style instead of substance.

Instead of wasting the board's time, I spent a large portion of our board meetings describing my activities, my thinking on important issues, and the direction I was taking on vital management decisions. I know other CEOs crowd their agendas with housekeeping items and resolutions that need to be passed, but I kept that to a bare minimum. I used these occasions to speak my mind and confirm that the board and I were still in tune with our goals and objectives on divestment, acquisitions, or strategic issues. We had real give-and-take in those meetings, instead of me and the operating committee making a slick presentation and then expecting the board's instant approval. The directors welcomed the give-and-take because they felt like partners—and they were. I wanted their input and I got it.

Boards that fail are the ones that have umpteen committees because the directors *think* they are being paid to be in the everyday running of the company. It's fun for directors to play the boy CEO, but it's not their job. When board members—particularly the professional directors and failed CEOs—see their role as managers and elbow their way into operational details, such as hirings and firings, marketing and product development, they cause companies to fail.

Not only is it counterproductive to operate so many committees but it's costly, too. When I arrived, Scott paid its directors $45,000 each annually, plus 2,000 stock options, plus pension, plus $1,000 per committee meeting and another $2,000 for the committee chairman. And it seemed like almost everybody chaired at least one committee!

If you could be on a committee, get your travel reimbursed, and get paid $1,000 per appearance, wouldn't you do it as often as you could? If you're going to be paid that kind of money just for showing up, doesn't that create a desire for more meetings?

What's more, it was common for Scott to pay directors the same fees for telephone meetings as it did for face-to-face gatherings.

At Scott, we dealt with this, in part, by simplifying the board's committee structure from sixteen to just three: compensation, nominating, and audit.

When I started making deep cuts in Scott's assets and staff, we found that at least two of our directors—the ones I would call professional directors—focused on lesser issues, rather than the major issues facing the company. "They're just trying to be good directors in the only sense they know," another director told me.

"But," I said, "we're facing major problems that demand a new direction." The two directors in question subsequently left.

•••

The Scott board I inherited also included a politician and a think-tank policy specialist. The politician had been a United States Representative for twelve years. He left Congress in 1991 and was recruited to join the Scott board.

On the surface, the politician seemed like the perfect board member for modern times: an accomplished, industrious statesman and a self-made member of a cultural minority. But his attendance record at Scott board meetings had been pathetic. He had been late to many meetings, left early, and skipped others altogether. In fact, he missed the meeting at which the board approved hiring me.

I told the board, "With his attendance record he doesn't belong on this board!"

Maybe we could have handled it more diplomatically—there were certainly those who advised us to be delicate. The politician and I subsequently had some heated telephone conversations. During one, he protested, "I have advised kings and presidents, and I don't have to listen to chief executives!" To which I answered,

"I've worked for two billionaires. To them, kings and presidents are footnotes!"

Several board members saw the problem as I did, but until I arrived, nobody had the nerve to come right out and say so. He resigned soon after.

By the end of 1994, some key directors and I concluded that another board member was not in tune with the new direction of the company. This man, the head of a Washington, DC, think tank, wanted to study everything at length before he would agree to act. But I wanted racehorses, not plow horses. He left the board as well.

•••

I initiated the change of directors in agreement with a core of board members—Gary Roubos, John Fort, Peter Harf, Richard Lochridge, and Bill Andres—who wanted what I wanted: to increase shareholder value above all else. I'm sure if you talk today to the people we removed, they would say that all Dunlap did was come in and fix this business up and get ready to sell it. Got his money and ran.

My answer? They should have done it themselves when they had the chance—seventeen years in the case of one director. Then the company could have saved $100 million and I could have spent eighteen months fixing some other destitute company.

Of the original board of thirteen, seven eventually departed. The others were Vice Chairman J. Richard Leaman, Jr., who left because we sold S.D. Warren, the business he represented, and Jack J. Crocker, former chairman and CEO of SuperValu, who reached mandatory retirement age and stepped down. A man of sound principles and experience, I was sorry to lose Crocker's counsel.

In early 1995, we put up new nominees for the reduced board and Gary Roubos quickly interviewed them in New York before the next scheduled board meeting in February. He accommodated me by coming all the way home from Bali, where he was on holiday. Those who were not going to be renominated would not be present, but my proposed slate of newcomers would be. They were:

- Gilberte E. Beaux, former chairman of the board of Adidas and Sir James Goldsmith's Generale Occidentale.
- Mark Davis, head of mergers and acquisitions for Salomon Brothers.
- Howard Kristol, the senior litigation partner with the New York firm of Reboul, MacMurray, Hewitt, Maynard & Kristol.

There would be no further changes in the Scott Paper board of directors. And when Scott merged with Kimberly-Clark in December 1995, Fort, Roubos, and Harf, chairman and CEO of Joh. A. Benckiser GmbH, joined the newly merged Kimberly-Clark company's board of directors to finish what we started.

•••

Directors are responsible for seeing that a company has proper management in place. They should monitor management to ensure it does what it is supposed to do. If not, the directors should take corrective action.

The main role of the board is to hire and fire the chief executive, and to set his compensation. The biggest way that a board impacts a company is to hold the CEO to a very high standard. Boards should be absolutely certain that companies are run properly from a fiduciary, legal, and moral standpoint. Boards should participate in approving or disapproving overall strategy, acquisitions, and major capital expenditures. But it is *not* the role of the board to get involved in day-to-day operations. People who think they can attend four, six, eight, or even twelve meetings a year and know how to run a company are totally deluding themselves. Boards don't run the company, but they better be damn sure that management can.

Directors often forget where their loyalty should lie—to the shareholders—and often act to protect themselves and the person who gave them a board seat, usually the acting CEO. Their sole allegiance must belong to the shareholders, the men and women who invest their hard-earned money in the company. Now, at long last, we see proactive boards dumping ineffectual CEOs who fail to perform.

Management runs the business and is responsible for setting, formulating and executing goals. My unhappiness with the original Scott board was fed by the view, among some directors, that they were somehow equals with management in decision-making. Every business issue, large or small, became a subject of board debate.

•••

With a strong, independent-minded outside board of directors in place at Scott, it was time to pursue an idea that had been on my mind all the way back to the Lily Tulip days: paying directors in stock instead of cash, pensions, and other benefits. That went hand-in-hand with another plan of mine: requiring directors to buy stock.

Boards of directors have all the perks in the world. They get paid obscene fees. They even get pensions. I don't think any director should have a pension. They're not employees, for God's sake. A pension assumes they're going to be there forever.

Reader's Digest Association, for example, gives outside directors a pension. Some automobile manufacturers give their board members a new car every three months; directors of certain airlines get unlimited first-class travel for themselves and their families. Many companies justify these perks as the price of competition to attract the "best" directors.

This is a great social disease: the boards can do well, but the company can fail. It's one of the corporate world's last dirty secrets.

Directors ask: "Why should I take a risk?" Why? *Why?* If you're a director of a company, you've got the opportunity to influence that company. If you don't believe in it to the point you're willing to take a personal risk, you shouldn't be on that board.

I have a lawyer friend. He said, "I've never lost a case." "Never?" I asked, impressed. "Nope," he answered, "I always got paid; lots of my clients lost." And that's a director compensation analogy. Directors, like lawyers, get paid regardless of their company's performance. The clients, the shareholders, can lose everything.

When I interviewed for the Scott job, I floated the idea of paying directors in stock and found many board members receptive. At least one, William A. Andres, former chairman and CEO of Dayton Hudson Corporation, had already been taking his directors' fees in stock from as many of his other boards as would accommodate him. I told the board how we had started the process at Valassis Inserts, Kerry Packer's Michigan-based coupon printing business. At Valassis, a privately held company at the time, I convinced the board to accept at least half of its compensation in stock. The company did extremely well, the stock followed, and everyone was happy.

If shareholders look at a proxy statement and realize the directors don't have any stock, it should leave a bad impression. If the company's such a good investment, why don't the directors invest? And if you go on a board, that should mean you think you can contribute, so you should put your money where your mouth is.

Many directors do buy stock, but I think that if director compensation is based entirely on stock rather than on cash, they'll be 100 percent committed to the company. A large economic stake goes a long way toward motivating a director to really pay attention. It sends a strong message to the shareholders that their interests are paramount.

Most people on boards don't *want* to invest in their companies; they want a free ride. They want options; an option is a free ride. How can you lose on an option? It goes down, you don't exercise. It goes up, you exercise.

What kind of contribution will the directors ever make if they don't have a vested interest in the company's financial success? They've got to show that they believe in the company, that they're willing to stand behind their choices.

I understand the other side: If you have nothing at risk, why not be on a board? You have nothing to lose.

Look at most boards today. Many directors have been in place for years and own just 100 to 200 shares of stock. That's nothing! And yet they get paid $50,000 to $100,000 a year, plus pensions, plus options. Many don't even exercise their options, let alone buy stock. When you look at the proxy and it shows their holdings, it usually shows only their options or restricted options.

They very rarely have reached into their own pockets to buy shares. If the company goes bust, what have they lost? Nothing. They got paid. It should be on every proxy in America this coming year. Any director who isn't willing to be paid 100 percent in stock doesn't believe in the company.

At our July 19, 1994, meeting, I put my initiative before the Scott board. "Executives are buying stock, employees are buying stock," I said. "I want you to be paid 100 percent in stock. We'll pay your documented expenses to get to the meeting, because that seems reasonable, but that's it. If the stock goes up, all right, you've done a great job. If it goes down, you take the hit. Send a message that we're going to be a shareholder-value company. We're here to make money for the shareholders, first and foremost. Show the world that you're willing to take a risk!"

To their everlasting credit, they did, voting to cancel all director compensation except stock equity. They then picked up their checks for that meeting's fees and handed them back. All the previous arrangements—the retainers, committee fees, pensions, stock options, and so on—no longer existed. In a matter of minutes, we made corporate history.[2]

Although we didn't put it in writing, I made it clear how I expected this new system would work. "Ladies and gentlemen," I said, "I don't want you taking this stock and turning around and selling it." They were not restricted by contract. But they did have to notify our general counsel if they were going to sell. And if they did, their actions would be viewed as not being supportive and we would have asked them to leave.

So how does the concept of directors receiving equity as compensation work in action?

Scott Paper stopped paying directors their pensions and options. We told our new directors to buy 1,000 shares. We then paid each Scott director 1,000 shares of stock annually, valued the first year on July 19, 1994, the day the new compensation arrangement was

---

[2] Technically, of course, we couldn't implement it that quickly because we needed shareholder approval. We put phantom shares into a parallel account so their compensation thereafter was based on the stock's appreciation. Directors weren't getting actual shares but the equivalent of the shares, and we subsequently put a plan in place to issue them shares.

approved, at $53.25 (pre-split). By the time we merged with
Kimberly-Clark in December 1995, the value of the first year's
compensation had more than doubled, increasing from $53,250 to
$120,000 per director.

Our directors loved it, but more important, our
shareholders loved it because the board members began thinking
like shareholders. They were no longer just picking up a check
at the end of a meeting.

If you're a director of a corporation you believe in, you should
thirst for equity compensation. For instance, instead of getting
$60,000, you could get $100,000. And nobody would care
because the shareholders would be rewarded accordingly. I have
no problem with directors or executives making huge sums of
money, as long as the shareholders do. If the shareholders
don't, the executives shouldn't either.

I thought paying directors in stock was the most natural
thing in the world to do, but the next day[3] my phone was
ringing off the hook. As it turned out, only one other
corporation in America was doing this, The Travelers.
Travelers' outside board members receive a guaranteed $75,000
worth of stock annually and no other compensation.

Our announcement drew a spectacular response. Harvard
Business School Professor Stuart C. Gilson was inspired to
study our entire restructuring.[4] Even someone I never agree

---

[3] We put out a press release the next day, announcing this new development in
director compensation. In support of our move, the release quoted Tom Neff,
the Spencer Stuart executive who brought me to Scott and who had written a
March 25, 1991, op-ed piece on director compensation for *The Wall Street Journal.*
Neff counsels boards of directors and recruits outside directors, and he began talking up
compensation reform a few years ago. When we first met, he gave me a copy of his
Journal article. Before me, his success had been limited to convincing two boards he
served on in the early 1980s, Macmillan Publishing Company, and Lord Abbott Mutual
Funds, to at least provide the option for board members to take their compensation in
stock rather than cash.

Our release also quoted Stetson University College of Law associate professor named
Charles M. Elson, who had written a more recent piece on the subject, "Executive
Overcompensation—A Board-based Solution," published in the *Boston College Law Review*
in September 1993. Abbreviated versions ran in *The New York Times* (July 18, 1993) and
The Wall Street Journal (September 27, 1993).

[4] "Scott Paper Company," Report #N9296048, December 8, 1995, by Professor Stuart C.

with, Sarah Teslik, executive director of the Washington, DC-based Council of Institutional Investors, said we did the right thing. She wrote an essay for her newsletter titled, "Let 'Em Eat Stock," supporting the rationale for directors to be paid in stock equity instead of cash.

We jump-started a revolution. And as shareholders and shareholder-rights advocates used Scott Paper as their mascot, Charles Elson, an associate professor at Stetson University College of Law, in St. Petersburg, Florida, asked me to be a "celebrity" spokesman for their movement. Before me, he and the other activists were a voice in the wilderness. Their intentions were good and well meaning, but they didn't have a champion.

Elson became involved in this issue during the late 1980s, a time when controversy erupted over the big paydays being handed out to chief executives, whether they produced for their companies or not. He wondered, "Where does that overpayment come from?"

He studied the potential correlation between director stock ownership and performance. Using *Business Week's* annual list of the highest paid, overpaid, and most reasonably compensated executives, Elson compared companies where the outside directors had substantial stock holdings to those where directors had few or no shares. He found that the more stock the outside directors held, the less likely it was that the company was overpaying its CEO. And the converse was also true: the less stock held, the more likely the company was over‐paying the chief executive. An additional study he made found a similar link between good corporate performance and substantial outside director stock ownership. Elson explained his findings by suggesting that stock ownership aligned the interests of the outside directors with the shareholders, rather than management.

Taking the next step, Elson applied the lesson to director compensation. He reasoned that if directors received $30,000 a year in cash, why not give them the equivalent value in stock? Within a few years, each director would have at least a $100,000

Gilson and Research Associate Jeremy Coli, Harvard Business School.

stake in the company, which, his research showed, was the equity threshold that makes a difference in attitude. He published the result of his study and recommendations in two law reviews and the op-ed pages of *The Wall Street Journal* and *The New York Times.*

Elson raised many of the questions that have long perplexed me with regard to boards: Why don't boards get rid of the chief executive when the time—and the CEO—is ripe? Why are chief executives allowed to go on, year in and year out producing woefully inadequate results? And when boards do make a change, why don't they go out and get the toughest, smartest executive who can do the job? Why do they get an executive who belongs to their country club? Why don't they get the best possible person? Why? Because in many cases, it's *disruptive.* That person is going to hold them to a new, tougher standard, and they don't want it.

You bring in an outsider—like I was, at virtually every company I've turned around—and there will be contrasting styles and contrasting results. Most boards don't want that because it'll be a contrast that people can use to compare to the status quo. Dramatic change is a condemnation of the board itself. All of a sudden this new person comes in and does all the things that should have been done for years. What the board should do is say that's the right thing to do and aren't we clever for doing it.

When Scott Paper was about to tell the world about our dramatic change in director compensation, I passed along Elson's *Wall Street Journal* story about compensating directors in stock to our public relations man, Pete Judice of Burson Marsteller. When he contacted Elson and mysteriously asked permission to quote him in a press release for an unnamed company, Elson surprised Judice.

"I don't know what company it is going to be," the law professor told the PR man, "but tell them their stock will get at least a point bump when they announce it."

He was wrong. The stock jumped $2.125. "It could have been sheer coincidence," wrote *Tampa Tribune* business columnist Mickie Valente, "but there are likely many companies who would like to test that theory."

Judice called Elson back the day after the announcement. "Would you like to have lunch with Al?" he asked. Elson quickly agreed, and we flew him to Philadelphia.

Over lunch, Elson offered me a proposal. "If *you* promoted director compensation in stock, I think we could make a lot of companies do it," he said. "When I wrote about it in *The Wall Street Journal, I* heard from consultants, but no CEOs. When Scott announced the switch, everybody wanted to talk about it."

His strategy was to encourage the powerful pension funds to vote against directors who have no stock and tell them to start demanding stock ownership. I agreed that it would have a big impact.

Elson arranged for me to kick off the inaugural Nichols Foundation Prominent Speakers Series at the Stetson Law campus in St. Petersburg, Florida, on February 2, 1995. He also coaxed the *Journal's* chief management reporter, Joann S. Lublin, to act as moderator for the question-and-answer session. Elson and Lublin didn't see eye-to-eye on the director compensation issue; she doubted most directors would accept stock in lieu of cash or that, if they did, it would change anything. The two of them had many friendly arguments on the subject.

Lublin was unconvinced that this was the start of a revolution. However, during the Q&A session, she asked me about it.

"While in principle it seems like a good idea," she said, "I wonder if in practice paying the board in stock really will be that good of an idea for the companies long-term? Paul Lego, the former CEO of Westinghouse, said he thought it was not a very good idea for directors to be paid only in stock, or to be required to own a certain number of shares. Because, he said, it may not always be the corporate interests that are the directors' interests. And you don't want the corporation's future and the corporation's decisions to be dictated solely by the directors' pocketbook."

I paused a moment for effect and considered the question. Paul Lego? The same CEO who in 1992 announced he was taking a $1.5 million pay cut after his company lost a staggering $1.1 billion, only to receive monster stock option grants of 700,000 shares, worth four times what he gave up?

"Just for clarification," I asked, "is this the same Paul Lego who all but tanked Westinghouse?"

"Right," she said, and the auditorium shook with laughter.

Toward the end of February, 1 was in Chicago participating in a Russell Reynolds Associates panel discussion on the topic "Boards of Directors: The Next Generation." Also on the panel: Jewel LaFontant-Mankarious, a lawyer with Hollub & Coff in Chicago and the first woman Deputy Solicitor General of the United States; William D. Smithburg, CEO of Quaker Oats; and Nell Minow, a principal of Lens Inc., and coauthor of *Watching the Watchers: Corporate Governance for the 21st Century* (Blackwell).

If there was ever another Al Dunlap in the business universe, it would probably be Minow. Without ever having met before, we clicked immediately. While LaFontant-Mankarious and Smithburg represented the staid, traditional notions of how a corporation and its board should operate, Minow and I were the iconoclasts at the opposite extreme, each of us alternately challenging them. "How dare people go on boards and not hold any stock!" we said, over and over again.

What I remember best about Minow's performance that day was her advice to anyone on, or about to join, a corporation's board of directors. "I want you to write this down," she told the audience. *"Do not hire Bill Agee!* We know two things about him. One is: He is out of work. Another is: He is very good at selling himself. These should be red flags! When a CEO says he can run the company perfectly fine from Pebble Beach, *that is* a red flag! When there is a life-size portrait of the CEO and his wife in the lobby, *that is* a red flag!"

I laughed along with everyone else when she said that. Agee's unparalleled ability to land and sustain a string of CEO jobs—his performance at Bendix left a great deal to be desired, he took some time off, and then did serious damage to light-rail transit manufacturer and bridge contractor Morrison Knudsen—has been one of my own favorite examples of the behavior of many directors.

Agee first came to prominence and became a household name in America following personal indiscretions while he was CEO of Bendix. His relationship with Mary Cunningham, a woman he hired as his executive assistant and then quickly promoted to vice president for strategic planning, made front page news around the country. She quit first; he was forced out when his ill-considered takeover attempt of Martin Marietta backfired and a beaten-up Bendix was sold to Allied Corporation.

Agee and Cunningham divorced their respective spouses and were married in 1982, amid all the chaos around them. When he was banished from Allied (now AlliedSignal), they disappeared for several years before resurfacing at Morrison Knudsen.

The Morrison Knudsen directors, all cozy with Agee at the wheel, seemed to fall asleep in the backseat. The CEO and his directors bonded and enjoyed board meetings usually held anywhere but near the company's headquarters in Boise, Idaho, a place where they and their shareholders might get a sense of how badly Agee was running the company. It was reported that Agee and his wife used the company jet for sightseeing trips to Yugoslavia, the Vatican, and the French shrine at Lourdes. After three years of living in Boise, Agee and Cunningham moved to Pebble Beach, California. But it was a period of time before some of the directors apparently realized he was running the company via remote control from his golf course mansion. And even when they figured that out, the board didn't see anything wrong with it. It was not until the stock lost 58 percent of its value from 1992 to 1995 and the company was in dire straits, that Agee was shown the door.

Minow and I bonded after that panel discussion and have been friends and confidants ever since. Her company, Lens, was started by Robert A.G. Monks in 1992. It invests in underperforming companies and makes their lives very difficult until they turn around. Of the seven companies Lens invested in from 1992 to 1995—Sears, Roebuck & Company, American Express, Westinghouse Electric, Eastman Kodak, Borden, Scott Paper, Stone & Webster—all seven replaced their CEOs.

After the fifth CEO change, Minow wrote an article for *Legal Times* in which she referred to executive musical chairs as "the Queen of Hearts School of Director Performance." "Off with their heads," she wrote, encouraging more boards to dump floundering chief executives. "The shareholders are angry and we have to do something."

Sometimes, she concluded, the company has to be changed. But always, the board has to be changed. And by replacing the CEO, the directors camouflage the real problem.

Her guerrilla boardroom tactics are alarmingly simple. Lens believes that "the board of a poorly performing company can demonstrate credibility only by choosing directors who have a proven record of making money, and who will make a full commitment to board membership, including a significant investment of their own money."

Lens buys a couple of million dollars' worth of shares—a mere fraction of what the company has out. But through the shareholder activism of Monks and Minow, Lens creates visibility for its notions of fixing companies. That, in turn, generates credibility with the powerful institutional investor community. Besides making money for itself, Lens's mission includes advising large institutional shareholders on how to make better use of their rights as shareholders. They believe, rightly, that institutional shareholders, as fiduciaries, are obligated to provide support for anybody who is willing to take the initiative.

Of all the companies Lens invested in, it made the most money on Scott Paper. Lens's major contribution to Scott was made before I arrived. It shone a bright light on problems with management and on products that needed to be corrected. It had put the company under a microscope and supported us when we did the things that were necessary.

•••

As a result of my high profile as an advocate of paying boards in stock, I was invited to serve on the National Association of Corporate Directors (NACD) Blue Ribbon Commission on Director Compensation.

Twenty minutes into the nineteen-member commission's first meeting, I raised my hand and said, "You guys are missing the point! The real issue is aligning the interests of the shareholders and the directors."

William W. Adams, former CEO of Armstrong World Industries, tried to cut me off.

"I disagree," he said. "There is no study that shows a direct link."

"I agree," said Harvard Business School Professor Robert

Stobaugh, chairman of the commission.

That's when I introduced Elson and his studies. He passed out copies of his research linking board stock ownership, reasonable executive compensation and heightened corporate performance and we literally felt the dynamics of the room change.

I'm not one to compromise on the big issues, and this was one of the biggest. I insisted directors be paid 100 percent in stock and that they must be required to buy X number of shares when they go on a board. Others protested and said, at most, it should be a mixture.

The final report, released June 19, 1995, wasn't all I had hoped for—the commission endorsed compensating directors *predominantly* in stock, not totally—but it was still the most controversial stand ever taken by an NACD Blue Ribbon Commission.

It recommended the following "Best Practices":

Boards should:

1. Establish a process by which directors can determine the compensation program in a deliberative and objective way.

2. Set a substantial target for stock ownership by each director and a time period during which this target is to be met.

3. Define the desirable total value of all forms of director compensation.

4. Pay directors solely in the form of equity and cash—with equity representing a substantial portion of the total up to 100 percent; dismantle existing benefit programs and avoid creating new ones.

5. Adopt a policy stating that a company should not hire a director or a director's firm to provide professional or financial services to the corporation.

6. Disclose fully in the proxy statement the philosophy and process used in determining director compensation and the value of all elements of compensation.

So, by the end of 1995, Scott Paper and The Travelers were no longer lone voices crying in the wind.

Campbell Soup Company adopted all of the NACD principles

and put them in its proxy. If you join the Campbell Soup board today, you must dig into your own pocket and buy 3,000 shares of stock, and you will be compensated annually for your work with 1,200 shares of stock, no cash. Pensions and medical benefits for independent directors were eliminated. Now, like its stockholders, the Campbell Soup directors are at risk.

As of early 1996, Texas Instruments, B.F. Goodrich, Digital Equipment, Alexander & Alexander Services, Johnson & Johnson, Warner-Lambert, Bell Atlantic, Brunswick, Armstrong World Industries, AMP, Asarco, IBM, and dozens of other corporations had adopted part or all of the commission's recommendations. At the very least, many others—including ITT—were immediately emboldened to drop director pensions.

Chapter 15
FEED A COMPANY, STARVE A CULTURE

LESSON: SEEK OUT AND FREE THE GOOD
PEOPLE. GIVE THEM THE OPPORTUNITY TO
FLOURISH FROM WITHIN.

Every corporation has a culture. How do employees and executives act? How do they deal with problems? What type of leadership do they provide? How are they compensated? It's all a matter of culture.

Value creation should be an important aspect of corporate culture. Those who create value move ahead; those who impede it should be left behind.

People who create value have a fire in the belly. They're never satisfied with what is; they're always imagining what could be.

Some companies, however, define their culture by only hiring executives and managers from certain universities (Ivy League schools such as Harvard and Princeton, for example) or regions. They're putting out a sign that people without a certain social pedigree need not apply. This sort of corporate in-breeding—the same ideas, the same themes generated by the same type of men and women—only reinforces cultural stagnation by hiring the same type of people with the same training and roots. They all see business from the same perspective rather than being challenged by different ideas and points of view and by people never satisfied with the status quo.

When he first hired me, Sir James Goldsmith said, "You know, dear boy, you've made a good deal of money on the Lily-Tulip deal, and if you do well with me you'll make a great deal more money, but it won't change you. It'll never matter how much you make from me, because you have a fire in the belly."

•••

The people who succeed are the ones who rise above the common denominator. At American Can, the vice chairman believed that fashion packaging for shirts and nylons would be a great business. I headed a group assigned to study it. I titled our presentation, "The Other Side of the Street Is a Blind Alley." It concluded that fashion packaging would be a bad move. Everybody in the group went numb at the thought of rejecting a notion belonging to the vice chairman. They said, "If you present this, we'll be fired!" Furthermore, they wouldn't put their names on the report! So I was the only one whose name was on it when I gave the presentation. The vice chairman was sitting in the room, which went absolutely silent when I was done. Everybody thought, "That's it, he's fired." Then the vice chairman spoke. "Al," he said, "I've been trying to get to the bottom of this. Thank you for a great presentation."

That's an example of a point in my career when I wasn't a chief executive but I took a position that was far out—and in the company's best interests. I bucked the prevailing culture, and American Can was a better company for allowing my journey outside the invisible lines. I look for the same willingness to buck the conventional wisdom when I choose people to trust as members of my inner circle.

At Cavenham Forest Products, an upstart young executive named Russ Carson once challenged me on an important point. Skeptically, I said, "Oh, Russ, why didn't you say this before I got here?" That's just what he was waiting to hear. He pulled out suggestions he had written long before I arrived, that were suppressed by the previous culture. I was impressed. When I left the company, Russ got my job and the CEO's chair.

Newt White is another example; he refused to give in to Scott's decaying culture. As senior vice president of Scott's Away-From-Home business, he was successful under the old regime because he divorced himself from the parent company and its culture. His business did its own thing, whereas the consumer guys were dying. He was one of only two senior executives to make the transition from Scott's previous management to my own. He may not have needed me to discover him, but I certainly gave him greater freedom than he had ever known before.

At Lily-Tulip, the financial reports were always screwed up and I had a great deal of difficulty understanding them. But there was always this one analyst whose reports made a lot of sense, Russ Kersh. I talked to him and he made sense, so I promoted him. He has been my right-hand man ever since, from the Goldsmith days through Scott Paper.

John Murtagh started his legal career in 1976 with a private law firm in Toledo, Ohio. One of the firm's clients was Owens-Illinois, before and during its sale of Lily-Tulip to KKR. He, personally, didn't work on any of their business, but when another lawyer from the firm joined Lily-Tulip, he invited Murtagh to follow him in 1981.

During the first few weeks when I was on the scene, Murtagh was out in the field working on labor issues. Checking in with the office by phone, he heard his friends and coworkers nervously talk about the holy terror stalking the executive suite.

When his field work was completed, Murtagh returned to the office only to hear that the three-person legal department was being downsized and he would be out of a job.

Murtagh is a resourceful, easygoing fella who would never let a thing like being fired ruffle him. He started packing his things and set up a job interview for the following week. That should be the end of the story, but it wasn't.

Murtagh was called into a meeting with Lily-Tulip's director of purchasing, Jack Dailey, the CFO, director of sales, and myself. He didn't know why we wanted to see him.

He sat down and I began talking to him. But he looked at me funny. "That's not my name," he said, as I addressed him. We hadn't met before because he been out of town. "Then who *are* you?" I asked.

He told me he was a junior attorney in the legal department. I realized Murtagh was not the lawyer I was expecting, the one I was keeping on, but I decided to keep him talking. I liked his attitude and besides, I was impressed by what he had to say. "What do you know about this?" I asked. "What do you know about that?"

"Wait a minute," he protested. "I just got told that tomorrow I'll be fired. Why all these questions, what difference does this make?"

"Ah," I said, laughing, "don't be too hasty." So I told him, "We're thinking about keeping you instead of your boss." He said, "What do you want to know?"

The next day, Lily-Tulip's infamous "Black Friday" when we let a lot of people go, Murtagh stayed and I defied conventional wisdom, firing his supervisor instead.

Russ and John didn't sink to the lowest common denominator when change came to Lily-Tulip, and they've been my leading change agents ever since.

Russ is tough, smart, and loyal. I put a high premium on loyalty. That doesn't mean just keeping people who agree with me. I recognize loyalty in people who speak their minds and tell me when they think I'm doing something wrong. Russ will do that; so will John. If everybody in a corporation was doing these things, they'd never get Dunlapped in the first place. These two young men found a comfort level with what I do and how I do it.

•••

In my first week at Scott Paper, I called a meeting of all the senior managers, not just the executive vice presidents. I wanted to see front-line management. I made everybody stand up and say what they were going to do for the company.

One guy stood up and started talking about what he had already done for the company.

"I don't care what you have *done,*" I said, making an example of him. "I want to know what you are going to do for me, now and in the future!"

He looked at me, dumbfounded.

"I'm not prepared to talk about that," he said.

"Then sit down," I said.

Needless to say, at every meeting thereafter, everyone was prepared to literally say what they were going to do to help the company. And the man who had no answers stayed on and found the answers.

Culture can also be defined in less obvious ways. We were a global company, so Scott Paper executives often needed to fly halfway around the globe. But instead of going alone, they traveled in groups. Someone who was going to London never had to worry about being alone; there was always a superfluous entourage right behind. It made the lead dogs feel more important having their pack in tow. (I stepped up the use of videoconferencing whenever possible.)

The great corporations have a rolling culture that is very much akin to a takeover mentality. They run their businesses as if hostile new owners just took over. They make the cuts, they're innovative on the product side, they don't keep operations that stand still. They don't care what the structure looks like. All they want to do is use the assets profitably, and they're not hung up on self-preservation. They're focused on the success of the company.

Prior managements at Diamond, Crown-Zellerbach, Lily-Tulip, and Scott had the opportunity years earlier to do the same things we did. Why didn't *they* make the tough decisions? Why didn't *they* restructure? Why didn't *they* sell off assets that didn't fit?

Culture!

Each of these companies had created a culture in which initiative was stifled, not praised. Employees weren't encouraged to be aggressive. Management played it safe, doing things the same way from year to year. And it was killing them.

A company should build on tradition, but try not to live on it. If you live on tradition, you die on tradition. But if you build on tradition, it is a sturdy stepping-stone to the future.

If you have a great culture, nourish it, sustain it, grow it. If you have a bad culture, don't just put it in remission; kill it. Otherwise, just like a disease, it will ultimately come back to kill you.

I have no desire to protect a culture, the corporate entity, or the in-place management. I don't think any of that's important. What's important is deploying those assets in the best possible fashion. Build where you can build. Shut down operations where they should be shut down. Sell where and when necessary.

A culture reflects the way things are; you have to change it to be the way you want it to be. Instead of continuing things the same way as they ever were, I set up a different culture at Scott, a culture of change, of accountability, of profitability.

Under any good management scenario, employees who are not capable of what they've been doing should be let go. People who get let go should be people who are not performing a necessary function, or have not been effective. Critics within and without will say, "Gee, they got rid of so many people." But your basic security in the world is your own ability to produce, your own ability to make a contribution. And if you're really good, people will want you.

•••

Some cultures are even more dysfunctional than others. During the years I spent working for Goldsmith, we received a call from Drexel Burnham Lambert, on behalf of Pan Am's labor unions. The unions had seen the writing on the wall for the famous carrier and were looking for a miracle—or at least a white knight. They wanted to know: Would Sir James consider buying Pan Am?

Jimmy, as pro-American as Europeans come, told me, "I want to do this, Al. We must save Pan Am."

We took a team—composed of myself, Kersh, Don Burnett of Coopers & Lybrand, compensation and benefits attorney Chris Sues, and mergers and acquisitions specialist Mark Davis, then of Salomon Brothers—and spent almost a month camped out at the Pan Am Building, reviewing their situation. We each had our own field to investigate.

When you walked in the lobby of the Pan Am Building in midtown Manhattan, it was just fabulous. But the offices and hallways were terrible; carpets were torn up and badly stained. I imagined that somebody came in every morning with a razor blade and cut up the rugs, somebody else came along with electrical tape and taped the rugs, then somebody else came by and spilt coffee on them. Based on what the corporate headquarters looked like, you couldn't help but worry about the condition of the planes.

When most corporate cultures are in ruins, it isn't apparent to an outsider or to the naked eye. Pan Am was the exception.

Our first meeting there was with Pan Am's chairman, who told us how wonderful everything was. He introduced us to some key people and we asked for some space in which the five of us could work with due diligence.

"We'll bring a couple of our own secretaries and equipment," I said. "What we need from you is a little conference room and maybe two offices."

"We have some space on the seventeenth floor," he said. I told him we'd take it.

"Well, I can't just *give* it to you," he stammered. "The manager on that floor might not like it."

That's how we found out Pan Am no longer owned the famous Pan Am Building. It just owned the sign. His hesitation—his *inability—to* assign us office space could have stopped the deal on the spot.

"Never mind," I said, "we'll work out of Fin Fogg's offices at Skadden, Arps. But I want you to know I have an interview this afternoon with *The New York Times* and if this comes up, I don't want you to be surprised."

I took two steps toward the door and I had the space.

We were pretty optimistic for the first two weeks, and then the bad news started coming in waves. Our research proved nothing short of depressing. We had begun our task full of anticipation, knowing Jimmy wanted this company and expecting Pan Am to be something special. In the end, we were all in for a crash landing.

Everything we examined was wrong. We found employees reading books on the job instead of answering phones, issuing tickets, or whatever their jobs were. We learned that $1 million a month in spare parts were unaccounted for out of a maintenance facility at New York's Kennedy Airport.

The Pan Am Building wasn't the only thing that was the airline's in name only. For all practical purposes, it had no assets. Everything was leased. It had a business making money in Miami, but that was a building cleaning service. The Boston-New York-Washington shuttle was making money, as was another shuttle in West Germany. But everything else was losing its ass.

Pan Am had a ticket office in the building's lobby; the rent was about $100 per square foot. Anyway, one of the fellows on our team was flying to England for a weekend, and we wanted him to fly Pan Am. He went down to the lobby for a ticket. Two hours later he returned, ticketless. He couldn't get anyone to sell him a ticket. They were all on the phone, reading books, doing their nails, or just plain disinterested.

Upstairs, Pan Am's executives didn't know their own cost structure; it was terribly mismanaged. They had only one antiquated computer center for the entire airline. If it went down, there was no backup.

One day we were working in the conference room and somebody got up to use the rest room. But when he tried to open the door to leave the conference room, the knob came off in his hand and we were stuck for thirty minutes. Nothing with the name "Pan Am" attached to it worked very well anymore.

There was terrible strife within management, where senior executives were undercutting each other's authority. And the company had horrible union relations. It took eight unions to move luggage from the street to the plane.

I remember one time a Pan Am captain called in from Kennedy Airport in New York and I could hear a marketing person screaming at him. Then he slammed down the phone. "I am not taking that crap from these captains any more!" he raved. "He's telling me he doesn't have any passengers and I am not going to take that harassment!"

Here's the rest of the story: I sent someone to check on the situation and found that the plane had been dropped from the computer—that's why there were no passengers!

No authority ruled anywhere in the company; there were plenty of excuses and no responsibility, no pride in the service that Pan Am provided. All this in a company that not long before was the No. 1 airline in the world.

It showed that there isn't a company in the world that bad management can't destroy.

Because Jimmy wanted so badly to hear some kind of options for saving the airline, we outlined a rough plan. We would lay off 7,800 people, including 38 percent of management, and move the headquarters out of the Pan Am Building in Manhattan and take it south to Miami. We'd also move maintenance to Miami, where the weather was good year-round and we could cut better deals with the unions. Pan Am had another problem: It was flying to places nobody wanted to go. We were going to dump little-traveled routes and concentrate flights to Europe, South and Central America and the Pacific.

Costs were grossly out of control, Pan Am had no strategic direction and management was improperly spending capital it didn't have.

That's when Chris Sues discovered the airline had unfunded medical and pension liabilities of $1.2 billion. That blew the rest of the equation out of the air: Pan Am had a negative net worth. No way we were going to recommend Sir James take this on.

"Jimmy," I said, "a year ago, we could have fixed this, but they are already bust, there is no pulse."

We packed up our bags, thanked our hosts, and beat a hasty retreat.

There were ways Pan Am could have saved money, but once we knew about the pension liabilities, it was clear that the airline was terminal. Needless to say, nobody there agreed with us. Management said *we* didn't understand the business. We knew better. Pan Am, despite its international brand name and remarkable history as an aviation original, wasn't even worth the attention of the bargain hunters.

Six months later, Pan Am was effectively out of business.

•••

In a dying company, the steady hand of the old culture will not save it. Part of my strategy in such a situation is to paint a bleak picture of the status quo and make sure that everybody knows the old culture wasn't successful.

Newt White liked to tell people that my approach "was to pee all over the old culture and point out the issues and the reasons it was not successful." That's shock therapy to get people to realize a need to change. I play hardball, but nobody working for me will miss the point: This is a new environment and a new way of doing business.

In certain circumstances, one of the quickest ways to get that point across is to move the corporate headquarters.

I've lived in seventeen states and three countries during my business career. I have moved many corporate headquarters because that is the ultimate way to change their culture. Moving sends a signal to employees that a new headquarters, in a new city, means a new way of doing business. By selling Scott Plaza in Philadelphia, we killed the last vestige of the old culture, which was pulling the company closer to an early grave.

Another bonus to relocation: There's nothing like being in a place where you're wanted and treated with respect.

I moved Scott Paper to Florida because the city of Boca Raton and Palm Beach County—which beat out Atlanta, Dallas, Greenville, South Carolina, and Charlotte, North Carolina—gave us an incentive package that helped defray the cost of the move. Our Florida hosts made reasonable concessions to us, the building was a good fit, the quality of life was attractive, there was no state income tax, and it was an easy place for recruiting quality people.

Here's an even better reason for relocating: I moved Lily-Tulip to Augusta, Georgia, because we had a large plant there. I wanted my people to be able to go from headquarters to a plant in minutes, not days. The only reason Lily-Tulip headquarters was ever in Toledo was because that's where its former parent company, Owens-Illinois, was headquartered.

When Lily-Tulip relocated, many people moved with us from Toledo to Augusta. We also found some terrific people in Augusta to replace the people we lost.

The move changed the company—for the better. It bonded us emotionally as people who had collectively survived a trial by fire and grown stronger from the experience. It also made us physically closer. When we were in Toledo, our people were scattered all over the map. When we moved to Augusta everybody pulled together. It created a camaraderie that could never have been as important and vibrant in Ohio.

•••

When I took over Diamond International for Sir James in 1987, management moved so slowly it was like watching grass grow. Each year they did as they had done the year before. The culture conditioned employees to always feel comfortable; they weren't forced to question everything they did or to act aggressively. There was no sense of urgency.

The company's land operation was a sleepy little company run by well-intentioned people who had not been exposed to aggressive market practices. Before us, they hadn't used their purchasing muscle, hadn't streamlined their administration, hadn't updated their equipment. And they weren't using the most profitable lumber mix.

Diamond was the house that matchsticks built, as a friend once put it. It was a quick fix, compared with other companies I restructured. It went from a loss to a $2 million positive cash flow in less than a year.

We threw out the old ways of doing things—the stagnant decision-making, dull-witted strategies, and steady-as-she-goes-into-oblivion management mentality. Improvement came from: a 10 percent improvement in productivity, due largely to a new incentive system: nearly $1 million in increased woodcutting efficiency: and a more cost-efficient and profitable mixture of woods.

We split Diamond into its component parts and sold pieces to operators who then prospered with them. In the companies we kept, some people rose to the occasion and did well for themselves. Others left.

I promoted a man named Art Larsen to forest manager for Diamond, and he caught on to my tactics in a big way. Instead of just going through the motions, he sought out higher and better uses for land, including real estate sales and recreational leases, and turned his foresters from custodians into merchants. They looked for outside business, everything from managing other people's lands for a fee to buying, selling, and brokering wood. They grew everything from blueberries to Christmas trees and radio towers, searching for every possible way to make money.

Cash flow from Diamond lands increased fivefold. In 1985, the California properties alone generated $3.8 million in operating cash flow. In 1986, they hit $6.8 million, and in 1987, $14.7 million. This increase came even though the volume of wood being cut on the lands remained static. It was a simple result of better resource management, which occurred when we showed the culture there was a better way of both responsibly managing Diamond's lands and increasing profitability.

The next step was assigning executive vice president Phil Lader (who later joined President Bill Clinton's Cabinet as director of the Small Business Administration) to assess Diamond's land holdings.

Sir James had so much land between Diamond and Cavenham—almost 4 million acres at one point—that Lader and I presented him with some 100 development plans for different sites around the country. We identified 165,000 acres that had genuine real estate potential for residential or commercial exploitation. But in the end, he convinced us that the real estate business was iffy at best and the returns were too speculative. Instead of going into development—as Lader expected we would—we decided to simply sell the land and let somebody else take the risk.

Based on this decision, Lader's job evolved and he with it. Instead of going into high development mode, he spent the next year as planner, evaluator, and strategist for selling the lands. And in retrospect, given the late 1980s crash in the American real estate industry, it was exactly the right decision at the right time. Through wisdom, providence, or just plain luck, Jimmy and I once again called the market right.

Lader marketed property to conservation groups and developers alike. "Get the fair market value," I told him. "I don't care who pays it." I told him that if it was sufficiently important land to be preserved then there should be enough people in the private sector willing to make charitable contributions equal to what a developer would pay.

Many of the high bidders for Diamond lands were indeed major conservancies. Others might have argued that these groups should have gotten a discount, but I said, "We're selling this asset as it is right now. What they do with it is their business." And in many cases, the environmental groups were able to use some very innovative fundraising devices.

We shook the sleepiness out of Diamond's eyes. We literally cast off the deadwood of a do-nothing forest products corporation and bolstered employees who comprehended a new culture that combined preservation with capitalism.

•••

Scott's culture was fairly congenial. Too congenial. Decisions took time because too many people were weighing in with opinions at every step. Everybody felt a need to be involved in everything, making it difficult to get anything done quickly.

The old culture discouraged challenges. If Mary had an idea for changing or improving her business, Jerry didn't challenge her on its merits because then she might do the same to his proposal next week. The review process was terribly flawed, leading to fiascoes such as the $300 million investment in a co-generation plant in Mobile, Alabama, or $350 million on a third coated paper machine for S.D. Warren in Maine. Those expenditures should never have occurred. The old culture allowed $650 million to be spent, making it impossible to find the money to support further development of new products such as pre-moistened toilet paper.

Scott was a consensus organization, a culture where, if executives weren't invited to a meeting, they felt left out— whether they belonged there or not. Their names on the copy list were a sign of importance.

There was endless debate over substantial issues, and equal debates over nothing at all. No one ever raised a voice, cut off debate, and said, "Here's the decision—go forward!" And when there was a decision, it could always be brought up again—there was never closure on the issues.

I prefer a culture where you can walk down the hail, get a decision made, and move on with business. At the old Scott, you had to write memos and touch base with different people so they were comfortable with even the most insignificant decision. It was a friendly, collegial environment that collapsed because it was completely unfocused on its reason for being: Making money.

This was a 115-year-old company whose traditions had survived through thick and thin. After a certain point, management became less a cadre of proactive leaders and more one of sedentary caretakers. I wanted to totally change Scott's culture, from one of accepting mediocrity, blaming everyone else for its problems and just getting by, to a responsible business that overcame obstacles with a high level of discipline and accountability. It was also an inbred society. I was the first outsider in its history to be given the corporate reins.

That change was long overdue.

Even in a thriving company, it often takes the eyes of an outsider to spot the obvious and bring business back to the correct path for the long journey ahead.

It is easier for an outsider because an outsider doesn't get caught up in internal politics, doesn't get caught up in the traditions, doesn't get caught up in the culture.

If you grow up in a culture, you will think and act the way that culture expects you to think and act. But an outsider examines the culture, makes a face, and says, "Why do you *do* things that way?" If the best answer is, "That's the way it's always been done," that's no answer at all. Business is dynamic. If it doesn't change, it becomes obsolete. A new structure, combining key people from inside the organization, with special talent from outside, will give leadership direction to all of its people.

If employees see their leadership exhibiting certain negative behaviors, the rank-and-file will say, "If they can be irresponsible or waste the company's money, then I can do it too." If they see executives spending thousands of dollars on nothing, will employees really try and save the company 50 cents here, a dollar there? If they see the executives blow it, they say, "What's the use?"

Leadership sets the cultural expectations and limits. Can the company be truly cost-conscious if the chief executive surrounds himself or herself with opulence? Does that inform the shareholders that this person is an appropriate guardian of their career investment? Does it send the right message to Joe and Judy Paycheck about why there will be no raise in pay this year or why job layoffs are coming?

You must wipe out enough of the old culture to be able to see the new culture. You must establish a new culture with people who have a different mindset and who will operate in a different and better way. It is like applying electric paddles to a corpse.

Change starts at the top. If you sit back and relax, the old culture will get you.

We restructured and downsized the Scott workforce within weeks of my arrival so I wouldn't grow accustomed to or even familiar with the old way of operating. It also sent the message that there was no such thing as business as usual.

Our behavior set a tone of urgency. Act quickly, be direct. The consequence of not being direct and not acting quickly is far greater than any consequence you may suffer by virtue of being direct. Yet, amid the chaos and confusion of layoffs, we looked for ways of reinforcing our commitment to the workforce that remained.

Everybody changed. We managed differently, spending far less time in meetings. The decision-making processes became crisper, clearer, and faster. We had fewer people, which meant fewer people making decisions. There was training and upgrading of skills because people were given more to do and more responsibility.

Some people can't make the shift. They don't like the new philosophy; it's too harsh. We had a number of people who opted out, people who were used to a more paternalistic, socialist business environment.

Many older companies have found themselves in the same boat as Scott Paper. They've become more welfare state than business enterprise. Scott had the worst of both worlds. It was like a welfare state and it wasn't profitable.

•••

Other steps topping my list of culture-shaking improvements include reassessing compensation plans, rewards, and recognition, and refining the company's goals and objectives.

If people balk at something and say, "We've tried that before," that's the kiss of death in my book. They're a disease; cut them out. Meanwhile, seek out and free the good people from the bureaucracy. Give them the opportunity to flourish from within.

Ironically, most employees who stayed with Scott Paper until the Kimberly-Clark merger didn't want to go back into a potentially bureaucratic environment where they wouldn't have an opportunity to be entrepreneurs, make decisions, and make things happen. For them and me, that was one of the most beautiful—and least heralded—of all the good things that came out of the Scott restructuring. Our people knew that they had autonomy and an ability to get things done under my management team that they didn't have before and may never have again.

Chapter 16
IMPRESSING THE ANALYSTS

LESSON: EVERY BUSINESS HAS A MESSAGE
TO SELL.

Scott Paper had an organized campaign to impress on the investment community the tidal wave of changes enveloping the company and the value we were creating. But the methods we used could be applied in almost every situation in which you need to sell yourself, a product, or a company.

In the paper business, as in many industries, what we do is judged every day by investment analysts who specialize in a certain field—forest products, retail, commodities, or technology. They study a company's annual and quarterly reports, break down the numbers, assess the current performance, and make predictions on what the future holds.

With time, some analysts grow apathetic in their jobs; others get complacent. So many companies, their CEOs wearing their Sunday best and a smile a mile wide, flashing convoluted flip-charts and running dog-and-pony shows—it's a wonder they get any work done at all!

But the folks at Brown Brothers Harriman & Co. won't soon

forget the show I put on for them at their New York offices on October 26, 1994.

That's the day paper industry analyst and manager Kathryn Felton McAuley invited me to address her firm. The very proper and uptight old money firm had a packed auditorium waiting for me, and I literally worked the room from back to front, shaking hands and saying,

"Hi, I'm Al Dunlap and I'm here for assertiveness training! Kathy McAuley says I'm not assertive enough!"

I was quite animated that day, delighted to let some of the starch out of the firm's traditionally stuffed shirts. Kathy would always call me "the flamboyant Al Dunlap"; I thought I'd go in and show them why.

"It is very nice to be here with the blue blood of the blue bloods," I said. "I know you are used to investing in stodgy old firms but now you will have an opportunity to invest in a real company—if you have the courage."

I challenged their tolerance to the legal limit, but God bless 'em, they took it all in stride.

The only moment of uncertainty was when someone rudely interrupted my presentation on Scott's commitment to cost cutting and increasing shareholder value.

"What makes you think *you* can do it?" the man asked snidely. The room grew silent as I paused and stared him down.

"We *will* be successful because I *say* we will be," I said plainly,

bringing an enthusiastic burst of applause and shouting.

Afterward, I was in the bathroom washing my hands, talking to Doug McCartney, head of the firm's domestic private banking group. I glanced away long enough to notice that their paper towel receptacle said "Scott." I started to smile and pulled out a paper towel.

It was not a Scott product.

Angry, I pulled out all the paper towels. Then I went into one of the stalls and immediately knew that, despite what the containers said, the toilet paper inside was also not ours.

I gathered up all of the illicit paper products, opened the bathroom door and threw them into the hall.

"I make toilet paper and you people buy *lousy* toilet paper!" I roared. "For God's sake, look at the amount of money your shareholders have made on my stock, and you have this crummy toilet paper! I want to see you buying better toilet paper."

I carried on that way because I knew that the one way I would get attention in such a staid organization was to be outrageous. McCartney was impressed. He went out and bought more shares.

But poor Kathy McAuley was mortified. Surrounded by institutional salespeople and portfolio managers, she stood there and just stared at me in disbelief. Later, she laughed about my performance, but at the time she thought she'd be fired just for inviting me.

Little did she know how many times in my career I had pulled a stunt like that—or how effective it was.

Back in the Lily-Tulip days, I was at a meeting in Don Burnett's office at Coopers & Lybrand, and his staff made the mistake of serving coffee in Dixie cups.

"I am offended by your use of these cups!" I said. "How much money does *Dixie* spend on your firm annually?"

Dramatically, I snapped the snaps on my briefcase and started to leave. They stopped me at the door and promised it would never happen again. It didn't.

Another time, while I was running Scott, I went to the Windy City for a lunch meeting with the chairman of First Chicago Bank. There was a box of Kleenex in the next room and I put it in the center of the dining room table.

"How can I have lunch with you?" I said, stricken by their betrayal. "It is embarrassing that you think so little of my business that you don't even stock our products! Why don't you use Scotties?!?"

I have always believed that if someone wants your business but doesn't have the good sense to at least pretend to use your product, you should make an issue of it. The point is that if you are working for me, you should support me. If you are not supporting *me,* why should I support you?

•••

There has always been debate about the appropriateness of a

proactive investor relations strategy. Many people feel publicly traded corporations should simply do their job and the results will be reflected in press releases and annual and quarterly reports. The analysts will pick up on those, and the stock will move accordingly. This school of thought holds that having a chairman on the street, talking to analysts, is a waste of time.

And many chairmen prefer it that way as well. They don't like being asked a barrage of detailed questions by strangers and outsiders. And more often than not, they don't know the answers, so it's embarrassing.

I believe, however, that the CEO's role includes many things. To me, a proactive investor relationship strategy is among the highest of priorities.

Putting good management in place, ensuring a strong strategy, spending capital wisely, and staying on top of operating results—these are all important. But I also think communication is equally important, whether it is with employees, customers, the board, shareholders, or the financial community at large. Investor relations is intended to convey management's intent and management's belief about the future. Investors, whether stockholders or lenders, can only make an informed decision about the company's securities when *they* are well informed. If we do not communicate what we believe in and expect for the company, how can anyone truly make an informed decision about us? If we have plans for the future that we haven't shared, I'd say we are cheating the investors of an opportunity. We are better off conveying broadly what we are trying to do rather than doing it quietly.

Being proactive sends a signal that the CEO is concerned about shareholder value and he or she will spend time with the people who own the company. If I worked for a private company with only one shareholder, I would certainly tell that person what is going on. Techniques may differ, depending on the number of shareholders, but we still have that obligation.

In dealing with Wall Street, we must be prepared to appear before people during good times and bad. To be consistent, we must be there both times, not just when it suits us. If a CEO or chairman doesn't meet with Wall Street for several months at a time, the financial community will lack confidence in what is going on in the business and become more inclined to sell. That could affect the stock price.

Scott's previous management apparently saw things differently, preferring to stand in the spotlight when things were good, hide in the shadows when they weren't.

When I took the Scott Paper job, Russ Kersh, John Murtagh, Basil Anderson, and I spent considerable time discussing how the spin on our plans would be read by the financial community and how best to handle it. We knew from our days at Lily-Tulip that the public relations of a publicly held company were vastly different from a private operation such as Goldsmith's, and we wanted to be ready.

We had absolutely zero confidence in Scott's internal communications department, which, when I was hired, told the press I was Australian!

That's why—and in keeping with our philosophy of outsourcing as many functions as possible—we eliminated our in-house communications department and interviewed outside public relations firms, settling on one of the world's biggest and best, Burson Marstellar.

The firm's basic charter was to represent Scott Paper and me, specifically: my ideas, plans, and implementation strategy, telling the Scott story step by step, day by day, as we transformed Scott from a failing company to a dynamic, reinvigorated powerhouse.

Using Burson Marstellar as our agent, I made myself available to the media. Pete Judice managed our press contacts and personally introduced me to the press, setting up hundreds of print, TV, and radio interviews.

It was a high-risk strategy, to say the least. I put myself out on a narrow ledge; we would either scale the heights or fall back to earth and make a mess. But, from experience, I knew that favorable publicity and the attention that I could bring to the company would be powerful messengers. Information we disseminated to the press and financial community alike would be very helpful in achieving our objectives for Scott. I instructed Judice to be aggressive with the press and gave him direct access to me. If someone wanted an interview, he had only to call my secretary and set it up. No intermediaries, no committees to weigh the impact or to debate what I should or shouldn't say.

If I was traveling to New York, I would call Judice and say, "Pete, I am going to be in the city next week. Who can we get together with and tell the Scott story?" He would then arrange interviews around my business schedule for the trip, a breakfast or lunch here, an office visit there. In three days, we sometimes squeezed in eight interviews. I never got tired of telling our story.

Besides dealing directly with the press, I also made frequent presentations to the investment community. Typically, I would be accompanied by our CFO, Basil Anderson, and our director of investor relations, Mike Masseth. I would open by talking general strategy, followed by either Basil or Mike discussing the hard numbers. I generally tackled all questions, but if there was something I didn't know, Basil or Mike would jump in. Their role was to make more credible the broad strokes I painted. If I said, "Of course this company will continue growing," they would provide the specifics as to why we thought growth was possible in the Pacific or Europe, how we stacked up against competition, or, really specifically, why one of Scott's products would succeed vs. one of Procter & Gamble's.

A typical meeting would be forty-five minutes to an hour, and I sometimes did as many as four in a day.

There were two different types of meetings. In large groups of twenty or more, I would stand and give a speech, offering a twenty-minute update on the company, then I'd take questions. More effective, I believe, were the dozens of small office meetings we organized and attended, where we would be seated at a desk or conference table and answer questions over breakfast or lunch.

When I prepared for a meeting with analysts, I prepared diligently. I got with our financial and investor relations people and challenged them to think of every question someone might ask me. "Ask me something that you think will rankle me," I'd say. "Ask me something that may embarrass me. And be tough as hell." No staff member was ever fired for pressing me in private so that I was prepared for rough going in public. They got me up to speed, knowing everything I should know.

We targeted two types of analysts, the sell siders at the major brokerage firms—such as Linda E. Lieberman at Bear, Stearns &

Company, George Adler at Smith Barney and Kathryn Felton McAuley at Brown Brothers Harriman & Company—and the buy side analysts. The buy siders do essentially the same type of work as the sellers but make recommendations to the portfolio managers within their own firms as opposed to making recommendations that go across all different companies.

Our strategy identified the key sell side analysts. We wanted to get them sold on Scott by convincing them that value would be created. Once assured, they spread the word more effectively than any story in *The Wall Street Journal* ever could.

We also targeted certain institutions such as Lazard Frères, Fidelity Investments, Oppenheimer Fund Management, Soros Fund Management, and Tiger Management, and met with their representatives.

The point was that we wanted to reach as broad an audience of potential investors as possible, some of whom we could reach directly, some indirectly.

We looked at ourselves geographically, studying where we were strongest. Financial institutions in New York, for example, owned significant quantities of Scott stock, but their counterparts in Boston didn't, so we chased the money in Boston. If an investment manager owned stock in the paper industry but not Scott, we looked at that as a potential market. We were convinced that if they were prepared to invest in our industry, they couldn't do better than to invest with us.

•••

The day after Scott's June 3, 1994, annual meeting, analyst Kathy McAuley published the report that first referenced my intention to focus "like a laser" on developing the right strategies to grow the company.

One of the ironies of my relationship with Kathy was that she once worked for St. Regis Paper, a company that Sir James Goldsmith raided in the mid-1980s, albeit unsuccessfully. But the Goldsmith raid put the company in play, and she always teased that, because of that, she had reason to dislike me.

During a private luncheon with her some time after my command performance at Brown Brothers Harriman, I told Kathy about my introduction to her firm. When I was hired by Sir James Goldsmith in 1986, he had given me a large advance on my future salary. It was the single biggest check I had ever received. But the check was drawn on a bank that I had never heard of. So I went to Jimmy and said, "Are you sure this check is not going to bounce?" And Jimmy laughed and said, "My dear boy, that is where the blue bloods bank. It is *not* going to bounce." The bank was Brown Brothers Harriman.

Kathy had recommended Scott before I started there, but had pulled her recommendation in the late 1980s when the company started going through a big expansion program. The stock dropped, so she had a good track record in terms of correctly calling the company's fortunes, negative though they may have been. About six months before my predecessor announced his retirement, she decided that Scott had probably hit bottom and was about due for some improvement. At that point, she replaced her "Sell" recommendation with "Buy."

But when several months passed between the resignation and any hint of a successor, Kathy grew nervous that the board of directors literally couldn't find anybody willing to take over Scott.

When my name was finally announced, she and everybody else shook their heads. "Al Who?" My name rang no bells because I had effectively been overseas for the previous five years.

A research check, however, showed that many of the companies I had previously run were turned around with enormous benefits to the shareholders and were then sold. That intrigued her.

She made the trip down to Philadelphia for the shareholders' meeting, which is where we met for the first time. When the day was over, she couldn't wait to write her report. The train back to New York had barely left the station when she started scribbling. Overnight, Scott became a stock that she wanted to aggressively promote.

•••

Across town, Bear, Stearns analyst and managing director Linda Lieberman's early endorsement of Scott Paper under my aegis established a tremendous amount of industry credibility for her and put her young career in high gear. And while many people thought about taking their quick profits and getting out, Lieberman continued saying, "Buy." Those who bought were handsomely rewarded, reinforcing her reputation.

She deserves tremendous credit for her courage in taking a chance on us, making educated observations, and writing leading-edge reports.

Linda came right up to me at the 1994 annual meeting and was impossible to miss. She was wearing a bright red suit that a blind man would have had trouble missing. No doubt about it, she wanted to be seen. More importantly, she also asked good questions. I immediately liked her and thought she was very smart. At the end of the meeting, she wished me well and said she would be watching us very closely.

As events unfolded, she was frequently on the phone, asking questions, telling us what she heard on the Street. She attended analyst meetings and press briefings, becoming an absolute expert on Scott Paper. Through Linda, huge funds such as Soros, Tiger Management, and Brahman Capital invested heavily in us.

She held meetings at Bear, Stearns where potential investors could meet me, and those who followed her admonitions to invest made huge sums of money with us. Linda rode the Scott deal all the way, interfacing with billions and billions of dollars worth of funds.

One day, in early January 1995, I flew out to Scottsdale, Arizona, for a Goldman Sachs & Company investment conference. They talked about our stock but it was apparent their analyst didn't have a clue what was happening at Scott.

"If you want the real story," I said, standing up, "why don't you talk to Linda Lieberman at Bear Stearns?"

They were shocked and appalled.

But hell, I told dozens of people that if they wanted an objective view of Scott, they should call Linda.

Lieberman, McAuley, and Smith Barney's George B. Adler were top-rate and followed the company better than anyone. They caused hundreds of millions of dollars to be invested in Scott and made their clients huge sums of money. They gained prestige for their company and for themselves as analysts.

"Linda," I said one day, "you are doing a fabulous job. I hope the people at Bear, Stearns are taking good care of you."

She assured me they were, but I wanted to be sure. I went to her firm and impressed on her supervisors how much I thought of her work. "Here is a young woman who I think is fantastic," I said. "She has made hundreds of millions of dollars for people and I certainly hope she is well taken care of."

I even wrote a follow-up letter. Linda, although somewhat embarrassed by my fawning, later said it didn't hurt.

•••

George Adler was an entirely different character from Lieberman and McAuley. A managing director of Smith Barney, he had been around the paper industry for forty years. He was cynical; he had seen companies come, he had seen them go.

And while he made positive forecasts for Scott during my time there, I don't think he really believed in the revolution until we were over the palace walls.

Adler asked very hard questions at the analyst conferences. One day, much to our surprise and delight, he caught fire and became a real believer. And because he was such a tough guy, when *he* truly believed, that convinced many more people who had been on the fence. It was significant because Adler's audience, the retail trade or general public, was quite different from the institutional investors to whom Lieberman and McAuley spoke.

When our stock first shot up like a rocket in mid-1994, Adler briefly lost his newfound faith. He played it by the numbers and almost mechanically lowered his rating of Scott from a "Buy 1" to "Buy 2," which infuriated me. I was so angry I couldn't call Adler directly to tell him what I thought of his action, so Mike Masseth did it for me.

"Al wants you to know that that was the stupidest thing you could do!" Mike said, quoting me precisely.

The next time I saw Adler was at a New York Stock Exchange meeting for analysts on June 14, 1994.

"I'm sorry you feel the way you do," Adler said to me, "but we have a rating system I'm required to follow."

"Then you must change your rating system!" I said. "Or you have to raise your earnings system."

The whole issue was forgotten when the Kimberly-Clark merger was announced a year later and Adler immediately and heartily endorsed it.

•••

We obviously enjoyed regular communications with the analysts and the portfolio managers. We put out press releases to communicate with the world at large, generating newspaper, magazine, newsletter, and online articles, TV and radio reports and discussion. Meanwhile, the analysts were forming opinions, spreading their views, interacting with the portfolio managers and the press—all this taking place because we generated it, creating very important results.

Is there a direct, instantaneous, causal relationship between analysts' reports and the stock price going up a point on any given day? The relationship is more subtle than that, but essentially, it all revolves around communications. Analysts say to their firms, "These are our best ideas for where you should put your money" and they are compensated if the investment transactions funnel through their firms.

Not every announcement set off a domino effect, nor was it expected to. I think we anticipated market reaction well. For example, when we announced a new venture in China, where Scott would spend $6 million today against long-term potential, it was exciting but not the kind of thing likely to move the stock price in the near term.

Likewise, individual asset sales such as S.D. Warren and the co-generation energy plant in Alabama contributed more to a cumulative, snowball effect than a daily impact. The more important element of those sales was the message they sent: We were getting out of those businesses and focusing on consumers.

If you come up with a brand new program, Wall Street won't give your stock price a 100 percent credit for it today. But the Street will give it some credit, and as the company demonstrates progress, it will increasingly earn more and more credit.

Having this understanding of and relationship with Wall Street was important to me, because when it comes to a company's stock price and its daily fluctuations, I believe there is always someone accountable. If the stock goes up, there is a reason. If the stock goes down, there is also a reason. Someone in my organization should know the reasons—or know somebody who does.

I pay great attention to the hourly ups and downs. That's my report card to the shareholder. If the stock goes down by an eighth, it's hard for anyone to explain; but five points, and somebody better know what's going on.

There is a profit-to-earnings (FE) ratio on every stock and the FE—the price per share divided by earnings per share for the past twelve months—reflects both the short and the long view of the company. If it didn't, every company in the same industry would have the same FE. It is like a barometer, or like feeling for somebody's pulse.

The stock price drives me. You can fool the market for a short period of time, but you can't fool it forever. Ultimately, Wall Street reflects the future, not just what we do today. Wall Street is always trying to understand if what has been announced constitutes normal earnings or good earnings. Can they be sustained? Will they grow? If the analysts and brokers want to know, so do I.

If our stock price falls, I can get upset about it, but the more practical response is to find out why. Sometimes we discover the reason is that a competitor is bringing out a new product that analysts believe will have an adverse impact on us. And if it is true, then we should react quickly and decisively. For example, if a competitor of Scott Paper was introducing toilet paper with perfume and that product is likely to command a large market share, we should consider doing the same thing. Or at least have a strategy ready to counteract it.

What we shouldn't do is change our strategy based on this hour's stock price. We will put in place and implement a strategy that doesn't change unless there is something wrong with it, or unless we find a better way to implement or enhance it. The stock market's meandering contains information. Our job as managers is to interpret and apply it.

It may be that there is misinformation about the company, or that a competitor is talking about us in a negative way. That happens.

•••

The job of sell side analysts is to do financial research on an industry and, based on that, predict its future. In my case, they wanted as much information as they could develop about who Al Dunlap was so that they could try and figure out what the Scott restructuring would be like. What would I likely do to turn the company around? What was my track record? Where was I before? How successful was I?

Our own shareholders were wondering the same things. The analysts were scrambling to offer their best-guess advice as to whether or not Scott would be a good investment under my guidance.

Because I had been in Australia, there was not a good and current dossier on me, which created a mystique. The Australian press had covered me aggressively, but their work was not easily accessible. And because Sir James Goldsmith's companies were privately held, there were no publicly accessible shareholder reports and public stock prices.

What the analysts did hear from people who knew me was, "Fasten your seat belts for the greatest roller-coaster ride of your life."

Analysts are the first line of defense for shareholders, and most of the ones covering Scott did an excellent job. They got into the trenches, asked tough questions, and used their implicit right to challenge me in their search for information the investors couldn't possibly find out for themselves.

I did everything I could to make their jobs easy, following the same script as at Lily-Tulip. Change the names and everything else was the same. I was totally accessible to the analysts who followed that company. They loved me, they loved the stock.

At one Lily-Tulip analysts meeting I attended, someone said to me, "Lily-Tulip had a great first year as a public company, but it was an aberration. You can't possibly continue this."

"If you believe that," I retorted, "go follow another company and tell your people to sell their stock tomorrow."

Even before that, when we took Lily-Tulip public, we did a twenty-three city road show promoting the initial public offering. One of the stops was in Boston, where I had a private meeting with top honchos of Fidelity Investments, including Peter Lynch.

One man said, "This company has only just recently been turned around and we're not sure it can last. Why should we buy stock on the public offering?"

I kept telling them why I believed in it, but I wasn't making any headway. By the end of the meeting, I was steaming mad.

"Listen," I said, grabbing my coat to leave, "this company is going to be enormously successful and quite frankly, I don't give a damn if you buy stock. And if you don't buy the stock, the hell with you!"

And with that, I walked out.

The next day, guess who came in for a gigantic share?

They said they tried every way they knew to back me in a corner, but the harder they came at me, the harder I went back at them. Apparently, when I told them I didn't give a damn and walked, that's when they put their order in.

During the Lily-Tulip public offering, there was talk that the executives and KKR insiders should sell some of their stock and get a taste of sweet success. I said, "We can't do that"—even though I didn't have any money and could have used the proceeds myself. We had a big argument about it. I said that selling would be a serious mistake; if we, as insiders, sold out, why should an outsider buy in?

The same argument came up years later during a meeting for Scott Paper in Houston. We were there trying to calm concerned investors about the pending Kimberly-Clark merger. I said, "We are supposed to be clever fellows and we haven't sold a share."

"What would you sell it at?" somebody asked.

"I'll consider selling at $60 (post-split)," I said. Everyone but me laughed. We ended up just over $60 (post-split) when the merger closed. Now the same people say I set too low a target!

•••

Mike Masseth's job as director of investor relations was saved because Basil Anderson spoke up for him early on. The two of them had worked together before I arrived, and Basil told me they had developed a solid working relationship. Even through Scott's bad times, Mike had built up real credibility with the analysts and investors on Wall Street because he didn't try to gild the lily; he didn't paint a picture of something other than what it was. And, like Basil, Mike was also an expert on the paper industry. He made it his job to keep the rest of us informed about what the competition was doing.

The role of somebody in Mike's position is one of providing balance. When the news was bad in recent years, his job was getting word out that Scott was trying to do things to improve but without a lot of success. He got high marks from analysts for giving them the truth, and they could make their own calls based on that. His consistency, whether the news was good or bad, won him the respect of a tough bunch of critics. No doubt his handling of certain issues helped temper response to Scott's often less-than-sterling performance. When earnings didn't meet expectations, that was particularly difficult to do.

When we met with investment firms, the percentage of people who subsequently bought our stock ran close to 95 percent. When people got a chance to look me in the eye, hear my views on doing the right things to increase shareholder value, and see credible executives such as Mike and Basil back me up, it was like I was a faith healer.

I remember when Basil, Mike, and I met early one morning with Neuberger & Berman. We felt it went well, but they were noncommittal as we left. An hour later—about the time of the market's opening bell—Mike coincidentally had a meeting with a specialist of the firm through which all of Scott's stock trades were followed and kept in balance. Neuberger & Berman was buying stock right before Mike's eyes.

Later, we discovered they were buying stock even as we were getting on the elevator.

That was almost uncanny because it is usually near impossible to find out who is actually buying and selling stock as it happens. In this particular instance, the stock specialist told Mike that Neuberger and Berman had been a big buyer that morning.

•••

On June 3, 1994, Scott stock was selling for 48-1/2. Did the multitude of analysts who wrote glowing reports in the wake of our annual shareholders meeting have an impact? Yes.

By June 14, another significant day in terms of my relationships with the financial community, our price had risen to 51-1/8. That was the day Scott sponsored a meeting with analysts, at the New York Stock Exchange Board of Governors Boardroom, and held a dinner that evening for sell side analysts.

The Exchange was an unusual meeting site because companies don't often hold meetings there. It's very inconvenient because guests must go through all sorts of security to get in, but that sent yet another message that we meant business.

I hit on many touchy subjects at that meeting, including my ideas for incentivizing boards of directors through stock equity—before Scott actually did it. I also discussed setting time limits for directors—five years and out; keeping previous, failed CEOs off the board; one-year restructuring plans; and how shareholders, not directors, own our companies.

Some of the sell side analysts later asked me, "Where have they been hiding you?"

The dinner crowd was tougher because sell side analysts have big egos, even bigger wallets, and little sense of humor. On the other hand, they made perfect fodder for me because I love tweaking the pompous and imperial.

I surprised many in the group by revealing that I had begun my career at Kimberly-Clark as a management trainee and had brought things nearly full circle by taking charge of Scott.

I had just finished describing my twin $2 million purchases of Scott stock—the first time many people there had heard of it—when one of the brokers challenged my investment as unimpressive.

"From some of the things I have read about you," he harrumphed, "I understand you might be worth somewhere between $50 and $100 million. Is this really a significant commitment on your part?"

"I don't know about you," I said, barely letting him finish, "but every dollar is significant to me and I treat every dollar like it is my brother. *I* think it is significant. Can you show me another executive who has dug into his own pocket and bought stock without any guarantees from the company?"

Analysts like that one test and provoke us to make sure that we have a bona fide level of commitment and belief in what we are doing. But they're still annoying!

•••

Linda Lieberman was among those at the NYSE meeting. The next morning, I attended a small breakfast meeting at Bear, Stearns, attended by Julian Robertson, an institutional money manager from Tiger Management. Robertson, a fine Southern gentlemen, sat quietly through much of the meeting, asked two questions, and left. I thought I had blown it. But the next day, he put in his first big order for Scott shares.

In two weeks, I already knew I liked Linda, but organizing this breakfast with Tiger impressed me and earned her my respect. She was a player. And Bear, Stearns started trading massive amounts of stock, accounting for perhaps 30 percent of Scott's trading volume. The firm and its clients made a fortune with us.

The second time I visited Bear, Stearns, maybe two months later, Linda set up a larger meeting with about twenty people. During the course of my presentation, I warned the analysts and brokers that they had better have Scott toilet paper in the rest rooms because if I went in there—like I did at Brown Brothers Harriman earlier the same morning—and they didn't, we were not going to do any more business together. Not only did they have Scott brands, Linda told me they always did.

In September 1994, our stock was continuing its upward move and Linda wrote a report that mused, "What now?" In many ways, she accurately projected Scott's future in that document, revaluing the whole company following the sale of S.D. Warren and outlining an exit strategy. Either sell the company, she advised, or divest it piece by piece. Linda gave us a twelve- to eighteen-month window and set an uncannily accurate target share price of $105 (pre-split).

So extraordinary was the report that Linda asked me to read it before it was published.

"I want your feedback," she said. "It is not getting printed unless you are comfortable with it."

She had nothing to worry about; I loved it and told her so. "How can you always be ahead of the pack?" I asked her.

Any other CEO in the world would have called her boss, Allen "Ace" Greenberg, and threatened to never do business with Bear, Stearns again over such a presumptive report. Knowing Greenberg, for whom I have the utmost respect, I bet it earned her a raise. He runs a first-class outfit and his ideas correlate to my own: be tough, incentivize, and be fair.

Being around Linda also introduced me to several other people at Bear, Stearns—my kind of people. Hungry, aggressive young kids, who didn't go to the right schools and didn't come from the right places, but were still headed for the top.

•••

Scott Paper stock had already appreciated 50 percent or more by the time Bob Jermain took it seriously.

Jermain, a managing director of Soros Fund Management, didn't buy his first shares until we split the stock. He bought in at $35 (post-split), but still did OK because the stock topped $60 the day of the Kimberly-Clark merger.

His interest was another product of my relationship with Linda. She had been wooing him for some time when he finally called Basil Anderson and asked for a meeting with me. Basil warned him that we had an amazing hit rate in terms of people who didn't own the stock or didn't own much, substantially increasing their holdings after such a meeting.

Laughing—he thought Basil was joking—Jermain came to Philadelphia the next day.

All the way down on the train, Jermain fretted that his trip was going to be a big fat waste of time. He had studied our stock and, despite the fact that it had gone up substantially, it appeared expensive on trailing earnings, the earnings a company has earned in the past, compared against anticipated earnings in the future. He had also met many high-flying managers who talked big and produced a whole lot less.

Usually, on Wall Street, a brokerage firm will manufacture a great corporate fairy tale about anticipated earnings. Then the analysts meet the company's management and hear that, "This could happen" and "That might happen." What they heard from me was what we were going to do in a specific time frame and how we were going to do it.

"What will you do on the cost side?" Jermain asked.

He was surprised how ready we were for that question, ticking off our intention of selling big assets such as Scott Plaza and S.D. Warren, and smaller prizes such as Scott Health Care and our share of the Cabin Bluff Partnership, a hunting lodge, conference center and 38,000 acres of timberlands in Canada.

Over lunch, I told Jermain about the two times I had personally bought Scott stock out of my own pocket. That got his attention, as it did everyone else's, but what riveted him was the $10 million investment my senior executives had subsequently made. That just didn't happen in his experience. He was also turned on by the way we had restructured director compensation.

If we thought Jermain left the meeting excited, we didn't know the half of it until a few weeks later. That's when he told us he was buying Scott stock in large volume from the train on his way back to New York. He didn't want to waste another minute! In fact, his boss, billionaire financier George Soros, put the stock in his own account.

In the months to come, we met with Jermain more than a dozen times, establishing a tight, friendly relationship. He eventually amassed more than 5 million shares (just under 5 percent of all of our outstanding shares) and became one of our largest shareholders.

But not everyone was razzle-dazzled by their first encounter with me at Scott.

Another potential investor thought the company had a good program when he visited Scott before I came on the scene. He thought there was some good stuff about to happen, but he didn't buy the stock then. And when I was hired, we spent time together on several occasions, but he still wasn't convinced. So he didn't buy.

A loud and boisterous guy with what some might call an abrasive personality, he put on a fireworks show not unlike my own. He made his views known and asked penetrating questions. He came to the 1994 annual meeting, saw us at a couple of other forums, invited us to his own office, but still couldn't get himself quite comfortable enough to pull the investment trigger.

This was one conservative investor. When the stock hit the low $60s (pre-split), he finally decided to buy. Don't cry for him, though; he still doubled his money.

When he finally came on board, it was extremely gratifying for me and Basil because he had finally seen the light.

There were other doubting Thomases, too. Among the analyst community, there are always people who buy based on leadership. When they finally bought in, others followed. There is always a lead steer or two, certain influential Wall Streeters such as George Soros or Warren Buffett. When they act or recommend something, others naturally follow.

A small investor doesn't have access to the information or resources Soros does. But because he has bought, so will the little guy.

Many people asked us, "Why should I buy now? The stock has already been run up."

We answered that kind of question by patiently explaining our programs, our strategy and what we planned to do in concrete terms. What people wanted to know was where the growth would come from. If we could explain our strategies in terms of new products, their likely impact, and further cost reductions, analysts could go back to their offices, take out their computers and figure future cash flows in the brightest light.

The way I put it to them was this: The best is yet to come, and Mickey Mouse could have done what I have done so far.

Financial people live in a tight-knit community. Information gets around, and people look at what a Buffett or Soros is buying or selling. When Soros bought Scott, that convinced a herd of others. A Bob Jermain might tell his friends, "I was just down to see Al Dunlap and he is for real." Word of mouth is an important form of advertising in the investment community.

Brahman called after Jermain visited with us. "We hear that we should be looking at your company. We'd love to visit with Al— is tomorrow OK?" Literally—tomorrow. These were people to whom time is money and they want to be able to make their investment decisions *now*. So we went out of our way to be available and give people access, in our offices or theirs.

•••

Scott was doing very well and getting better. Our margins were expanding. We had a return on equity of 20 percent, we grew our sales by 20 percent, and operating margins increased by 20 percent. We tightly managed capital. The company was generating a tremendous amount of cash flow. *Free* cash flow, money that was available for spending for growth, more than our immediate capital needs—plus, we still had more assets on the market. To create value, we had to redeploy those funds somehow. We couldn't just generate cash and park it in a bank.

So the next key strategic question for Scott was what to do with a strong balance sheet or with the cash. The options included giving it to the shareholders, buying back stock or paying huge dividends. Another direction would be to make acquisitions within our newly redefined core business. A third option was to find some way to grow internally in related businesses. I didn't think there were enough opportunities for us to do that. So it came down to giving it back to the shareholders or acquiring something.

Giving it back to the shareholders says, "I can't do better than you can do with this money." And while that was possible, we felt we *could* do better, so we looked at acquisitions.

We looked at Champion, Kimberly-Clark, Fort Howard, and James River, as well as other consumer product companies. Other prospective mergers didn't make sense because they combined dissimilar businesses for the sake of bigness.

We felt that a combination with Kimberly-Clark would be the best because of the nature of their product line. Geographically, where we were strong they were weak. They were strong in the United States but not in Europe, where we had more clout. Kimberly was dying in Europe. Scott had a great European operation. Most of the analysts said this was a godsend for Kimberly to get Europe squared away.

In terms of products, Kimberly-Clark was strong in brand

names such as Huggies diapers, Kleenex facial tissues, Kotex and Lightdays sanitary pads, and Depends adult diapers. They had reentered the bathroom tissue market in the United States and were expanding in bathroom tissue in Europe.

Putting together Scott Paper and Kimberly-Clark was strategically the right thing to do. The weaknesses of one could be shored up with the strengths of the other. We could fully load up one truck instead of having two half-empty on the road.

A hostile takeover appealed to my ego—the junior management trainee returning victorious—but it wasn't financially practical. We would have had to pay a premium to their shareholders. Then Kimberly-Clark would have had to be restructured to generate synergy for our own shareholders and return the value of the premium paid. It could have been done, but why? If we voluntarily joined forces as a pooling of interests, no premiums had to be paid and all the existing shareholders of both companies could benefit from whatever synergies there were.

This was definitely the best option.

Mark Davis of Salomon Brothers helped us think through all the different strategic alternatives. Meanwhile, Dillon-Read was working with Kimberly-Clark and we got a call that Kimberly-Clark would contemplate a merger at somewhere around market price. We said, let's talk and see if everyone is serious about it. The first contacts between the companies were exploratory conversations conducted by Salomon Brothers and Dillon-Read.

At the very first face-to-face meeting of principals from the two companies, Russ Kersh and John Murtagh represented Scott in Atlanta. They immediately recognized Kimberly-Clark's interest as genuine, and we moved forward quickly from that point. Our board enthusiastically approved going to the next step, which was setting an exchange rate for the merger. This was the guaranteed value at which Scott Paper shares would be exchanged for Kimberly-Clark shares.

Settling the exchange rate was the only heated moment in the entire negotiation. John and Russ had instructions from me that if Kimberly-Clark didn't meet our threshold, they were to walk out. And they would have, too—if it hadn't been raining.

The Kimberly-Clark side moved much slower than we did;

they had more people to consult on major decisions. With us, I gave John and Russ their instructions, and they were free to represent the company from that point as they saw fit. The problem in this case was that they couldn't say whether the Kimberly-Clark side wasn't empowered to make a decision or was engaging in show business as part of the game.

Russ and John desperately wanted to do the deal, but Kimberly-Clark hadn't met my threshold price. I said, "Come on home, we are not doing this deal." Russ objected; he wanted to give them more time. Besides, he said, "It's raining. Let us at least stay until it stops raining."

Nobody will ever believe that I, the guy who stood to make $100 million from the merger, was willing to walk away from the table and go back to building Scott. If the driving force was the money, I had the deal done. I could have given just a little bit, it was done. Everybody who was going to make a lot less than me—it was a lot to them—wanted to do the deal. Russ said, "Al, look at what we are going to get!" I said, "It is not that; we've got to do even better by our shareholders. Pack up."

Before they could leave Atlanta, they got a call at the hotel from the Kimberly-Clark people who said, "Let's finish what we started." They offered to split the difference—making each Scott share worth .765 per Kimberly-Clark share—and I said, "Do it!"

When it came down to due diligence, Kimberly-Clark thoroughly investigated all of our productivity and cost-efficiency claims. No doubt they suspected things were overstated or done with smoke and mirrors. But we kept getting word back that they were amazed that we actually did the things we said. They learned from the way we did certain things in our paper mills and said some of the stuff we had done in some of the production facilities was just beyond what they thought could be done. I assume they will try and apply these lessons in their own organization.

When we went public with the impending deal on July 17, 1995, I suffered a moment of panic. What if Wall Street didn't understand the upside of the deal and rejected it? If it failed to win the market's support, I would lose support and sixteen months of rebuilding confidence in Scott would be lost. That was the risk I faced if I was wrong. It would have killed me personally—and my credibility and everything I had worked for. Everyone still would have made money, but I would have lost every bit of the goodwill.

Fortunately, any initial reluctance on the Street was soon forgotten. Kimberly-Clark stock immediately shot up $4-7/8. David G. Santry, a senior vice president at Oppenheimer Capital, one of our major shareholders, told *The New York Times,* "It makes really good sense from a strategic point of view. I think it's good for the shareholders." The headline in *The Wall Street Journal* about our deal was, "Stockholders Can Benefit in a Merger, Even Without a Fat Takeover Premium." And *Advertising Age* wrote, "It frequently makes more sense to buy than build from scratch"—a word of encouragement to wary Kimberly-Clark shareholders.

The merger was my final gift to our shareholders.

As the paperwork was being completed between our two companies and the deal ran through the regulatory gauntlet, I thought back to 1963 when I started my career with Kimberly-Clark as a $650-a-month management trainee in New Milford, Connecticut. My first pay raise was $35 more a month. And now here I was, thirty-two years later, and Kimberly-Clark was paying me $20 million not to compete with them for the next five years! Twenty million not to do a damn thing, when they had paid me $650 a month to work my ass off.

I reflected on all of that and thought about myself as the architect of this great merger. It was almost overwhelming, and more than a little humorous that this little trainee came back as chairman of their big competitor, engineered this whole thing, and they were paying me all this money not to work.

It shows the training program works.

•••

As well as Bob Jermain did in buying Scott stock, he—like much of Wall Street—was nonetheless skeptical about the true motivation for the structure of our merger with Kimberly-Clark. That kind of skepticism immediately nudged Scott stock down (post-split) from $51 to $49, and then pushed it even further back to earth, at $43.

It was a tax-free exchange, a merger of equals. Everybody came out on top. But Wall Street was put off because there was no premium in it. I was severely criticized.

Our stock had already been up 168 percent. I repeatedly told the financial community, "Kimberly-Clark is buying a company that just went up 168 percent in the last twelve months. They obviously believe there is still more growth potential. I believe once the market recognizes it, there will be a premium."

There was still handwringing and criticism that I should have held out for a premium. I disagreed then and I haven't changed my opinion today. I was a major shareholder and I believed it was the right thing to do, even if it took the market a while to understand it. I was right; we ended up with a 32 percent share price increase from the date of announcement to closure.

When Jermain phoned me to discuss the merger, he referred to it in a derogatory manner as a "take under," which he described as the opposite of a takeover. A take under was what happened when the stock traded lower than before a merger announcement.

I tried to reassure him.

"This is a natural progression," I said, "of all the things that have already come to fruition."

I reviewed the synergy between Scott and Kimberly-Clark and how the cost savings that could be derived from putting us together were enormous. "Wall Street has no idea how large this will be," I said. "Many people have already lost money underestimating me."

Jermain was still wavering. What bothered him was that he had met Wayne R. Sanders, chairman of Kimberly-Clark. There was nothing wrong with Sanders, Jermain said, he just wasn't me. In a short period of time, Jermain had become accustomed to the way I handled his investment and wasn't yet at ease about slipping into bed with Sanders.

"I have had meetings with Sanders, too," I said. "He knows that he is taking over a company with a mindset deeply entrenched in shareholder value and cost-consciousness. I believe that he will do the right thing. And if he doesn't, the shareholders will be at his heels. And I am a shareholder."

He only started coming around when I pressed the point that I was keeping all of my money from the deal in Kimberly-Clark stock, more than $80 million, making me one of Kimberly-

Clark's largest individual shareholders. "I'm going to be very active in telling their board to do the right thing by shareholders," I said. "You can bet on that."

He was not the only shareholder concerned about the plummeting fortune of Scott stock after the announcement. But he decided not to sell. And, more importantly, he convinced the people for whom he works not to sell.

Now we both had a great deal of money and credibility on the line. Jermain had only been with Soros for six months, and his credibility had been called into question as the market originally interpreted the merger news, but he stubbornly stuck by us.

I have no doubt that other brokers and analysts thought twice about selling off their Scott stock, wondering why Jermain had stuck with us. If he believed the merger would work, many others no doubt reconsidered the implications of the deal as well. Their premium then came: the 32 percent run-up of the stock after the announcement of the merger.

Chapter 17

FIGHTING WORDS

LESSON: IF EVERYBODY IN THE
CORPORATION WAS DOING THIS, THEY'D
NEVER GET DUNLAPPED IN THE FIRST
PLACE.

Dunlap (dun-lap) *Vt* [after Albert J. Dunlap (1937-)]
1. To turn a company around at lightning speed. 2. To focus on
the best; eliminate what is not the best. 3. To protect and enhance
shareholder value.

Word has filtered down from the board of directors to the
executive corridors and beyond. Your company will soon be
Dunlapped.

Are you a dead duck?

Thousands of people who have been Dunlapped have had
great success in their lives. Yet thousands more were fired. How
can you avoid being a casualty?

If you go with the flow, you'll ultimately drown in the
undertow. Long before you get Dunlapped, work as if I might
move into the corner office tomorrow. Even if you're buried in
office politics, do the right things. Don't be afraid to be a

maverick. Differentiate yourself from other people. State your views. Write memos. Put your opinions out there in living color. Don't just tell the next CEO who comes along that you actually had these views, prove it.

Your ideas will never see the light of day unless you communicate.

I learned the importance of standing out from the crowd from my own first-hand, on-the-bottom-looking-up experience. After two years as a management trainee with Kimberly-Clark, I went to my boss and said, "Kimberly-Clark and I are at the crossroads." If he was offended by my presumptive behavior, I never heard about it: a week later, I received a more substantive assignment.

And when you see change, don't run in the other direction. Don't be a spectator when it starts. Prove you have been or can be a catalyst for change, and you'll ultimately be part of the group running the corporation after it's been Dunlapped. If you have spent your life acquiescing and not fighting, not making your voice heard, you'll be gone.

I come into a company like an absolute whirlwind, demanding change and not interested in excuses. I'm not like anybody you have ever worked for in the past.

To exist and thrive around me, people must be willing to experience and relish change and challenges. Those two things frighten some people off. But the reason for wanting to stay is the benefit of seeing the results of the change—the change that you helped make.

Because of the speed with which my job must be done, I definitely come into new situations with preconceived ideas. I form strong and fast opinions about people. But I am not intransigent. I will listen to reason. In a public forum, I don't like to be interrupted, but I will almost always listen to private counsel and consider idea and options. Learn the difference between being a "Yes" person and listening carefully and picking a spot for discussion. And once a final decision is made, it's time to stop talking and start implementing.

•••

When an Al Dunlap comes in, make yourself visible. If you truly believe you can do the job, ask for the opportunity. There's nothing wrong with walking into someone's office and saying, "I can do this job, I want to be part of the team." It's refreshing, because so few people have the guts and courage to do it.

Those whose jobs will be eliminated in a restructuring should still consider the outcome philosophically, and have enough confidence in themselves to know they will have opportunities somewhere else. A company is not your high school or college alma mater. Don't get emotional about it.

Those left behind, meanwhile, will have broadened responsibilities and will learn to do more—and more quickly—in the newly lean organization. They will become increasingly valuable as better trained employees, so they are not afraid to end up somewhere else.

Fewer people will be doing the same amount of work. You will spend less time processing and more time implementing. There will be more decisions made, more rapidly and by fewer people. The focus will be on implementation.

Show no fear; anticipate, anticipate, *anticipate,* and be prepared at all times. When I pick up the phone and call you to my office, know what I want to discuss before I tell you. When I ask a question, know the answer or where to find it in a hurry. Be ahead of me and don't waste my time arguing. Be committed to the program.

If it's your own career you are really worried about, then that's not going to be enough motivation in this environment. You must be determined to work on behalf of an organization that needs your complete support. You must be concerned with the greater good and remember that the shareholder is king.

If your performance is good and you have the support of the people I depend on, you'll stay and thrive, and you may be given more responsibility.

Finally, take pride in what you do, in where you work, but never lose sight of the end goal: making money. If we don't make money, we won't last another day in business.

•••

If you are a good, loyal, motivated employee I will be the best boss you will ever have. My decisions created sixty-two millionaires at Scott and fifteen at Lily-Tulip. Good people have done brilliantly under my leadership. If you don't believe me, here's what the senior executives of Cavenham Forest Industries put on a plaque given to me *after I* had moved on:

In recognition of A. J. Dunlap...

For leadership and contributions to Cavenham.

And with appreciation for teaching us to challenge what is and to continually seek what can be;

Demanding more of us than we thought possible;

Providing us the freedom to perform and showing us that excellent performance today is the foundation for the highest achievements tomorrow.

That was presented *after* the company was merged with Hanson PLC and I no longer had any control of these people.

I cause people to achieve more than they ever thought they could achieve. The process is painful. Sometimes, it's ugly. But in the end, it's worth it.

PART V

WHERE DID I GO?

Chapter 18

HELL FROZE OVER:
KIDS AND ANIMALS CHANGED ME

As I enter the rest of my life, I look back on the great men and women that I worked with and all that we accomplished in multiple corporations that we turned around across three continents.

And despite a whirlwind of criticism and controversy in the press, I can't think of much I would have done differently.

Sorry if you thought I would think differently almost 20 years after the original publication of *Mean Business*, but I still stand by my four principles and the way that I have executed them.

And yet I have changed.

•••

My life up until the point I retired in 1998 was always so busy.

My wife, Judy, and I lived in 17 states, three countries, and traveled to 39 more countries. I hardly ever had any time to be me. And that was fine, because I had this burning desire to accomplish something in business.

My mother, who was such an unbelievable force in my life, said, "Son, you're going to make something of yourself." As a result, I was always more focused than anyone else I met.

Sir James Goldsmith said, "My boy, you have a fire in your belly that will never go out."

What I accomplished in business gave me credibility, and – it may sound crazy at my age–allowed me to live up to the expectations my mother set for me. But now my parents have passed and all of those great, great, great businessmen whom I cherished have left us as well: Sir James Goldsmith and Kerry Packer died; Ben Nobbe and Ely Meyer are gone. I had to move on, too, into uncharted territory for me.

So when the inevitable day arrived that I was not fixing damaged corporations anymore, I thought, what am I going to do now?

•••

When we first relocated to the Central Florida city of Ocala and Marion County, Judy and I hardly knew a soul. It's a community of haves and have nots, but we were hardly the wealthiest or the most charitable. The people we met, from Wal-Mart to the country clubs, went out of their way to make us feel welcome.

We moved slowly into the community and found the peace we sorely desired here. It's quite tranquil and we come and go as we please. A lot of wealthy people who live here do so with understated elegance, which we've come to admire and appreciate. We stayed somewhat private for a time as we came to know the area's resources and needs. Little by little we felt our way forward and decided what we wanted to do and how and when we wanted to do it.

The first opportunity was a call from someone who had read that I came from a poor family back in Jersey and asked if I would speak to children at a local charter school that all came from an impoverished background like mine.

Because of where I started and what I made of my life, they thought that I could relate to the kids.

JUDY DUNLAP:[5] **The kids loved him. They had so many questions and he stayed and answered every one of them, encouraging them to reach beyond their surroundings, to reach for a hand up, not a hand out.**

Word got out after that experience. Our doctor is on the board of

---

[5] I had this book pretty much to myself for almost 20 years. It only seemed fair to give my wife of 46 years, Judy, a few words in this updated edition. You'll know she is talking because her comments will be in **bold**. *Like Judy.*

the YMCA of Central Florida in Ocala and he told us about the organization's hope of expanding its programs to more of the same type of kids to whom I had spoken. Most of these youngsters were on subsidized Y memberships because their families couldn't afford to join.

A luncheon and auction was held to kick off the YMCA fundraising drive. A local car dealer walked to the podium and said he would match the first $10,000 in donations. He figured it would take several months for the community to reach that amount.

The auctioneer, jokingly, said, "Does anyone want to give $10,000 right now?"

Judy and I talked it over quickly, looked around the room, saw no other hands go up, so I raised mine.

The car dealer said, "*Really?*"

At first he thought I was being a smart ass.

"For heaven's sake!" he said. "I didn't think I'd have to pay this money for months!"

Everybody laughed, but I wrote my $10,000 check right then and there.

Judy then got to know the Y a bit better by going there to work out. She was extremely impressed by the facility's professionalism and the results she got personally.

•••

We became involved in funding and hosting an annual Christmas party for 100 underprivileged children from across Marion County.

The school system chooses the children and we put it on in conjunction with the county sheriff's department, which brings out the canine unit, police horses, and even a helicopter. These are the poorest kids in the county, those who would otherwise have no Christmas presents.

There are magicians, clowns and face-painting, as well as lunch and a movie.

The event ends with each boy and girl receiving a bag of the year's hottest holiday gifts—and a large stuffed animal—given to them by Mr. and Mrs. Santa Claus.

All of the sheriff's deputies help out, and when the kids leave, it's as emotional for these tough, tough men and women as it is for Judy and me.

When we first started sponsoring the kids' party, I saw a little boy wrapping some of his food in a napkin and putting it in his pocket.

"You don't have to do that," I said.

He said, "I'm going to take it home for my little brother."

We realized that there were families going hungry at Christmas, so we started sending each child home with extra food for the holidays.

Judy's father was a bartender and her mother worked in a supermarket until she retired. We both come from poor backgrounds, so to be able to do something like this for these kids is so rewarding.

•••

JUDY: When somebody like Al retires, you wonder, "What are they going to do?" Now I look at him and wonder when did he ever have time to *work*?

Together, we filled the hours and the days with all kinds of unexpected things, some fun, some serious. Al has changed a lot in his senior years. He loves country music. He *never* liked country music. He likes children. He never really had time for children before because he was so busy trying to be successful and he always gave 120 percent to the job. Now, however, we can and do enjoy being around kids.

The one thing I'm most happy about is that I talked Al into doing our philanthropy now while we are alive to see it bear fruit.[6]

We sat down and talked a lot about what was important to us and we realized it was medicine, education, and animals, so that's where I've concentrated what we're doing.

---

[6] **JUDY: It just made sense to me—why not do it now when we can actually see the good our wealth can do? We can enjoy what's happening with it.**

I had another approach to that. I was having a coffin made with pockets to put my money in, and then she said she was going to cremate me, so I said, "Alright, alright! We'll do it your way!"

•••

For the last few decades, one of the constants in my professional and personal life was my love of and affinity for animals.

Judy and I once lived in a heavily wooded area of Ridgefield, Connecticut. I was traveling all the time and my wife said, "I'm a little afraid to be home by myself all the time, Al. Maybe we should get a dog?"

I grew up a poor inner-city kid who never raised any animals. Having a dog in our home was a big decision for me, but if it was going to make Judy feel safer without me, I was ready to give it a try.

That's when we bought our first German shepherd, and we've since raised seven of them. They get bad press sometimes–as I have – but they are fantastic creatures, and we love the shepherds.

I've got to tell you a true dog story.

It was 2003, during the week between Christmas and New Year's, and we were still commuting between Hilton Head, South Carolina, and our new place in Ocala. One of our dogs, Cadet, had gotten older and infirm. The vet said it was time to put the dog down; there was nothing more he could do but provide a peaceful, respectful end.

"Al," he said, "we've done everything we can do. If we prolong her life beyond right now, we are not doing it for the dog. We'd be doing it for you, and that is wrong."

It made sense, but I never got over it.

Judy and our chief of staff, Sean Thornton, were crying and before I knew it, so was I. Not knowing what else to do, I lay down on the floor and cuddled Cadet in her last moments of life and cried. Watching me was a foreign student, there on an internship.

I said, "This is embarrassing. I was a paratrooper for heaven's sake, and I'm crying like a baby."

"Mr. Dunlap," he said, "it's all right to cry. I cried when I lost my dog, and I think I'm pretty tough, too."

"Yeah?"

"I'm an exchange student," he said, "but back home, I'm in the Israeli Special Forces. We think we're pretty tough, too. You go right ahead and cry. Nothing wrong with that where I come from."

It never gets easier, as any pet owner knows, but the thing that has gotten us through–because no one wants to put a dog down–is calling the breeder at Kingston Kennels in Great Britain and knowing it'll be about three months before he has a new dog ready for us. So we grieve for three months, but always knowing we're getting a puppy, you know–a new dog is coming. I always tell people if you're going to have another dog, the best thing to do is get it right away.[7]

We looked around and realized we never did any of the things with animal rescue that we had always admired in other people. We moved constantly while I was active as a CEO and, in the years that immediately followed, we split our time between Florida and Wisconsin and did quite a bit of casual travel, something we never had time for previously.

As Judy and I started settling on a year-round home we concluded Wisconsin was too far and there wasn't enough available land in Boca Raton. Ocala, Florida, however–the horse capital of the world–was a place where we could buy a large piece of land and live out our dream of being around more animals.

We bought a farm and gradually expanded it. We love this land and have taken every opportunity to expand our property by buying whatever became adjacent to it. The farm is now up to 100 acres.

Putting the land to use in a way that put us in greater contact with the animal kingdom was almost an accident. In retirement, animals in need always seem to find us.

I've always said that I respect predators because they have to get their own meals. They can't call room service.

But abused and neglected animals can't get their own meals. They have been put in captivity and rather than be treated with respect and love, they've been mistreated. That greatly affected us.

Since relocating to Ocala, we've rescued more than 75 animals, and it gives us great joy. As we took in these poor animals that were afraid, we nourished them, and gave them the finest

---

[7] When a Marion County Canine Unit Sheriff's Deputy was killed in the line of duty a few years ago, the heartbroken family was afraid they would lose their specially trained dog as well. We stepped in and bought the sheriff's department a replacement dog for "Justice," who was allowed to retire and stay with the late deputy's family. In subsequent years, we bought four additional dogs for the Canine Unit.

veterinary care. We have seen them develop and regain their strength and purpose. It's a wonderful, wonderful thing, and it gives us enormous satisfaction–as great a satisfaction as turning around some of the largest corporations in America.

In my heart, the greatest animals are still my shepherds because they are absolutely an integral part of our life, sharing our home. But now we've got all these other animals as well. It has been a great undertaking for us, and we've done it on a huge scale. We've built barns. We've built paddocks. We've built shelters.

When we walk into the fields, many of the animals recognize us and respond to our greetings. We can pet them, and they'll go "*Meeeeeeee*" That's what an animal does. And the pride and pleasure it gives us is indescribable.

Down the road from our original property, Judy always stopped to give a carrot to a retired, eight-year-old racehorse. When we had the opportunity to buy the adjacent property on which the horse lived, the owners told us they intended to put it down. We said, "No horse, no deal." It was a big deal to us. Today that animal– Judy named her Sweetie Pie–is fantastic. The vet says it's in as good a shape as any racehorse in Ocala.

That really opened our eyes to the fact that there are animals out there that people don't want, that people will kill or neglect regardless of what's right for the animals.

Speaking of saving innocent lambs from slaughter, our next rescue was, literally, a lamb.

The landscaper for our property has a daughter who is a member of the local 4-H Club. In her first year, she raised a lamb as part of her commitment. The thing is, the kids raise these animals and then take them to a livestock auction. She found that a lot harder to do when the time came than she–or her parents–ever expected.

One day she came to our farm, crying, and said, "Mr. Dunlap, please save my lamb, Snow White!" She asked us to give it a home and we purchased it at the auction.

Six years–and six lambs–later, our farm is home to a growing flock.

Then I heard from a rescue organization down the road about a pair of miniature donkeys that were being abused. They said, "You've got some beautiful land. Would you consider taking them in?" I said, "Absolutely."

We named them Patton and MacArthur because of my military background.

Patton became ill one day and was in terrible intestinal distress. He couldn't get up because his belly had blown up like a balloon. Sam Nunez, our farm manager, came to me and said, "Something's wrong with Patton. Get the vet, Mr. D, get the vet!" It broke my heart to see Patton that way, so I told Sean to do everything he could to save Patton.

The vet came and said Patton had some kind of an intestinal blockage–not unusual with miniature animals, we've since learned. Sean and Sam rushed him to a thoroughbred horse facility in Ocala–Peterson & Smith Equine Hospital–that is world-renowned for its equine care.

They examined Patton and confirmed the vet's initial diagnosis of a blockage.

1.   "Do you want us to take care of him?" the doctor asked.
2.   "What will you do?" Sean asked.
3.   "We'll have to put him down, of course."
4.   "Can he be saved?" Sean asked.
5.   The doctor said, " If this was a thoroughbred horse, we would do an operation."
6.   "So?"
7.   "It's a *donkey*," the doctor said. "It's a *very* expensive operation."

Sean has worked with me for more than 20 years, first as my bodyguard and now as my chief of staff. He didn't need to call me to know what to do next.

"Let me tell you something," Sean said. "If I have to call my boss and tell him that there's something we could do to save this donkey but you only perform it on thoroughbred horses because it's expensive... well, *I'm* going to be the one that's going to need an operation."

They gave Sean a dollar figure to do the surgery.

"Do it," Sean said.

The doctor said, "Do you want to clear that with Mr. Dunlap

Sean called and I said exactly what he told them: "Do it."

The operating room there was as sophisticated as any I've ever seen at the Mayo Clinic. At least ten people were in the surgical theater–doctors, nurses, and anesthesiologists–all working on Patton. They put him under, opened him up, removed his stomach and intestines, found the blockage, and then put him back together again.

It was amazing.

Incidentally, one of the surgeons was Irish.

He said, "I'm from Dublin, Ireland. You know, I never did that on a donkey before."

"Well," I said, "I'm from New Jersey,[8] and if anything happens to my donkey, you swim with the fishes."

The surgeon laughed.

"You ever hear of the IRA? Would you like to wake up with a bomb under your bed?"

Great surgeon and a great sense of humor. I always admired people who could give it as well as they could take it.

Some time later, we took in a big, white donkey we named Hannibal. He was in rough shape when we got him. Now he's gorgeous. Hannibal and I have had a great relationship. When he sees me coming, he goes "*Errrrrrrrr*," and I pet him. After Sweetie Pie, he was the next big animal we adopted.

Then came the donkey we call Legs. His legs were so thin when he got here that we didn't feel they could support his body. We weren't sure he would ever survive, but he did.

And when a local petting zoo went under, nobody wanted to take in their goats. So, naturally, we did.

Judy and I also have given homes to a multitude of ducks and 18 beautiful Baldwin Black Angus–also rescue animals.

A researcher from the University of Florida came out to check the marbling of their meat. He marveled over the health and general condition of the Angus, assuming we'd soon be ready to sell them for beef.

"What are you talking about?" I said. "They're my pets!"

The guy couldn't comprehend that I had made a dozen Black Angus into pets.

"They're worth thousands of dollars! " he argued.

---

[8] When I graduated from high school in New Jersey, I say, jokingly, you got three things. You get your diploma, you get a switchblade, and they enroll you in the first stage of witness protection.

I said, "I named them, for God's sake. I'm not going to *sell* them."

The researcher just shook his head.

"I don't understand," he said.

We're totally different than the horse farms. Every animal here is a rescue. We give them the best veterinary care, the best food, the best everything. We don't make one penny on them. The animals here will never be sold for food, labor or anything else. They will live out their lives here in peace.

I look at this land and this farm and it's the final fulfillment of my dreams.

Chapter 19

THE HEART OF A LION

A young lady was kidding around with me in Sam's Club recently.

I said, "How old do you think I *am*? I'm 59!"

She looked at me, paused for a moment and said, in all seriousness, "I don't know who you are, but if you're 59, you better get a new doctor!"

•••

As anyone who has been through it knows, retirement isn't all sunshine and lollipops.

Judy and I have each endured life-threatening health scares over the past two decades. And those situations have certainly contributed to our joint desire to live every moment to its fullest and direct our wealth to the causes we find most satisfying while we're here to see the results.

I had an undiagnosed cardiac arrhythmia that landed me in an emergency room on three separate occasions with defibrillator paddles being applied each time to keep my heart pumping.[9]

It all started on one extremely dry, hot Florida summer day, the

---

[9] It may surprise some of my critics to learn that I have one of those, but the doctors have seen indisputable truth that my heart exists!

kind that leads to wildfires set off by a combination of dry tinder and heat lightning. I came home that afternoon from playing tennis and there was a great deal of acrid smoke in the air around Ocala.

JUDY: He said, "I feel like I can't get a breath."[10]

That happened a couple of times over the next month and we went to our home in Hilton Head, South Carolina, where we were expecting a houseful of guests at 3 p.m. But at noon, Al got that feeling again, so Sean called our doctor in Ocala. He said, "Get Al to the emergency room immediately! Don't ask him, just put him in the car and I'll call the hospital there."

It turned out my heart was beating 155 beats per minute.

The ER doctors hit me with defibrillator paddles, admitted me overnight and they got it under control–temporarily, as it turned out.

The problem recurred two more times.

JUDY: His skin was getting gray. He was sleeping all the time, all day long. Didn't have any of his usual energy.

Our doctor sent me to the Mayo Clinic in Jacksonville, Florida, for an exam. I was diagnosed with an atrial flutter–the precursor to atrial fib–and the doctors there suggested that I should have an ablation performed.

JUDY: Al had to have two procedures. First they sent a camera into his heart to make sure he didn't have any blood clots. When he cleared that first hurdle, the doctors told Al explicitly all the things that could go wrong with the ablation surgery.

They gotta tell you what could go wrong.

JUDY: So they told him and Sean and I thought, "Oh, jeez."

He told me, "Al, we could accidentally puncture your heart, and you could die. Or we could burn out too many cells, and you're

---

[10] I was having trouble breathing, and do you know what they originally discovered? The doctors came to me and said, "Mr. Dunlap, we found all these feathers in your nose. Does your wife have a feather pillow?" I said, "Yeah, as a matter of fact, she does. Why?" They said, "Well, Mr. Dunlap, we think that's the root cause of your breathing problems. She's putting the pillow over your head at night."

JUDY: I had to get a new personal trainer because I wasn't strong enough to hold it down long enough!

going to die."

JUDY: It was pretty frightening. But he had the surgery, and he has been great ever since.

As for Judy, she needed some work done on her teeth, which led to a sinus condition. The doctor did a CT scan, and when he saw the result, his response was, "Oh, my God! I've got to get this woman out of here. This is serious."

Our local doctor sent her to a specialist in Philadelphia, which was when an X-ray uncovered a massive tumor in the front of her head.

JUDY: Every doctor, when they saw the X-ray of it, went crazy.

They said I should put her down. So, I said "Okay, doctor. I gotta take your advice."

JUDY: The oncologist thinks that I was either born with it or I got it when I was very young because my brain has grown around it and adjusted to it. He said, "Nothing will probably ever come of it. And even if you decided you wanted to do something about it, *well*, if you were my wife, I wouldn't touch it."

They wanted me to have it checked in six months and they would see if there was any growth. I said to Al, "I am not having it checked again because if it is growing there's nothing I can do about it. I just have to live my life, and if it's what we all think it is, it's nothing."

You lose a wife. That's tough. But the minute it appears in the paper you get so many calls from these single women! I mean, it's easy.

JUDY: It never stops, folks. He goes on and on like that all day long.

•••

Everybody has a moment in their life when they take their health more seriously than they did in their youth, so now you know what motivated us to take action, not just for ourselves but also for the sake of the general public.

The world-famous Mayo Clinic is headquartered in Rochester, Minnesota, with satellite hospitals in Phoenix, Arizona, and

Jacksonville, Florida.

One day it occurred to me that I had never really done anything sufficient to memorialize my parents. Judy and I have had some wonderful experiences with the Mayo Clinic and we decided to send some of our resources their way.[11] As a result, the Jacksonville offices of the Clinic now sport a plaque referencing my parents that says:

To Albert and Mildred Dunlap, who gave their son all the opportunities they never had in life.

The Clinic bought Luther Hospital in Judy's hometown of Eau Claire, Wisconsin, and we decided, in conjunction with them, to build a cancer center there. Previously, if you lived in that area and you had cancer, your only treatment option was to go all the way to Rochester. It was an added cost on top of the medical treatment itself, and caused patients to often be separated from family at the time in life they most needed love and support.

The Dunlap Cancer Center at Luther Hospital is the most gorgeous cancer center you'll ever see. It is decorated in a happy yellow, with lots of wood from the state's Northern Woods, and the whole chemo treatment area was built looking out over Half Moon Lake.

JUDY: When I go back to Wisconsin for a month every summer, they always call me and set up a lunch with the doctors and administrators at the cancer center. They bring me up to date on how it's growing and what's new in cancer treatment.

In 2013, they took me on a tour and when we came to the chemotherapy treatment area, it was full of people. Barbara J. Eidahl, the administrator who runs it, said, "We may not be able to go in there today because it is so busy." And I said, "I understand."

As we started moving on, a nurse came rushing out and said, "The patients want Mrs. Dunlap to come in!"

Some of them recognized me as the blond woman pictured in

---

[11] As of July 2014, we have made gifts of more than $5 million to the Mayo Clinic.

the lobby and wanted to meet me and thank me for bringing cancer treatment to this sometimes remote area of the country.

I cried when several patients told me their stories and how much difference the facility has made in their recovery.

One more thing we did for the cancer center was to underwrite a lovely flower garden that the treatment rooms look out upon. We have a woman who takes care of all that, and she tries to outdo herself every year before I get there to visit. It is named Ginny's Garden in honor of my mother, Virginia Stringer, who loved gardening.

Chapter 20
FLORIDA STATE UNIVERSITY;
WHERE THE HELL IS THAT?

I was still running Scott Paper in Philadelphia in 1995 when I was invited to do a college speaking tour that included stops at the business schools of Harvard, Yale, and several other Ivy League universities.

Along the way, somebody said, "Would you also consider speaking at Florida State?"

I said, "Where the hell is that?"

We hadn't relocated Scott to Boca Raton yet, so although I had heard of FSU, my knowledge of college geography was limited. But I accepted the invitation and soon found myself in Tallahassee, the state capital.

And then I opened my smart mouth. My lead-in line was, "Geez, I'm impressed! I didn't know you had classrooms. I thought you just had athletic facilities!"

Judy and I were introduced to the Seminoles' head football coach, Bobby Bowden, as well as the college president. We thought they and all the kids were terrific, and that started a great relationship.

As I write this in 2014, we have donated $10 million directly to Seminole Boosters Inc. and triggered a state match of an additional $5 million for a total of $15 million.

The first donation, in 2006, went into building three new outdoor football practice fields[12] and a 50,000-square-foot student success center.[13] It houses classrooms, a career resource center, meeting rooms, offices, technology accommodations, and job interview rooms. It is a place where leadership and community service are taught and encouraged, and the professional staff helps current and graduating students get jobs. We felt it was a necessity when we discovered that recruiters visiting the school's campus had to conduct interviews with prospective job candidates in the basements of existing buildings. If I was an executive and I was interviewing a young man or woman for a job at Google or Xerox and our time together is relegated to some basement, I would be turned off. The kids' chances were reduced before they even sat down to talk. With our gift, the school built a facility with brightly lit, state-of-the-art interview rooms.

"People from more than 40 countries have come here to see how we do career services," said Janet Lenz, one of four professors comprising the Center for the Study of Technology in Counseling and Career Development within The Career Center.[14] "And our staff has visited more than 4—from China to Tasmania to Ireland to Greece—to help people redesign their career services to be more effective in reaching a wider population."

JUDY: We are thrilled because the kids love to talk to us about their experiences at The Success Center. They are enthusiastic and love to pick our brains. Most of all, they're happy there. One girl came up to me and said, "If I could sleep in this center, I would."

It's already the most visited building on campus.

JUDY: That makes it all worthwhile. Keeps us young, too, being around the kids. We never build a building just to put our names on it. We wanted it to be useful.

And finally, Judy and I gave another $5 million toward a 92,00-square-foot, state-of-the-art indoor football practice facility.[15] It

---

[12] The Al Dunlap Football Practice Complex.

[13] The Albert J. and Judith A. Dunlap Student Success Center.

[14] http://news.fsu.edu/More-FSU-News/24-7-News-Archive/2013/November/Visiting-career-services-practitioner-praises-Florida-State-Career-Center

[15] The Albert J. Dunlap Athletic Training Facility.

was built over one of the existing outdoor fields. FSU joined a corps of other elite college football programs that already had year-round, elite athlete facilities or have plans to build one in the near future including Alabama, Auburn, Georgia Tech, Virginia, Virginia Tech, Tennessee and Louisiana State University.

"Al and Judy Dunlap really made this project happen," said Seminole Boosters president Andy Miller.[16]

One of the completely unexpected results of our relationship with FSU was when then-President Dr. Eric Barron invited Judy to give the Spring 2013 Commencement Address to graduates.

We had spent a lot of personal time with Dr. Barron and his wife, Molly, in Tallahassee and as our guests at the farm. They're wonderful people.

JUDY: I was stunned when he called. Al has spoken at the school several times, but Dr. Barron said that they would like to give me an Honorary Doctorate of Humane Letters and asked if I would be the commencement speaker.

I wrote a speech and practiced it at least once every day, either to the dogs or to the cat or to Al. Al himself is such a great speaker. So many people stand up before a group and they read their remarks from a printed speech or a TelePrompTer. But my husband can speak with just his bullet points and note cards. I thought, "I want to do that," but you have to really prepare. You don't want to memorize because that can put you in a world of trouble. So I practiced every day.

One day I was giving my speech to the dogs, and Cadet got up and walked out.

I thought, "Uh-oh. Maybe I goofed up somewhere."

The dog actually shook my confidence. It's so funny, because they would lie there and look at me when I was talking. I suppose they thought I was talking to them.

Finally, the big day came. I was seated on the stage at the Donald L. Tucker Civic Center with the other dignitaries, school administrators, and student speakers. It was a very

---

[16] JUDY: In recognition of our large gifts, the Seminoles Boosters gave us a wonderful, life-sized sculpture of Al and me and the dogs and the cat. But Al had them make the female head screw on and off – just in case.

special moment in my life.

I saw Al off to one side, and then I spotted my family, which had flown in from Wisconsin, seated up in the president's box. I just thought, "How wonderful to be here!" I was the kind of kid in school that, when I had to give a talk in class, I would sit and get myself all worked up and hope against hope that the teacher wouldn't call on me to give it, but once I got up there and started talking, it all felt quite natural.

I have a strong faith in God, and I believe that He has directed my life, and the things that I'm doing now in my life are things that He wants me to do. Because of that, I feel totally relaxed and at ease about what I've been up to for pretty much my whole life. And, you know, I don't know what's in store, and I don't know what else He wants me to do, but I'm here to do it and happy to be of service.

At one point in her brilliant speech, Judy broke from her planned remarks.

"My husband used to love to play football, and so we built the Albert J. Dunlap Practice Fields here at the university. And last month we broke ground for the new indoor practice facility. Now Jimbo Fisher, I don't know if you're out there anywhere, but no more excuses! We want to see a national championship here at this great university! "

The moment was captured for posterity and immediately became a YouTube sensation, viewed and downloaded thousands of times. It proved especially prophetic when Coach Fisher did, indeed, lead the Seminoles to a last-minute victory over Auburn in the sixteenth and final Bowl Championship Series on January 6, 2014.

By the way, my wife is now *Dr.* Dunlap. I'm like a third-class citizen in my own family!

•••

On April 30, 2014, the Marion County Seminoles Club held a post-season meeting at the Golden Ocala Golf & Equestrian Club where Head Football Coach Jimbo Fisher publicly recognized the contributions Judy and I have made to FSU football. Gene Deckerhoff, the radio voice of the Seminoles, was the emcee of the event and it was a really wonderful night.

A few days before the party, we were at a red light when I noticed the car next to us had a big Noles magnet on a side door. Both of our car windows were closed, but I was trying to signal that we were FSU fans as well by pointing to her door and back to my door. She couldn't wait to pull away from the crazy old man.

Then I recognized her at the Booster Club meeting.

I chuckled loudly and said, "Hello, again!"

She said, "I wondered who the hell you were when you pulled up next to me at that light. I was terrified. I thought you were crazy!"

But then she said, "Come with me."

She introduced me to her son, who was an FSU baseball player.

"This is the guy from the stoplight that was going like this," and she imitated my hand motions from inside the car.

It was pretty funny.

Chapter 21

FAMILY MAN

JUDY: When Al came into my hometown of Eau Claire, Wisconsin, in 1966, restructuring wasn't even a word that was thrown around yet. But Sterling Pulp & Paper was a company that was in trouble, and he had no choice but to fire people to make it solvent again.

People said horrible things to my parents. "How can Judy marry this man? He's so *blah blah blah*!"

I told Al one night that people were making horrible comments about him to my parents, and he said, "Sit down. We're going to have a talk and if, after this talk, you don't feel that you can live with what I'm doing, then maybe we're not meant to be.

"I didn't come here to win a popularity contest," he continued. "I came here to save a company, and if I have to get rid of 20 percent of the people so that 80 percent of the people have job security, that's what I'm going to do."

The thing about Al all of these years–and I've been married to him for 46 years–all the nasty stuff that was ever written about him wasn't true, really. It wasn't *Al* that got these companies in trouble.

People are really surprised when they have an opportunity to meet him and spend time with him.

I can't tell you how many times I've hard people say to him,

"You're not at *all* like we thought you'd be!"

By the way, all these years later—nearly half a century—Sterling Pulp and Paper is the *only* major company that was in Eau Claire when he was hired that's still in business today.

•••

Russ Kersh, my long-time right-hand in business, was the first protégé I took on. Sean Thornton is my second. He was in drug interdiction for the U.S. Coast Guard for several years, then provided private security services for everyone from Pete Rose to Demi Moore.

He came to work for me in 1994 as my bodyguard and driver. When I retired, he stayed with Judy and I in those roles as well as personal assistant and today, chief of staff. We trust him implicitly. Only Judy knows me better—and I pay Sean well enough to like me a little better than Judy does some days.[17]

When Sean married Ann Marie Cooney in 1993, she became the next member of our expanded family and their two kids are among the best things that ever happened to Judy and me.

Our relationship with Kate and Sean Patrick is beyond special. They kiss me, they hug me. Judy says they are the grandchildren we never had.

We love them and we've tried to give them all the opportunities we never had growing up.

JUDY: Sean still works for us, and he and Ann Marie call us "Mr. and Mrs. Dunlap" or "Mr. and Mrs. D." But once their oldest, Kate, came out of the womb and started talking, she called Al "D." And then she started calling me "Ju-D."

Sean's mother lives in South Florida and Ann Marie's mother lives in New York (both of their fathers are deceased), so we're sort of surrogate grandparents to those children.

The relationship among us has grown and we're blessed.

---

[17] Besides, we found that a lot of the threats against my life were coming from my wife.

EPILOGUE

JUDY: I know what's important in Al's life:
No. 1. Business.
No. 2 and No. 3. The dogs.
No. 4. Me.
But being fourth in his life hasn't been too bad.
And now we've got a Calico cat.
JUDY: Yeah, right.
And how about Hannibal? Hannibal and I are pretty close!
JUDY: Apparently I'm moving off the list entirely.
Of all the things I've accomplished in my business career, do you know what I enjoyed the most?

Doing this book. I tell everybody that. It was the most enjoyable experience and I got to tell my side and the book is forever. Fame is on loan and then the loan runs out. A book is forever.

ACKNOWLEDGMENTS

{**1996 EDITION**} Writing *Mean Business* caused me to examine not only the elements of what makes a successful business, but what makes a successful individual. In my book, it comes down to one word: family. My wife, Judy, has been a loving, supportive partner and friend across three continents and four decades on one of the most thrilling rollercoaster rides imaginable. The family also includes our beloved dogs and constant companions, Brit and Cadet.

I only wish my parents, Al and Mildred Dunlap, were still with us to see what they created. They gave me something far beyond wealth—self-respect.

A business career as varied and global as mine could not go forward without an equally devoted business family. Two men in particular saw potential and became my mentors. Ely Meyer believed in me at a very young age and provided unheard-of opportunities. And my great friend the late Sir James Goldsmith taught me things no business school education ever could. I will forever be in his debt. The world has lost a giant among men.

Along the way, I have followed their example and chosen young people whose talents I helped develop. Russ Kersh was a junior accountant when we met, but I saw a fire and intelligence in him that I have relied upon for almost 15 years. He became my alter ego, a trusted business associate and friend. Attorney John

Murtagh was already sending out resumes the day we met by accident. But instead of firing him, I sent his boss packing. John's legal and personal counsel have been invaluable to me. He, Russ, and I formed an unbeatable trio. And we rounded out our team with Jack Dailey and Lee Griffith.

Several former business associates gave freely of their time in the preparations of *Mean Business,* reconstructing events, detailing negotiations, and providing documentation to my co-author and myself. We are grateful to so many of them, including Basil Anderson; Bill Andres; Bob Jermain; Dave Harris; Dick Nicolosi; Dick King; Dixon Boardman; Don Burnett; Doug McCartney; Evan Rees; Fin Fogg; G. Chris Andersen; Gary Roubos; George Adler; James Packer; John Fort; John Nash; John Nee; Kathy McAuley; Linda Lieberman; Loretta Roccanova; Madame Gilberte E. Beaux; Marguerite Hamilton; Mike Masseth; Nell Minow; Neville Miles; Newt White; Paolo Fortin; Pete Judice; Phil Lader; Russ Carson; Tom Hardy; Tom Neff; and Dee Valek.

Writing a book took me into one of the few corners of the paper business I had not yet conquered. I'd like to thank my friend, Fred Iseman; my agent, Andrew Wylie; my editor at Times Books, John Mahaney; and especially my co-author, Bob Andelman, for an exhilarating ride. I told them I wouldn't write a book unless it was the best and I think it is.

{2014 EDITION} In bringing my story forward these past 18 years, I've made many new friends and would like to gratefully acknowledge their support, including Florida State University Head Football Coaches Bobby Bowden and his successor, Jimbo Fisher; former FSU President Eric Barron and his wife Molly; everyone at Seminole Boosters Inc., including Eric Carr; and the Marion County Seminole Club.

Also, the management and staff of: Golden Ocala Golf and Equestrian Club; Country Club of Ocala; my neighborhood Sam's Club and Wal-Mart; Peterson & Smith Equine Hospital; Marion County Sheriff's Office; Trinity Catholic High School; the Humane Society of Marion County; YMCA of Central Florida; Boca Raton Resort & Club; and The Mayo Clinic.

Albert J. Dunlap
Ocala, Florida
July 23, 2014

{**1996 EDITION**} There are several people whose contributions I'd also like to acknowledge, starting with Russ Kersh and Basil Anderson, who took a very personal interest in the accuracy and quality found in *Mean Business*. On the production side, I am grateful for the long hours of transcription put in by Tricia Martin and early editing by Vicki Krueger.

Professionally, I am grateful to John Mahaney of Times Books, who recommended me for this project and then shepherded me through its most challenging moments. And my agent, Joel Fishman of the Bedford Book Works, has proven himself one tough SOB. and friend.

I also deeply appreciate the unstinting support and friendship of Al and Judy Dunlap, one of the most fascinating couples I have ever met.

Finally, I could not have survived this year without the love of my wife, Mimi, who endured my many absences and long hours with good humor and understanding.

{**2014 EDITION**} People sometimes find it hard to believe that Al Dunlap and I have remained friends for the past 18 years. I don't see what's so surprising: the man is loyal and true to his friends and the people who are loyal and true to him. We hit it off the day we met over a shared love of dogs and the fact we both grew up in New Jersey. In almost two decades we've only had one bad moment together and Al doesn't even remember it!

And in all these years, he has not only been one of my biggest supporters but he has also taken my daughter, Rachel, under wing as well. Which is pretty funny when you learn I didn't even tell Al that my wife, Mimi, was pregnant back in 1996 because I knew he would think I'd lose my focus on writing his book. He was stunned when I became a father right around the same time *Mean Business* was first published. (Somewhere I have a blackmail photo of Al making googly eyes at infant Rachel over luncheon in Boca Raton.)

A few people I'd like to acknowledge who have been important to me this time around: the management and staff of Dystel & Goderich Literary Management, including Jane Dystel, Miriam Goderich, and Michael Bourret; my transcribers, sisters Karen Napier and Jana Ward; the many people at Random House who smoothed the rights transition that made this new edition possible; Jessica Kaye and George Hodgkins at Big Happy Family, who steered us through the digital audiobook release; the folks at Amazon, Kindle and CreateSpace for print and e-book advice and guidance; and Sean and Ann Marie Thornton for, well, everything.

This was my first time guiding a book through all of the publishing phases by myself and it reminded me of all the mentors I've had over the years on the production side of printing, including: Anthony Scialiss; Ron Frantz; Raymond Martino; Al and Missy Martino; Mike Culotta; the late Tom Howland; and Tom Bartel. And thank you Aunt Bess.

Finally, thank you to Andrew Skwish for the extraordinary design of the cover and the new Mr. Media Books logos; Patrick and Jennifer Milberger for offering their input on early cover designs; my new No. 1 fan, Sallie Spinner; Rachel Andelman and Jared Wang for producing the video book trailer for *Mean Business* (watch it and more at http://www.MeanBusinessBook.com or on Facebook at http://www.Facebook.com/ChainsawAl); and Mimi Andelman for proofreading the new material contained herein. And you, too, my loyal canine companion, Chase!

Bob Andelman
St. Petersburg, Florida
July 23, 2014

ABOUT THE AUTHORS

ALBERT J. DUNLAP grew up in Hoboken, New Jersey, the son of a union steward. He graduated from West Point and after completing his military service began a thirty-seven year career in business that took him to seventeen states, Europe, and Australia. He has held important positions at many companies, including Sterling Pulp and Paper, American Can, Lily-Tulip, Diamond International, Crown-Zellerbach, Consolidated Press Holdings of Australia, and Scott Paper, to name a few. He lives in Ocala, Florida, with his wife, Judy, and two German shepherds, Brit and Cadet.
http://www.MeanBusinessBook.com

BOB ANDELMAN grew up in North Brunswick, New Jersey, and is the author or co-author of fifteen books, including *The Wawa Way* with Howard Stoeckel, *Building Atlanta* with Herman J. Russell, *Fans Not Customers* with Vernon Hill (founder of Commerce Bank and Metro Bank), *Keep Your Eye on the Marshmallow* with Joachim de Posada, *The Profit Zone* with Adrian Slywotzky, and *Built From Scratch* with Bernie Marcus and Arthur Blank (co-founders of The Home Depot). He also hosts the popular video blog Mr. Media Interviews. He lives in St. Petersburg, Florida, with his wife, Mimi, daughter, Rachel, and fiercely loyal terrier, Chase.
http://www.MrMedia.com

Made in the USA
San Bernardino, CA
12 August 2014